RULE No. 5
NO SEX ON THE BUS

For Natalie

RULE No. 5
NO SEX ON THE BUS
(CONFESSIONS OF A TOUR LEADER)

BRIAN THACKER

ALLEN&UNWIN

First published in 2001

Copyright © Brian Thacker 2001

Allen & Unwin
83 Alexander Street
Crows Nest NSW 2065
Australia
Phone: (61 2) 8425 0100
Fax: (61 2) 9906 2218
Email: info@allenandunwin.com
Web: www.allenandunwin.com

National Library of Australia
Cataloguing-in-Publication entry:

Thacker, Brian, 1962– .
    Rule no. 5—no sex on the bus: confessions of a tour leader.

    ISBN 1 86508 553 7.

    1. Tour guides (Persons)—Europe—Humour. 2. Tour guides
    (Persons)—Europe—Anecdotes. 3. Tourism—Europe—
    Humour. 4. Tourism—Europe—Anecdotes. 5. Australians—
    Travel—Europe—Humour. 6. Australians—Travel—Europe—
    Anecdotes. I. Title.

914.002

Set in 11/15 pt Minion by Bookhouse, Sydney
Printed by Australian Print Group, Maryborough, Vic.

10 9 8 7 6 5 4 3 2 1

CONTENTS

GOOD MORNING

'Good morning, everyone! My name is Brian, and I'm your tour leader on this 28-day coach-camping tour of Europe. Our Coach Captain here is Tony [*Or is it Terry?*] who'll be [*No, I'm sure it's Tony.*] driving us over 7000 kilometres through eleven countries, including Belgium, Holland, Germany, Switzerland, Austria...um...Liechtenstein, Italy, France, Monaco and Spain. We've got about a [*Gee... that blonde in row five is cute.*] two and a half hour drive to Dover [*I'll have to make a move early, before Tony (or Terry?) does.*] where we will transfer on to our cross-channel ferry and a four-hour trip to Oostende in Belgium. From Oostende we have about a four and a half hour drive to Amsterdam. We'll be stopping on the Belgian/Dutch border to change money and hopefully [*If you buggers don't piss-fart around too much.*] we'll be at Camping Bos, our campsite in Amsterdam, by around seven o'clock, where our Super Cook, Tracey, will be waiting for us with dinner [*It better not be bloody spag bol again!*]. By the way, if you have any questions at any time [*But please, I beg of you, no really stupid ones.*], don't hesitate to ask. I'll speak to you all again [*Shit, did I forget something?*] as we get closer [*Ah, it doesn't matter.*] to Dover.'

PROSTITUTES POTHEADS & POFFERTJES

Rule no. 2 in our crew manual reads: *Learn all names on day one.*

I confess: I am hopeless with names. Embarrassingly so. I've tried every technique known to man but I'm still buggered if I can remember names. I can remember utterly useless information like the capital of Burkina Faso, but I can't remember the name of someone I was introduced to only seconds before. I must have inherited this mental deficiency from my father, who'd call out to me across the backyard, 'Colin, Michael, Bruce...um...ah...Brian!' He couldn't even remember his own son's name. But he, too, could tell you the capital of Burkina Faso.

Sadly, forgetting people's names is not really a great qualification for a job as a tour leader. Having a shocking sense of direction and being impatient and prone to sarcasm don't help either. Yet there I'd be, a fully-fledged tour leader, standing on a drab London street at six o'clock in the morning with 42 very excitable young people, just about to embark on a four-week coach-camping tour around Europe.

Hey, I'm not saying I'm a bad tour leader. I mean, I never did win 'Tour Leader of the Year' but I always gave my passengers what I thought was a good time. Yes, I got lost a few times, fed the passengers a couple of dodgy meals, got a bit too drunk now and again and lost a passenger or two along the way but I did it all with a smile. I love Europe. I love its history, people, food, drink and on every trip I took, my love of Europe would rub off onto the passengers—even if for some it was only the love of European drink.

By the twenty-eighth and last day of a trip I *would* know *most* people's names—and if I forgot, I could always cleverly divert their attention by telling them that the capital of Burkina Faso is Ouagadougou (made famous in the Glen Miller song, 'Excuse Me Boys, Is That the Ouagadougou?'). However, by the end of the two and a half hour drive to Dover, I would be happy just to have remembered the names of those two in the seat behind me, Jason and...um...damn!

As soon as we stepped on board our ferry to Oostende, my driver and I would head straight for our complimentary breakfast in the truckers' lounge. This was a passenger-free zone. The time spent with passengers could often be quite intense. You were always the centre of attention. The life of the party. Even worse, you would be asked questions constantly. When any opportunity came up for free time away from the passengers, we'd jump at it, even if it meant sitting in a truckers' lounge surrounded by truckies shovelling down plates full of fried eggs, fried bacon, fried tomato, fried mushrooms, fried potatoes, fried bread and fried cups of tea. Even sumo wrestlers don't eat this much. No wonder so many truckies look like a Teletubby in a blue singlet. But at least truckies didn't keep asking me, 'What can we do on the ferry?'

Most passengers would head straight for duty-free to stock up on booze. 'Where can I get some beer?' was a frequently asked question throughout every trip, along with the incessantly repeated, 'Brian, where is the toilet?' Answering the first one, of course, only increased the frequency of the second. However, as a tour leader, I faced much tougher questions during a trip: 'If I ring Australia now, will my mum be home?' (No, I think she's out shopping with *my* mum.) 'Will my brother like this shirt?' (No, I think he'd prefer it in beige.) Or this really difficult one: 'How can you tell if the kettle's boiled?' (Hang on, first let's work out what that funny whistling noise is.)

The four-hour crossing would generally pass without incident. Most of the passengers would just wander aimlessly around the decks, but there are exceptions to every rule. One young Kiwi decided, after finishing his bottle of

5

duty-free vodka—in just over an hour, I might add—that he should entertain the rest of the bar by dancing stark-bollock-naked on a table. For the next two hours, three burly Belgian security guards combed the decks looking for our suddenly rather shy Kiwi friend who had bolted off into the bowels of the ship as they approached his impromptu stage. For someone who had played a lot of rugby and didn't have many brain cells left, his hiding spot was particularly clever. He had snuck into one of those kids' playrooms that are filled with thousands of brightly coloured plastic balls, then fallen asleep in the corner—totally submerged—while a bunch of three-year-olds played noisily around him.

Already I can sense that you are getting the picture. Twenty-eight-day tours of Europe are not for the faint-hearted. For tour leader and punter alike, they require stamina and single-minded dedication. You might think package deals are a trifle unambitious, but many of the people who take them have very high hopes. It's just that (on the 18–35 tour circuit, at least) those hopes are more likely to concern sex and drinking than cultural enrichment.

Arriving at Oostende, we would devote the next few hours to getting out of Belgium as quickly as possible. The package tours offered in the brochure promised the opportunity to visit anything from eleven countries in fifteen days to a more relaxing seventeen countries in 70 days. Inevitably the shorter trips involved a lot of, 'Quick everyone, if you look out the window now you'll see Luxembourg…whoops, sorry, that was Luxembourg.' Belgium too was one of these fly-by-countries. Now don't get me wrong here: there is nothing wrong with Belgium. On the contrary, it has some beautiful towns. Well, one beautiful town anyway. Brugge fully deserves its reputation as one of the most perfectly preserved medieval cities in Europe. It's like the Disneyland version of Amsterdam, without all the hippies, rubbish and 'Live Fucky Fucky' bars.

Perhaps Belgium's greatest asset, though, is that there are over 500 different varieties of beer. Since most of those are rather tasty drops, it's not surprising that Belgians are some of the biggest beer drinkers in the world. It might also go some way in explaining the work of that famous Belgian, Plastic Bertrand, whose classic 'Sarn Blarn Blue And Wah' (well, that's what it sounds like, anyway) doesn't even make sense to native French speakers.

However, there are a couple of frightening aspects to Belgium. One is the driving. Up until the mid-seventies, the Belgian folk didn't have to do a practical driving test. A Belgian could just waltz into the test centre, complete a written test and be given a licence right there on the spot. Then—this is the scary part—they hit the roads. I suppose those same people have had twenty years' driving experience by now, but back then the whole of Belgium must have been nothing more than a 30 000 square kilometre circuit for dodgem cars.

Another thing about Belgium that is possibly of even more concern is racing pigeons. Do you actually know anyone—a friend, family member or even a rather odd workmate—who owns a racing pigeon? Well, in Belgium there are 3.5 million registered racing pigeons. That's one racing pigeon for every three people. Yes, frightening.

Faced with the prospect of all those Belgians driving all over the road, pissed, trying to retrieve their racing pigeons, you can understand why we drive through the country as quickly as possible.

The border between countries is where we'd normally stop for money exchange. Given how prices vary from place to place (the cost of a cup of coffee in Sweden buys about a week's holiday in Greece), I would give the passengers a rough guide on how much money they'd need for each country. Inevitably I would get, 'Brian, how much beer will I drink in Holland?' (Think of a number, double it and multiply by ten.) My favourite, however, was the often repeated question on the German/Swiss border: 'How much *Swedish* money do I need?' I would try to explain: 'None! We're going into Switzerland and they have their very own *Swiss* money.' The passengers would look at me for a second, say, 'Ohhhh', and march straight up to the exchange counter: 'Yes, I'd like fifty dollars worth of Swedish money, please.'

Holland is flat and smells like shit. And I really mean that in both respects. The country is so flat that its highest point, Vaalser *Mountain,* is a staggering 60 metres high. You could reach the summit of this mighty peak in just over three and a half minutes.

While Dutch soil is quite fertile, it's not quite fertile

enough for the Dutch folk. So they cover the whole country in fertiliser made from...well, shit. Boy, did it stink. We'd race through the country with windows closed, only opening them every so often so we could marvel again at how much it stank.

On a coach-camping trip we would head straight to our campsite, just out of Amsterdam. However, on some trips we'd head straight into the centre of Amsterdam itself, eating our dinner on the way. These particular trips were on converted double-decker buses that in a previous life shuttled Poms to and from work at the time when every good Englishman wore a bowler hat and it was actually cool to like Cliff Richard. These rattly, noisy old beasts had been gutted and turned into cosy motorhomes sleeping twenty-four sweaty, smelly, sexually hyperactive people.

There were good and bad points about these deckers, as we called them. By far the best of the good points was that the passengers could sleep as we drove along. I mean really sleep, in a proper bed with pillows. The whole of the upstairs was decked out with bunk beds. Now and again we would do what we called a 'rolling start', where the bus would leave at, say, six in the morning while everyone stayed in bed. When people crawled out from under the covers for breakfast, we'd already have travelled four hours down the motorway—which was a necessity sometimes, because the old hulks (which have now been overhauled a second time and reborn as Internet cafés) were so bloody slow. Even worse, I might add, was the noise they made: at 60 kph they could be mistaken for an out-of-tune 747 coming in for a landing (which must have been rather alarming for homeowners along the route). Even with the stereo up full blast, the constant rumble from the ancient diesel engine was deafening. Trying to be heard on the bus microphone was almost impossible. During my fifteen-minute spiel on the history of that day's country, I could have told them anything. The one or two passengers who would even bother to try and listen would be staring intently, trying to pick up what I said.

'What'd he say?'

'I think he said that Holland is full of *eels.*'

'Oh, right.'

Pulling into camp was a delight. There was no setting-up of tents or blowing up lilos. It was all there inside the bus. Which was wonderful when it was raining or you simply couldn't be shagged putting up a tent. However, with twenty-four people sleeping on a bus, it was no Brady Bunch slumber party. Upstairs alone there were eighteen people sleeping in a room no larger than a four-man tent. With all that snoring, farting, coughing, bonking and rustling of plastic bags, sleep would not come easily.

Another great thing about deckers was that you could cook while driving along. On many occasions I sat in one of the comfortable seats with freshly baked scones and a cuppa spread before me on a large table as we chugged down the road. One of the two downsides to this was that the bus had no airconditioning, so when it was a sweltering 38 degrees, the last thing on earth you would want to do was put on the oven for a tray of hot homemade scones.

The other was that we didn't have an onboard cook (the camping trips did) so passengers would be rostered on to cook each night. Admittedly, I had some delightful concoctions conjured up by a passenger who was an apprentice chef at the Ritz or by someone brewing up their great-aunt's award-winning pasta dish. However, if I let the passengers cook by themselves the whole trip they would serve us up canned ham and pineapple pieces every night for dinner. So inevitably I ended up either cooking myself or overseeing people who consider a boiled egg a culinary masterpiece.

On the coach-camping trips our onboard cook would be waiting for us at Camping Bos in Amsterdam. I would call her—or him, for that matter—from the Belgian/Dutch border and a three-course meal would be waiting for the passengers when we stepped off the bus. On one trip my cook, whose name was Heidi, was your fair dinkum, you-beaut, bonza, dinky-di Aussie sheila from Adelaide—so naturally I told the passengers she was from a small village in Switzerland. I also told them she spoke only a little English and that they had to speak to her very slowly so she could understand. One by one, as they made their way to the cook tent after putting their bags in their shared two-man tents, they would greet the cook. 'Hello... Heid...ee...how...are...you?' they'd ask ever so slowly. Heidi would mutter, 'Yeah, not bad thanks, mate', seemingly undeterred by the passengers' odd behaviour. A passenger confided to me later, 'Gee, Heidi's picked up quite an Aussie accent from you guys.'

On a decker trip, the passengers' first experience of Europe—besides eating spag bol (or ham and pineapple if the passengers cooked) sitting just off the motorway, surrounded by fields, cows and that oh-so-pleasant smell of fertiliser—was not our lovely camping ground but a brisk five-minute walk straight into the heart of Amsterdam's red-light district. One of the very first Cultural Sights they'd see was the pros on show. Within the first hundred metres we'd come across large windows filled with even larger, mostly Indonesian women wearing the skimpiest of erotic lacy underwear, beautifully displaying their seven hips and trucky's arms. What an introduction to Europe, the supposed cultural centre of the world! (Incidentally, I can't help but wonder what demand that abundant supply of roly-poly women is meeting. There's no charge for looking, so there must be some men who fantasise about outpointing female sumo wrestlers and are prepared to pay for the privilege.)

The buildings in the red-light district are the same pretty, gabled seventeenth-century houses you find all over Amsterdam. Indeed, the area is really very picturesque, with all those canals and the brilliantly bright reflections in the water of the neon signs spelling out 'Live Lesbian Show Inside'. In the doorways of the live-sex-show bars would be tall, blond Dutchmen asking ever so politely whether we'd like to come in and see two women have sex with an orangutan, a whole set of ten pins, or something just as horrendous. That's bad enough, but then they'd go into such explicit detail about the unnatural act in question that watching it live would have been an anti-climax.

Back to those tall, blond Dutchmen. The Dutch really are an incredibly tall bunch. I remember reading the reason somewhere: back in the fifties or sixties, the Dutch were pumping some sort of growth hormone into the local cattle population to make bigger cows and therefore more meat. Apparently, when the Dutchfolk ate their somewhat overdeveloped slabs of T-bone steak, they too grew, spawning a generation of tall Dutch people. I never did believe this story, but I would tell my passengers anyway and watch with amusement as they stared wonderingly at Dutch people and approached any piece of meat they were served with extreme suspicion.

In between the professional ladies in the windows and the live-sex shows are the ubiquitous sex shops with the usual array of painful-looking contraptions in the window. One evening, with only a group of twelve, I took them into the imaginatively named SEX SHOP. ('Hey, there're 178 sex shops around here. So as not to confuse anyone, let's call ours...um...SEX SHOP.') It was empty, except for the tall, blond Dutchman behind the counter. Browsing through the delightful collection of magazines, I came upon a particularly tasteful number called *Fist Fuckers Monthly*. Now fair enough, there are people out there— a worry in itself—who'll buy a one-off magazine full of various fists being rammed up women's vaginas, but 'monthly'? The mind boggles. How many variations can you get? Fist in, fist out, fist with wristwatch in, fist with wristwatch out...it's truly frightening. With that in mind, I ambled up to the tall, blond Dutchman and asked, with the straightest face I could muster, 'Excuse me, do you have any books on Van Gogh?' He stared hard at me for a second then looked straight back down at his latest copy of *Fist Fuckers Monthly* and totally ignored me. Everyone, including tall, blond Dutchmen, hates a smartarse.

Less than ten minutes into the passengers' first taste of Europe, I'd walk my group straight into the Moulin Rouge nightclub. This was no normal nightclub. There were no disco balls or Donna Summer songs here. A tall, blond Dutchman would greet us at the door and then lead the group into the 'waiting room' until the 'show' began. The waiting room was actually a small cinema where, to the excitement of some and the utter horror of others, what looked like the movie version of *Fist Fuckers Monthly* would be screening.

After ten minutes or so I would drag the passengers from their seats and lead them upstairs to the nightclub, where we would be seated in prime position around a small stage. The lights would dim, loud pumping music would blare out, and a young, well-dressed, tall, blonde Dutchwoman would step up onto the stage and begin dancing. This would go on for a couple of minutes, then, in a fairly business-like fashion, she'd get her kit off and delicately push a rather large lit cigar up her fanny and, quite casually, begin to smoke it. Lying on her back with her legs in the air, she would puff out huge clouds of white smoke—including, I might add, perfectly formed smoke rings. OK, it sounds impressive (if unappetising), but I'd seen her do it all umpteen times. The only thing I still found embarrassing about it was that when she'd finished she'd walk directly past me, totally naked and smelling like the Cigar Bar at the Ritz, and say, 'Brian! How are you?'

Next to dazzle us with her crotchistic expertise would be the Texta Lady. She would go through the same five-minute disrobing before dragging one of the male passengers up on stage. Trying to act cool, he would smile nervously as she took off his shirt, blindfolded him and laid him down flat on his back. She would pull out a large black marker pen from her little black silk bag and carefully push it inside herself. Straddling the fellow—who had no idea what was going on—she would squat down and begin to scribble something on his chest. After a few minutes of jiggling about, she would undo her accomplice's blindfold and stand him up to reveal I LOVE YOU written across his chest. Reactions to this inscription varied. I had one passenger who was so proud of Texta Lady's display of undying love for him that more than a week and three countries later he was still sporting her message as clear as the day he got it. Others couldn't wash fast enough or scrub hard enough.

By this stage of the evening, different members of the group would be reacting to the show in very different ways. Some were, of course, just loving it. As a matter of fact, some of the lads were loving it just a bit too much. Even after the copious amounts of beer they had drunk, they seemed rather reluctant to go to the toilet. When they were finally forced to stand up at the end of the show, they would shuffle out bent double with their hands placed over their groins (such a strange posture, incidentally, that it is much more noticeable than even the largest lump in the pants). Quite a few of the passengers smiled and joked nervously to hide their shock, while some were just absolutely terrified. On one occasion a sweet nineteen-year-old girl from a small God-fearing country town in New Zealand was as white as a ghost by the second act. By the third act, she was in the toilet emptying her stomach of my lovely spag bol.

Act three was the very talented Candle Lady who would somehow manage to do cartwheels and headstands in the darkened room with a burning candle poking out of her fanny. Then, before the passengers—particularly the girls—got too bored with women inserting foreign objects, out came Darth Vader. Well, a big black man dressed as Darth Vader. The girls would show a sudden interest at this point and were very keen to see if the stories of large black men were true and whether Darth Vader's light sabre in his pants made that 'vvooosh' sound when he swung it about. He would peel off his robes to the accompaniment of John Williams' stirring 'Star Wars' music, then pull two giggly girls onto the stage and, wearing only a G-string, tease them with a spot of dirty dancing. Finally, he would simply turn around and, with his back to the audience, drop his underpants and give the two girls their own private viewing of his light sabre. By the look on their faces,

I think Darth Vader's light sabre must have been switched on and glowing a fluorescent red.

The second-last act was just that: an act. An assistant put a furry round rug—the kind you'd find in your sweet grandma's lounge room—on the stage and a couple in dressing gowns made their way to the stage. They casually dropped their robes and got down to the business. Boy, did they look bored. I was bored and I'd only seen them do it twenty times. They would do this half a dozen times a night. Every night. Every week. Eventually, mercifully, after ten minutes of jiggling about, he dismounted, picked up Grandma's lovely furry rug and left the room. Which was normally about the same time I did. I still have horrible nightmares about the final act, in which, on my first ever visit to the Moulin Rouge, I had taken a leading role.

Before I became a tour leader, I had to survive and pass a training trip, along with a bunch of fellow Aussies and a handful of New Zealanders. This tour from hell was a three-week, brain-numbingly intensive, definitively ghastly and exhausting experience. The trainers, who may well have done their training courses with the Gestapo, seemed to find great enjoyment in treating you like a piece of particularly sticky, smelly excrement. To be fair though, I can understand why. They did have to weed out those with no leadership potential, and having to retain our composure while being treated as if we should be flushed down the toilet was something we all went through several times a trip.

In our case, only three personalities of the fifteen wannabe tour leaders combined that mix of tinpot dictator, incorrigible smartarse and expert in self-preservation necessary to pass.

Amsterdam was the last city we visited on our training trip (we started in Paris), and on our second-last night I became the co-star of the final act. I was dragged—and I mean literally dragged—onto the stage by a 120-kilogram Jamaican lady with breasts the size of beanbags. I was joined by three other poor buggers, and to the strains of calypso music our rather large friend proceeded to take a banana, peel it and shove it up her more than ample fanny. As soon as she grabbed the first lad and made him bite the end of the banana, there was a frantic push and shove to be anything but last. Like every right-thinking person faced with that situation, I panicked...and ended up last in line. By the time she got to me there were barely two inches of banana poking out. Somehow, it got worse. To make my task even more horrifyingly difficult (not to mention difficultly horrifying), she blindfolded me. Not only did I have to try and bite less than one inch of banana but, being completely blind, I first had to find the banana. As I very—and I mean very—tentatively edged my way towards the abyss, my head was forcefully shoved down and all of a sudden I had a mouthful of banana. And that was not all. Let me just say that it took me two whole years before I could even look at another banana.

I'm sure you can now understand why, just before Big Mama made her appearance, I would make my disappearance and slink off downstairs to pay the bill. Meanwhile, one of my poor passengers would also discover the true meaning of a banana split.

After dragging the rather shell-shocked passengers from their seats, I would take them on a little stroll up Beautiful Street. The street itself is not beautiful; in fact, at only a fraction more than a metre wide and about fifty metres long, it is nothing more than a lane. It's nicknamed Beautiful Street because it's full of women on show and, let me tell you, there were no roly-polys there. These young women were stunning, and what astonished me is that they could easily have been strutting the catwalks of Milan or gracing the cover of *Vogue*. So why this? Drugs? It can't pay that well. A local once told me anyone can hire out a window and adjoining bed for a thousand guilders a day. I got out my calculator and tried to figure out the sums. It costs 'fifty guilders for a straight fuck' as a lovely young lady, who I'm sure was Claudia Schiffer's sister, informed me when I asked for a quote (and yes, before you ask, this was strictly for the purposes of research). So if you did three shifts of eight hours at, say, two tricks an hour, that's 2400 guilders, which meant each girl made about 500 guilders a night (A$500). I would suggest renting one of the windows to the female passengers to help them make a little extra spending money.

I'd stroll into Beautiful Street closely followed by 40 odd people, sniggering, pointing or just staring rigidly ahead in case they saw something Mother wouldn't approve of. There were always a few men walking through checking out the wares and, by the look of the many closed curtains, men who weren't satisfied with just window shopping. It was very weird, standing next to a closed curtain and knowing that only metres away a gentleman was getting his 50 guilders' worth.

After Beautiful Street the passengers would be given a couple of hours of free time before they were due back to the bus. There were always passengers who wanted to try Amsterdam's weedier side, so I'd point out a coffee shop I believed to be safe. More importantly, I'd tell them that if they were going to try 'space cakes'—which are like Granny's home-baked tea cake, only laced with hash—they should only have half each, because they were really strong. After all, how could I tell if they were two-bite screamers? The fact is that the cakes aren't really that strong any more. A few years back the coffee shops started making space cakes with a little less cosmic content, to protect their customers from themselves. It usually took forty minutes or so to get stoned, but they were finding that people would wait twenty minutes, think they hadn't taken enough, and wolf down another one. Inevitably the cafés would end up with a lot of very stoned people off their heads, donning cheesecloth shirts and listening to Neil Young. And you can't have that!

On top of this I would plead with my passengers that if they intended to buy exotic intoxicants, they had to sniff them, smoke them, eat them, snort them, inject them or shove them up their noses before we left Holland. On some borders—particularly the German/Swiss one—the border guards had spot inspections of the bus with their trusty German Shepherds sniffing for drugs. And the thing was that if they found any, it wasn't only the passengers who were busted, but the tour leader (that was me) as well. I didn't really fancy spending the rest of my life in a German prison eating sauerkraut just so my passengers could nibble on hash cookies for an extra day or two. So I'd plead with them a dozen times not to take drugs across the border. When even I got sick of hearing myself harp on about it (and the driver started threatening me with violence if I didn't let him crank up the stereo again), I would assume that they had understood.

But life, as we know, is never that simple.

One crisp, clear summer's day in the Swiss Alps, I walked behind the bus to find four of my passengers smoking a joint straight out of a Cheech and Chong movie. We're talking HUGE.

'Where in the hell did you get that?' I cried.

'Um…Amsterdam,' one groggily replied.

'WHAT?'

They had taken a couple of bags of Afghani Gold or Guatemalan Green or whatever across two borders, including one of the toughest in Europe: the German/Swiss border.

After sending my weedier passengers off for some brain food, I would take the rest of the group to the Last Watering Hole, a rather seedy bar with great music and cheap beer. Every so often, though, I'd get the chance to slip away by myself and head to the Sailor's Bar for a quiet drink by the window, watching the punters slip in and out of the pros-on-show shops. This was always an intriguing spectacle, but I was especially curious on the only occasion I noticed one of my very own passengers peering in the windows. When he finally found the courage to step inside, I took careful note of the time. Exactly eight minutes and seventeen seconds later he walked out. I figured out (my calculator comes in handy for a lot more than doing the accounts) that it cost him about six dollars and eleven cents per minute. But if you consider that he probably spent at least four minutes stripping off and getting dressed again, that's a rate of about...well, at any rate, it all adds up to a rather expensive way to unwind.

Getting lost was one of my greatest fears. Amazingly, I got a job as a tour leader despite having possibly the world's worst sense of direction. I mean, I get lost driving home from work. On my first trip to Amsterdam, after leaving the Last Watering Hole with 22 people trailing behind me, I got hopelessly lost. I thought I knew a short cut back to the bus and, in a scene reminiscent of Chevy Chase in *European Vacation*, I walked my group in a big loop through the back alleys of Amsterdam. Walking past the Oude Kerk (old church) for the second time, I stopped the group and, with a straight face, repeated the same spiel about the church that I'd given less than ten minutes earlier. The scary thing is that quite a few of the passengers didn't even notice.

Back to camp after their first, very long day, most passengers would still postpone going to bed in favour of making their way to Fred's Bar at the campsite. Fred the bar owner was tall (funny that!), but strangely enough not blond. (I figured he was probably blond as a kid and had just darkened with age.) Fred would refuse to serve people water, saying 'This is a poob. You drenk foocking beer in a poob, not vorter.' However, his favourite line was saved for closing time, when he would walk out from behind the bar brandishing a baseball bat and shout at the top of his lungs, 'OK, ve are clozing now, so can everybotty FOOK OFF! I vont to go home ant harv sex wiz my vife.'

Our first morning in Holland was always spent honouring the three tourist clichés: cheese, clogs and windmills. We would begin the day with a cheese-making demonstration on a farm about twenty minutes out of Amsterdam. This was followed by a cheese-tasting session where the passengers could try Gouda, Edam, Gouda with herbs, Gouda with pepper, Gouda with nettles, smoked Gouda, Gouda with Edam and Gouda with Gouda. Inevitably some of the passengers would buy big slabs of the stuff. Unfortunately, no sooner had they hidden it in the bowels of the bus somewhere than they would forget about it— forget about it, that is, until about 22 days later. Suddenly, in the stifling heat of the Mediterranean summer, they would begin to wonder why the back of the bus was smelling like Pete Sampras's socks.

Cheese was immediately followed by a clog—or

klompen as those wacky Dutchfolk call them—making demonstration. A young and (by the look of the drooling girls) handsome, tall, blond Dutchman explained in word-perfect English—while ever so casually hand-chiselling a clog with a dangerously sharp-looking instrument—how comfortable they are. He would calmly assure us that it only takes a couple of years of constant wear to break them in. Great deal, eh? Endure two years of hobbling about cultivating crop after crop of agonising blisters for the privilege of looking like Bozo the Clown.

I have to say that I am particularly impressed by the Dutchfolk's grasp of English, not to mention that most of them speak German and French as well. Mind you, they don't have a lot of choice when you consider that the only other places where they understand Nederlands (as the natives call it) are Surinam, the Dutch Antilles and the bits of Belgium where they speak Vlaams. We call Vlaams Flemish out of politeness to the Flems, but it is exactly the same language as the one we call Dutch out of impoliteness to the Nederlanders.

Only the most ambitious Dutch person would ever expect you to learn their tongue-twisting language. Written Dutch gives the impression that someone has got hold of a bag of Scrabble letters, shaken it around, emptied the letters onto a table and used whatever words came out. Try saying KONINKLIJKE LUCHTVAARTMAATSCHAPPIJ—not something I've just made up, but the name of Holland's national airline. Sensibly, the Dutch have shortened it for international consumption to KLM.

After cheese and clogs, it's off to the third cliché in as many hours: the Windmill. There we conduct that multinational tourist cliché (and integral part of any bus tour), the Photo Stop.

Actually, you are lucky to find any windmills at all in Holland now. A hundred years ago there were 10 000 windmills; now there are less than a thousand and only 200 of them are still working. We'd stop at two of those surviving windmills for our Photo Stop, which normally took about five minutes. Unless of course we had a group of Asians. Funnily enough, or not funnily as the case may be, they tend to not smile in their photos. With a face more appropriate to a funeral ceremony, they would stand perfectly rigid in front of every major monument in Europe. Plus a few walls, public toilet blocks, power poles and, well, anything at all really. The reason they took so long on their Photo Stop was that they would take a photo of each other, then one with a friend, then one with a total stranger's friend, and finally—and always—a photo standing with their tour leader. It's nice to know that there are about 10 000 photos of me in photo albums all over Hong Kong. I'm easy to spot: I'm the one who's smiling.

Next stop for the morning would be Vollendam, a Traditional Fishing Village. Yeah, right! When the Zuidersee was drained back in 1919, more than 1.5 million hectares were reclaimed from the sea and this land now houses over 100 000 Dutchfolk. Vollendam used to be by the sea but now sits on an inland lake miles from the coast. Deprived of its original industry, Vollendam now lives off tourists and is oh-so-cute-and-quaint. The locals still dress in Dutch national costume. For men, that's baggy black pantaloons fastened with silver guilders instead of buttons, red and white striped jackets, and little black fisherman's caps. The women wear seven coloured skirts and the most dreadfully twee white lace bonnets. Both sexes, of course, wear those podiatrist's nightmares, wooden clogs. Needless to say, this is not done for the tourists. Repeat, not. I wouldn't be cynical enough to suggest otherwise. You do have to wonder, though. It's just a little hard to believe that these same people who wear cute little outfits and lace bonnets also have shops full of *Fist Fuckers Monthly* and a crack squad of shift workers who insert strange things up themselves.

The main reason for our visits to Vollendam was to get our official group photos taken. Everyone had to wear the aforementioned national costume, and I have to admit that I enjoyed it immensely. Not the photo shoot itself, but getting dressed beforehand. The most deliciously gorgeous local Dutch girls would dress you and put their arms all around you to do up buttons, tie scarves around your neck and even put your pants on for you and fasten them up. I was smitten. It was lucky, I have to tell you, that the pants were very baggy.

The group photo would be taken in a studio with a rather tacky painted fishing village as a backdrop. Inevitably, the biggest and most yobbish of fellows would dress in the women's costume and take great delight in fondling each other's foam breasts. Everyone, and I mean everyone, was given something to hold on to. We were handed plastic babies in Dutch costume, plastic tulips, long plastic smoking pipes, baskets of plastic fish, posies of plastic tulips, accordions, bits of rope, fishing nets and more fucking tulips.

In the shop window of Photo Studio Zwarthoed there are framed photos of supposedly famous people who have subjected themselves to looking like total twats. I could recognise only one, and that was Jane Seymour (who did a great impression of a twat). I have no idea who the rest were. I went inside and asked one of the cute Dutch girls who they were and she told me they were famous Dutch people. Hmmm! Can you name one famous, *modern* Dutch person? I could only think of one. The footballer Dennis Bergkamp. And he wasn't there.

As our final Dutch excursion, we would double back and head into Amsterdam town itself. In most cities we visited on our circuit of Europe, we would take a walking tour. This would be led by the supposed authority on all things European and historical: me, the tour leader. Now, I consider myself a bit of a European history buff, but there are limits. On a three-hour walking tour of Rome, for example, one can't expect to remember every name and date, or the history of (and everyone who lived at or stopped for afternoon tea at) a particular site. So just before each walking tour started, I'd read through my prompt cards and away I'd go, hoping for the best.

Sometimes I still couldn't remember the exact date, so

I'd do what you would have done. I made it up. 'OK, everybody, this is the Niewukerk, which was completed in... [*a moment of panic*]... 1471.' This was close enough— it was built some time during the 1400s. Sixteen days into one trip, in the middle of my walking tour of Venice, I noticed a couple taking notes. I asked what they were doing and the fellow said, 'We're taking down everything you say for our parents, who are travelling around Europe in two months' time.' This will be interesting, I thought to myself. Mr and Mrs Williams will not only have a couple of bung dates, but also a few names even the locals wouldn't recognise. As we walked through the cities, the passengers would quite often ask me what a certain church was called. Some cities have hundreds of seemingly grand churches, and I can't be expected to know them all. Again, if I didn't know, I'd just rechristen them. 'Oh, that's the... ah... Santa Maria della Agnolotti.' I can just see it. Mr and Mrs Williams asking at the tourist office in Venice for directions to the Santa Maria della Agnolotti. Not unlike an Italian in Leeds asking the way to St Mary's of the Mushy Peas.

My walking tour would begin at Central Station and head up the main drag, Damrak. But first I had to try to get 40 passengers across the road without getting hit by a bike. The Dutch are renowned for being a tolerant bunch, with their lax attitudes on drugs and prostitutes and—the greatest show of tolerance of all—letting so many people wearing cheesecloth shirts across their border. But when it comes to bikes and bike paths, they have no tolerance at all. They will knock you down in a second if you put one foot on their beloved bike path. Even car drivers are scared. In fact, if a car hits a bike, no matter what happened, Dutch law says it's the driver's fault. There are 16 million bikes in Holland (more than one for every person), and 550 000 in Amsterdam alone. Everyone rides a bike. You see girls dressed in elaborate party outfits going out for the evening, businessmen in designer suits with their brief-cases strapped to the handlebars, or even your common or garden-type hippy. Strangely enough, they all seem to ride the same bike: a rather clunky looking contraption straight out of the 1940s. Why doesn't anyone ride a flash 20-speed Mongoose? I suppose the locals are always worried their bikes will end up in a canal, like the 10 000 that were pulled out of the canals in Amsterdam last year alone. Why so many? Maybe it's a case of too many space cakes or Heinekens and then—whoops!—missing one of the 1281 bridges that cross the canals. Or do people just steal a bike and, when they've finished with it, chuck it in a canal? During the 1960s, with all that peace and love shit going on, the city of Amsterdam decided to put hundreds of bikes, all painted white, in the centre of town as free public transport. Oddly enough, quite a lot of freshly painted brown, blue or black bikes could be seen around the streets of Amsterdam in the weeks that followed. All the white bikes had not so mysteriously disappeared. Funny that!

Early one Sunday morning I was standing in an unusually quiet Dam Square, at the end of Damrak, giving my spiel on the Royal Palace—the official residence of Queen Beatrice, who is neither tall nor blonde (she undoubtedly didn't eat the beef)—when a tall blond Dutchman sidled up to me dressed as, well, a tall blonde Dutchwoman. In fishnet stockings and all. Looking rather the worse for wear after a Saturday night that had turned into Sunday morning, he (or she?) rocked on his high-heeled shoes and stared blankly at my now slightly uncomfortable passengers. I paused in mid-sentence. She (or he) looked at me with glazed eyes for a second, shouted out something in Dutch, then waddled right through the middle of the group with her skirt tucked almost neatly into the back of her lace panties. I waited till he or she was out of sight, then summarised for the benefit of my shell-shocked little flock: 'Welcome to Amsterdam!'

The next stop was Anne Frank's house where, after I had finished my moving spiel on Anne and her family, we would all jump onto canal bikes. These painfully slow contraptions hold four people per bike and the front two cycle the thing. I would lead them through a series of canals, dodging cruise ships and barges on the way—which part of the 'keep to the right' rule do you think passengers couldn't understand?—to just near the Rijksmuseum. Once, however, I had to find two lost passengers who had not returned back to camp from the night before (that's another story), so I left someone armed with a map and in charge of leading the way. I made the horrendous mistake of appointing as my acting deputy a fellow with the IQ of a Surprise pea and, not surprisingly, he got the whole group hopelessly lost and at least two kilometres away from the Rijksmuseum. So what did he and the rest of the gang do? They simply pulled up by the side of a canal on the outskirts of Amsterdam somewhere, jumped out and abandoned the canal bikes. I had great fun trying to explain to the owners that I had no idea where their ten large and brightly painted canal bikes had got to.

While the passengers had a few hours' free time I would wander around. This was one of the main reasons I liked the job. The wandering. I had such a wonderful opportunity to get to really know a city. Amsterdam, for instance, I ended up visiting about 25 times. I'd hire a pushbike and ride through the suburbs and parks or sit in a streetside café and just watch the city go about its day. At the end of my free time I would meet the bus behind the Rijksmuseum and wait for the passengers to return after their afternoon in town. One time while sitting in the empty bus I was flicking through the local radio stations when I came across one that played nothing but birds tweeting. It did change, though. After ten minutes of yellow-breasted thrushes and the lesser-spotted starling, it would fade down like a song finishing, then would start again on, say, a tropical theme with golden-eared lorikeets and a startled whoop-whoop bird. Every now and again between tweeting a DJ would come on to say in that inimitable Dutch way, 'Flop de hoop, de flop floop de hoop, de flop'. Then the birds would start again. I left it on, ever so softly, as the passengers returned one by one and took their seats. I just watched them, with contained amusement, as their ears pricked up and they looked around, dumbfounded, trying to figure out how a toucan would come to be in a bus park in the back streets of Amsterdam.

The Dutch really are a wacky bunch. And I mean that in the nicest possible way, of course. On another occasion I was sitting in the bus waiting for the passengers to return when I heard this bad rap music (I know most rap music is bad, but this was really bad). It was coming from a telephone box in the square next to the bus. No ordinary phone box, I soon discovered, but a 'Rap Phone'. You walked in, shut the door, picked up the phone and, when you pressed the number one, you got a bass drum: *Booom*. Two gave you a snare: *Thump*. Three was a high hat, *Tsss*, and so it went. Just in case you didn't happen to be the proud owner of any rhythm of your own, you could hold down zero and get the whole rap beat thing. Then, picking up the mouthpiece you rapped into the phone. But the best part was that there were speakers on top of the telephone box and all and sundry could hear your—more likely than not—horrible attempts to sound black, cool and intimately acquainted with the less attractive parts of New York. Naturally, I had to have a go. I walked in, got the beat thing happening, said 'Yo, mudderfocker!' a lot, threw in a few 'pwartys' and 'cworfees' and a few more 'yoes', got bored in about two minutes and slunk back to the bus. 'How was that?' I asked my driver. 'That was cool,' he said. Yeah, right!

Why was it there? I had no idea. I asked the tall blond Dutchman working in the kiosk what it was all about. He just shrugged and said, 'It's some sort ov art sing, I sink.' Wacky Dutch, hey? Sitting back on the bus, I watched as mostly young, blond, tall Dutch kids took turns at making a dreadful noise. Finally, after a few minutes of peace— only disturbed by the mating calls of a pink-arsed finch—a little grey-haired old Dutchwoman (formerly tall and blonde) walked into the telephone box. Seconds later, out of the speakers came *boom, crash, boom, thump, tssss, boom, thump.* This was followed by a long pause, then the same combination again. Another pause, then she walked out looking rather dejected. This poor Dutch lady thought it was a real phone and was hitting the numbers totally oblivious to the fact that she was creating something that probably would have made the rap charts in the US.

In each country we visited we would try to include a 'national meal', like pasta for Italy and snails for France. So for our Dutch national meal that night we would naturally go to...an Indonesian restaurant. I don't reckon there is any authentic Dutch cuisine worthy of the name or, more importantly, worth eating. What can you think of? Well, there's space cakes, I suppose. And not only space cakes. You can buy space fudge, space doughnuts, space cookies, space raspberry tarts and even space lemon meringue pie. In fact, I wouldn't be surprised if you could walk into McDonald's and order a space Big Mac: 'Yes, certainly, and would you like space fries with that, sir?'

Just quickly, while we're on McDonald's, the one in Leidseplein was an amazing place to visit in the wee hours of the morning. It was full of people with the munchies. I was in there once, standing in the long queue, and heard a stoned guy in front order 'Four Big Macs, three fries and two apple pies, please'. They must be used to it there, because the pimply counter kid replied, 'Would you like three sundaes with that, sir?'

Back to the food. There are poffertjes, which are delicious little Dutch pancakes covered in strawberry sauce and icing sugar. But even though I easily manage a dozen for lunch, it doesn't quite pass as a sit-down dinner. Then of course there's the old Dutch favourite of tulip bulbs. During the Second World War, the Germans moved all fuel and transport from Holland to stop the Allies advancing and, in the process, stopped any food coming into the country. Fifteen thousand people died of starvation and what kept a lot of people alive was eating tulip bulbs. Some people subsisted on this culinary delight for a couple of years.

'What's for dinner tonight, honey?'

'Oh, I think we'll have broiled tulip bulbs.'

'Oh, goodie!'

But I don't think I could make the passengers eat tulip bulbs, no matter how nicely they were sautéed in a light olive oil with a touch of garlic. There's herrings, but I wouldn't force them onto my worst enemy. Finally, there's Holland's national dish: *Hutsepot*. This dates from... shit, I've forgotten... um, 1574 (close enough), during William the Silent's campaign to oust the ruling Spanish from

Holland. The turning point came in the town of Leiden, when Willy flooded the province, sailed his ships right up to the walls of the city and caught the Spanish troops off guard, sitting down for their evening meal. The stew pot left bubbling on the fire by the fleeing Spaniards became the symbol of freedom. That's all very well, but *Hutsepot* is traditionally made from meat, vegetables and prunes all mixed with lemon juice and strong vinegar, then boiled at length in fat and ginger. This delightful little concoction is eaten by the Dutch every year on 3 October. While the French have liberty as their symbol of freedom and the Swiss have William Tell, the Dutch have a pot of a rather questionable stew.

So that's why I'd take them out for an Indonesian meal instead. I'd explain how Indonesia had been a Dutch colony for a few hundred years and that what we were going to have was primarily a Dutch invention (just like the souvlaki was invented in Australia). Rijstafel is made up of twenty or more dishes served up with rice. Indonesian people born in Holland who have returned to their ancestral home are quite surprised to find that this style of eating doesn't exist in Indonesia. Later on in the trip I would also have trouble trying to explain why we were having Hungarian goulash in Italy, chicken and chips in Germany and gluggy vomit in Spain.

LEDERHOSEN
LAGER
& LUFTKISSENFAHRZEUGS

'Whatever you do, don't mention the war!'

That's the first thing I'd say to the passengers driving across the border into Germany. And I'd say it with a very serious look on my face, because it's not entirely a Basil Fawlty, jokey approach to international relations. Under the banner 'Topics to avoid in Germany', *European Customs and Manners: How to Make Friends and Do Business in Europe*—a book published in Britain as recently as 1992—lists: 'World War Two, and especially questions regarding what people were doing during the war, or questions such as "Are you married?"'

Hmmm, I wouldn't quite put 'Are you married?' in the same category as 'Didn't you or your forebears kill six and a half million Jews?'

Because of the EC's open border policy, the Dutch/German border is a doddle. You just drive straight through without even stopping. However, that's not the case on all borders. On the particularly nasty and time-consuming German/Austrian border for example, the procedure (according to the Crew Manual, our bible) is as easy as this:

1 Proceed to customs office on right-hand side.
2 Fill out Laufzettal form (Green Form) in office next to bus.
3 Proceed upstairs to counter (A) with a German flag.
4 Show passports and completed Laufzettel form.
5 After you have received a stamp proceed to (B) the Deutsche Zollabfertigung in building (D).
6 Collect and fill out German road tax form.
7 Go next-door to counter (4) on level (C) to KASSE.
8 Pay road tax in deutschmarks.
9 Leave office and report to German Border Guard (with green uniform) and get stamp.
10 Report to Austrian Border Guard (with grey uniform), SHOW PASSPORTS, LAUFZETTAL and ROAD TAX and [what the hell] get another stamp.
11 Report to German guard in sentry box (brown uniform), present Laufzettal, which they will retain. Show passports and road tax.
12 When OK'd, proceed through border.

13 If form incomplete or stamps missing, return to counter (A) and start again.

Simplicity itself.

As you can imagine, this little pantomime can take quite a bit of time. On one such occasion, after being away for 30 minutes because I didn't get stamp (B) in building (D) and had to go back to counter (A), I returned to the bus, got on the microphone and announced in all seriousness: 'I'm sorry it took so long, everyone. I accidentally mentioned the war, so they made me wait.' Most of them believed me.

One of the very few good things Adolf Hitler gave the world (besides wonderful material for 'Fawlty Towers' episodes) was the autobahn, or freeway as we call it—even if it was conceived for the sole purpose of moving German armies from one side of the country to the other. Today, to the obvious delight of white-knuckled businessmen in Porsches, BMWs and Mercedes (what's the plural of Mercedes?), there's no speed limit on quite a few of the autobahns. Although drivers are *advised* to keep below 130 kph, some are more than happy to cruise along at no less than 200. There was never any danger of frightening the passengers with Porsche-like speed on the old deckers. They barely (and rarely) made it past 80. When they did, not only was there the usual deafening noise, but the whole bus would shake uncontrollably, sending cups, plates and bodies flying all over the place.

Coaches, on the other hand, were legally limited to 100 kph. If the speedo went past the 100 mark, somewhere out of the dashboard would come a continuous high-pitched beeping noise. All the drivers seemed to have developed rather selective hearing when it came to this noise. On one occasion my driver, who was just breaking the century, kept the beeping going for over half an hour. Finally it had become so excruciatingly grating that I screamed, 'Chris, can't you hear that?!'

'Hear what?' he replied innocently.

'That bloody beeping noise.'

'Oh sorry, I didn't know it was doing it.' For five minutes there was silence, then: 'Beeeeeeeeeeeeeeeeeeeeeeeepp!'

Just think how annoying people's habits can become when you have to share a bedroom or bathroom with them, and multiply that effect by ten.

Not long after entering Germany we'd pass a sign pointing off the autobahn to the town of Ausfahrt. I'd tell the passengers Wilhelm Ausfahrt was the instigator and spiritual leader of Germany's unification in the 1800s and that many towns in Germany are named after him. As the kilometres passed by, so too would signs for the town of Ausfahrt. By about the tenth sign for a lovely hamlet of that name, a passenger would finally say, 'Gee, there's a shitload of towns called Ausfahrt.' I would usually wait a few hours before explaining that Ausfahrt is actually German for 'Exit'.

The whole of the Ruhr Valley seems to be criss-crossed with autobahns. In fact, the area has more motorways per square kilometre than anywhere else in the world. Where do they all go, I wonder? They seem to have autobahns to get onto autobahns, which eventually take you onto another autobahn, around the loopy bits (there seem to be a lot of them) and back to where you started. But as soon as you manage to leave the autobahn and head into the Rhine Valley, you can't help but be hit by its sheer beauty. It may be an over-hyped tourist trap, but every inch of the Mittel Rhine, which takes in 129 of the Rhine's 1320 kilometres, is the stuff of which postcards are made. The densely wooded, steep gorges are punctuated by terraced vineyards and magnificent castle after magnificent castle.

Driving along the banks of the Rhine, we'd pass through the fourteenth-century village of Bacharach—named after Burt, I'd tell the passengers—until we'd eventually arrive in Boppard, one of the many immaculate villages along the Rhine, full of half-timbered and gabled medieval houses. Waiting for us among the many cruise ships lining the mile-long promenade would be our Josef Weinhard cruise ship. Well, we hoped it would. One morning we arrived five minutes late, only to see our boat chugging away up the Rhine. The Germans will wait for no man (or tour group). The whole sad saga had begun after a mild panic at our Amsterdam campsite when a girl couldn't find her best friend. I said, 'She's probably picked up for the night', to which her virtuous friend snapped back angrily, 'No, she wouldn't do that.' Eventually we found her with Geoff—Fred the bar owner's son—looking very much as if she'd done what her friend said she wouldn't do. Her fellow passengers thought it was all hilarious until we missed the boat, but normal service was soon resumed. After a quick conversation between the cruise office and the boat, we raced down the Rhine in the bus and were picked up at the next town.

Always on hand at Boppard, to greet us on the gang-plank, was Captain Josef himself. You knew he was a real captain, 'cause he had a beard. Without the beard, he would have been a dead ringer for Captain Stubing, who definitely shaved far too often to be a real captain. Before arriving in Boppard, I would coach the passengers to bolt up the stairs to the open deck at the front of the ship (or the bow, or yardarm, or whatever the hell it's called). This is the prime viewing position and I'd warn them that the indomitable German tourists would try to get there first, even if it meant pushing us over, stamping all over us and shoving the weaker of us in the river. I'd explain that the German tourists are always easy to spot because the males of the species invariably have moustaches and chequered pants.

Now don't get me wrong. I think the German folk are normally a friendly, helpful, jovial bunch. It's just that when you put them in any form of a queue, they go stark, raving mad. I was once standing in the queue for a ski-lift in Switzerland during the German school holidays, so naturally the place was full of expert queue-jumpers. I was getting pushed and shoved and stamped on and kicked when, just off to the side, I heard an Australian accent. When you're surrounded by Germans, strine stands out like a German tourist without chequered pants, so I pricked up my ears. This young Australian bloke had turned to the German behind him and enquired politely, 'Excuse me, do you speak English?'

'Yes, yes!' the German answered enthusiastically.

'Good, then get off my FUCKIN' skis!'

I have long suspected that the Germans do a course at high school on how to push their way to the front of a queue, simply because they're so damn good at it.

The Brits on the other hand love to wait in line. You could gather a few friends together in the middle of an English town and just start a queue leading nowhere in particular. Within minutes there would be at least ten people standing behind you. And, gosh, do they queue neatly, unlike the Germans who form something akin to the queue for the last lifeboat off the *Titanic*. Another time at the snow (this time in France, during the English school holidays), I was on a particularly busy ski run queuing for a T-bar. The problem was that although the Brits were queuing two abreast, the run was so busy that the queue reached halfway up the *piste*. The Brits all around me seemed totally unconcerned that you'd get less than half a run before you had to join the queue again.

The Germans always seem intent on getting the best possible position, whether it's at the beach, the pool or a border crossing prior to invasion. And they'll get up ridiculously early to do it. After seeing the very crowded but breathtakingly beautiful Hanauma Bay in Hawaii, I decided to go back early the next day and have the beach to myself. I hired a moped and left at seven in the morning, knowing the first bus from Waikiki didn't leave till eight. I arrived at 7.30 to find the car park empty except for a couple of cars in the far corner. I was looking forward to being the only person snorkelling in the crystal clear waters among the vast array of brightly coloured fish, but it was not to be. As I filled out the hiring book for snorkel and fins, I noticed there were already fourteen names above mine for that morning. And—this is true—in the column marked 'Nationality', every single one had written 'German'. Plus there were already a dozen or so extra people with moustaches and check pants on the beach. They can't all have come in two cars, I thought. Some must have left their hotels at two o'clock in the morning and damn well walked.

With my passengers well versed on German queue etiquette and employing a few well-placed elbows of their own, we'd score the front seats on the boat. The passengers would then try to fight their way to the front of the queue for the bar, but they could forget that. When it comes to beer, there is no way on earth they would get in front of the Germans. They'd trample their own grandma to get to beer, if she didn't trample them first.

Through the boat's tinny speakers we would get a prerecorded commentary by Captain Josef himself. First he spoke in German which, through the tinny speakers, sounded unsettlingly like an excerpt from the Nuremberg Rallies of the Second World War. Then came his own English translation, which went something like this (to be recited in a Germanic monotone): 'Cuming up on ze left iz Burg Katz und next to dis iz Burg Maus, vitch said in Inglish is und cat und a mouse. Bose ver made in ze four-teens century. Ze reason for ze name iz ze two castle owners fought so often…like ze cat und ze mouse. Ha ha! Burg Katz voz mades by Count Vilhelm ze second Von Katzenellbogen vitch iz very funny…because it means in Inglish ze cat's elbow. Ha ha!' And so it went on.

I shouldn't really take the piss out of Europeans speaking English. I mean they're a darn sight better than us Aussies, who'd be lucky to know seven words in a foreign language. Most Europeans speak near perfect English. But I'm sorry, when the exception comes along I can't help myself.

I found this full-page ad from the German tourist board in an Australian travel magazine. It featured a stunning photo of a half-timbered house on the Tauber river in Rothenburg. Next to it, in huge type, was the copy:

'Germany's nicest places and buildings date back to when there were good old days. Magnificent stately homes and spine-tingling robber barons' castles hold hands with mediaeval towns. They draw one to a trip through Germany, where centuries are at home.'

I can't speak for you, but that certainly makes me want to pack my bags and jump on the first Lufthansa flight to Germany, where centuries are at home.

Back to our good captain who, in between bursts of less than animated commentary, would play Germany's gift to the music world—well, besides Bach, Beethoven,

Handel, Schubert, Brahms and Wagner. *Dickebacken Musik* ('fat cheek music') is nothing more than lots of tubas, bass drums and a room full of very drunk Germans singing at the top of their lungs. These joyous little polkas have touching romantic titles like 'Dich Grosse Säugling' (which has nothing to do with a sagging horrible penis but simply means 'you big baby'). The best thing of all was that you could buy a tape called *Captain Josef's Rhine River Party Time* at the bar. As Captain Josef himself so eloquently put it (every ten minutes): 'If you are enjoying zis music, you can buy my *Rhine River Party Time* tape vitch includz all zee nice songs you haz heard today.' The Germans could have used these tapes, and probably did, to torture Allied troops into spilling their country's greatest secrets. A few hours of that and I think I would have handed over my own mother for medical experiments.

Although I'm sure only a German could love it, not all *Dickebacken Musik* is entirely homegrown. On my first visit to one of the huge beer halls at Munich's Oktoberfest, I was watching the Germans swinging their beer steins in time to the *Dickebacken Musik* when they all suddenly went absolutely ga-ga. They jumped up on their seats and began swinging their fraus around, squealing with delight. The oompah band had started playing that German classic by John Denver (whose original surname was, after all, Deutschendorf), 'Take Me Homes to Country Roat'. I never did find out where Vest Wirginia was though.

By the end of the 90-minute cruise, some passengers would have somehow managed to get totally rat-arsed.

One time I had to stop a very intoxicated young guy from singing along to 'Roll Out The Barrel' with words of his own invention. They went something like 'Roll out the gas chambers, roll out and gas all the Jews'. As a tour leader, I really think we should have been allowed to whack passengers across the back of the head. Hard.

Some passengers would spend most of a 28-day trip in a beer-induced haze. (Usually less than half a dozen out of the 42 passengers.) They would tend to sit at the back of the bus, happily singing along to Cold Chisel songs. To be perfectly frank, I liked them. They were never too much trouble. Except for the odd moment, anyway. They didn't badger me with hundreds of annoying questions; they only ever asked one: 'Where's the bar?' And they were always the first to put their hands up to help unload the bus (or to lift some local's car off some narrow street and onto the footpath so we could get the bus through). Most of all, they were always good for a laugh.

Curiously enough, every trip seemed to have the same passengers. There would be the half-dozen bogans pissed at the back of the bus; two straight girls in glasses who sat at the front of the bus and asked stupid questions all day; the boring fellow that no-one spoke to the whole trip; the quiet girl who, all of a sudden on day fourteen, stripped down to her underwear, threw up on the bus and slept with the driver; the history buff who cross-examined me during my spiels ('Wasn't it 1378?'); and always just one odd nationality, like a Ukrainian or a Venezuelan, thrown into the mix. As tour leader I had to empathise with them all. One minute I'd have to be a bogan, then a history buff, then a Venezuelan.

Our first night in Germany was spent at Camping Platz Freidenau in St Goar, run by Herman the German. I'm not joking, that is what we called him to his face. Herman was (and hopefully still is) your stock standard German. He had a moustache (there must be a law in Germany stating that at some point in your life you have to grow a moustache—I think they have the same law for Italian women), he always wore check pants and he worked bloody hard.

During the day he'd run the campsite, taking bookings, collecting fees and so on. He'd also do work around the campsite, like putting up a new toilet block or restumping the main building. At dinner he'd be in the restaurant, cooking plates and plates of his scrumptious Jaeger schnitzel. He was also the waiter, and afterwards he'd clear the tables and head straight to Herman's bar. There he'd serve drinks, put on silly hats, which the Germans seem to find *incredibly* funny, and even down quite a few Jaegermeisters (a schnapps that tastes like the cough mixture your parents had to prise open your jaw to make you swallow). Herman would dance and crack plenty of those oh-so-wacky German jokes, and be the last to leave at some ungodly hour in the morning. At 6.30 the next morning, while my usually-glassy-eyed passengers and I were getting our act together for an eight o'clock departure, Herman would be in the kitchen cooking up serve after serve of bacon and eggs. What really had me stumped was when he found time to see his wife. Before I go any further, I should tell you his wife, Ursula, was a former Miss Germany and an absolute babe. I kept meaning to volunteer to fulfil any marital chores of the intimate kind, as Herman seemed unlikely to ever have time to fit them in. Just to help Herman out, of course.

Herman was one of the nicest people on the road. He would bend over backwards to help you (that's why I thought it would be nice of me to reciprocate with his wife). On one trip we left Amsterdam a day early to be in St Goar in time for 'Rhine in Flammen', a truly dazzling fireworks display for which all the lights of the town are turned off. Hundreds of rockets and flares light up the whole sky and pour out of the turrets of the Rheinfels castle high above the town. The whole shebang ends with a thousand giant candles sent floating down the Rhine. We weren't even booked into Herman's, but after a phone call that morning we arrived to *Jaeger Schnitzels mit Pommes Frites* already set out for us in the dining room. The minute we finished, Herman jogged us all down to the best vantage spot to see the fireworks on the banks of the Rhine.

As we were leaving early one morning on another trip, my rather clumsy driver decided to take out Herman's restaurant balcony with the top of the double-decker bus. Oh shit, I thought, but a calm Herman came out and simply said, 'Oh, vell.' By lunchtime he would probably have had it fixed and be already halfway through re-channelling the Rhine.

Next stop after St Goar was a 'hypermarket', which is essentially a faaaaaaaarking big version of a supermarket. Europeans love these mini-cities and will spend a whole day wandering aimlessly up and down the 328 aisles. They (the hypermarkets, not the aimless Europeans) sell everything and anything. I can just imagine Frau Hilda telling her husband, 'I'm just popping out to ze supermarket *mein Liebling*, to get some *Bratwurst und Sauerkraut*. Do you vont anysink?'

'*Ja*. Carn you get me *ein* four-berth caravan, *ein* pack ov rice boobles, *ein* pneumatic drill *und* forty litres ov beer?'

Wertkauf is one of the major chains of hypermarkets. The one we shopped at, just outside the city of Karlsruhe, is apparently the biggest in Europe. The car park itself is as big as Luxembourg. We would tend to do enormous shops, buying enough to last five days. With three meals a day for 40-odd people, we'd easily fill five or six trolleys. The cook would have prepared a list which we divided up between the cook, the driver and myself, each with our small group of helpers who were on cooking duty. The passengers, as part of their 'European experience', were rostered on to peel potatoes, wash dishes, clean the bus and help with the cooking. So the rosterees for that day became our shopping helpers, while the rest of the bunch managed—after 45 minutes in a supermarket full of everything you could possibly ever buy—to come back to the bus with nothing but beer, Coke and potato chips.

I knew of one driver who would try his very best not to take the passengers anywhere near a hypermarket for the whole trip. You see, he didn't want them to buy any beer. He'd buy slabs of the stuff himself, usually cheap shite from France called 33, in little cans worth about forty cents each. (Actually, they weren't *worth* anything like that, but that's how much they cost him.) He'd then resell them to the passengers for a dollar. He had his own fridge plugged into the electrics of the bus. When we pulled into a campsite in sweltering 32 degree heat, he'd make a killing. He was very organised and had a sheet of paper taped to the lid of the fridge with the passengers' names on it. Every time they took out beers, marks were put against their names. Every couple of days he would walk around and collect great wads of cash.

More amazing still, he would get his mum in Australia to send over large bags of ten-cent pieces—he'd make her go to the bank for this—that he used in German cigarette machines. As he regularly proved, an Australian ten-cent piece is exactly the same size as a German one deutschmark coin, worth about a dollar. So he'd buy packets and packets of cigarettes—not to smoke himself; he didn't smoke—to sell at a slightly reduced rate to the passengers. Again, he made a killing. The result of all these fiddles, I believe, is that he's just recently bought a $400 000 house in Sydney with the proceeds. Not bad, eh?

The money for food came out of a 'food kitty', which might be something like £5623 for a four-week trip. As tour leader, I would have to spend exactly that amount, not one pound more or one pound less. There was always plenty of money and the passengers ate like kings. Except,

I have to admit, on one or two occasions. Once I had only twelve passengers for a five-week trip, and on the last day I had promised them homemade hamburgers on the barbie. Checking my remaining funds—and the price of mince meat in Holland—I realised they would be lucky to get one burger between four of them. But, with a bit of ingenuity (and a packet of the Dutch equivalent of Weet-Bix), I made enough for two hamburgers each. By breaking the Weet-Bix up, softening them in a bit of water and mixing that mixture with the mince, I managed to make a large pile of big patties that the passengers devoured with cries of, 'Hey Brian, these are *great* hamburgers!' Which was lucky, as rule no. 10 states: *Maintain an acceptable standard of food.*

Every cent, rappen, pfennig, lira, centime and groschen had to be accounted for with some sort of receipt. I made the terrible mistake on my first major trip of letting my driver talk me into buying 48 large cans of beer during our supermarket shop. I would generally have a different driver on each trip, but for some unknown reason I did quite a few trips, including my first, with one driver: the tall, bronzed, handsome and charming (in a nice-sleaze-bag type of way) Kiwi, Kevin Kelvin. Or, as I told the passengers to call him, Coach Captain Kevin Kelvin. Kevin loved life on the road more than anyone I knew. He was always happy and never complained. It probably had something to do with the fact that he bonked himself silly most nights and found it quite easy to talk tour leaders into buying him beer. Admittedly it was only his second year, so he was still fresh. I'd meet drivers on the road who had been driving for up to twelve years. Quite a few of them had what was known as ODS (Old Driver Syndrome) and whinged and complained constantly. For Coach Captain Kevin Kelvin, though, nothing was ever a problem. We got on really well. As long as I kept him supplied with the amber fluid. However, this didn't come cheap. Coach Captain Kevin Kelvin assured me it would be alright, but there among all the grocery shopping, smack in the middle of the itemised supermarket docket, was '48 Bier'. The office promptly deducted the 84 deutschmarks from my pay at the end of the trip.

You couldn't get away with just buying beer on impulse. Beer in German is *bier*, in French it's *bière* and Italian it's *birra*, so it's easy to spot on a receipt. But I soon discovered there was a more subtle way to buy beer and thus go undetected. One time in a supermarket in Amsterdam (one we hadn't used before), I was standing with my cook, Heidi, at the checkout with our two-trolley-load of groceries when we both noticed the gentleman in front being handed his *non-itemised*, price-only receipt. Heidi and I looked at each other, smiled and headed straight back down the aisle. Fifteen minutes later we returned from our separate shopping sprees. I had beer, shampoo, a new toothbrush, some socks and a twelve-pack of 'anti-baby condoms' (yes, that's what they were called).

Our sheer and utter delight at this small coup stemmed from the simple fact that we got paid sod all for doing our actual jobs. A week's wages could just buy a two-course meal and a nice glass of house red in your basic run-of-the-mill Parisian restaurant, so even the smallest perks were gratefully seized upon.

We would try to shop as quickly as possible. I always thought it a tad unfair for passengers to spend what little time they had in Europe wandering around deli sections of supermarkets trying to find sliced mortadella. I, on the other hand, love deli sections in supermarkets. I'm fascinated with all the different cheeses, meats, stuffed olives and other delectable little tidbits, and can spend hours just drooling over them. The German delis, however, seem to be predominantly stocked with *Wurst*. And boy, do the Germans love their *Wurst*. There's *Bratwurst*, *Knackwurst*, *Kalbswurst*, *Blutwurst* (*Blut* is blood, erggh!), *Bauernwurst* and *Schweinwurst*, but my favourite is Munich's own *Weisswurst*. This, by tradition, should only be eaten between midnight and midday. So, after a night on the Löwenbräus, there's nothing better than waking up to a *Weisswurst* for breakfast. Oh, by the way, did I tell you *Weisswurst* is traditionally made from calves' spleens and brains?

I can speak reasonable conversational German. I mean I can't hold deep discussions on the socio-economic ramifications of unification, but I'm fairly confident getting by. One time I walked up to the large frau in the deli section—I think being large is a prerequisite for the job, but it might just be a consequence—and ordered '*Ein Hundert und Fünfzig Scheiben auf Schinken, bitte.*' She looked at me with total disbelief for a second and proceeded to give me 150 grams of ham. I had asked for 150 *slices* of ham (which is only two days' worth for 40 people). '*Nein*,' I said, '*ich möchte ein Hundert und Fünfzig SCHEIBEN auf Schinken.*'

Since she was staring at me in disbelief, I resorted to charades and eventually to plain old English and then plain old shouting: 'ONE HUNDRED AND FIFTY SLICES! SLICES!' Grumpy that I'd wrecked her nice simple job, where the most slices she'd ever had to count was probably about ten, she counted up my 150 *Scheiben* and mumbled something in German to her large colleague, which I think must have been something like, 'He must be harbouring at least 50 illegal immigrants in his basement.'

There was a little money-saving trick involving the fruit and vegie section that I'm proud to say I made up myself. The official procedure was to fill a bag with, say, apples and put it on the scales, press the button with the little picture of an apple on it and a sticker would appear with the weight and price, which you would then stick on the bag. But what I would do, and teach the passengers to do, was to grab a bag, put five apples in it, weigh it, get the sticker and—looking around to make sure no men in jackboots were watching—put another ten apples in the bag. This would be done with all the fruit and vegie shopping, and I was always totally amazed that the checkout fräulein wouldn't even blink an eye at an overflowing bag containing no less than fifteen apples when the price shown couldn't have been for more than four.

The fun part was trying to find your way out of the hypermarket, as the interior was equivalent in size to Tasmania. You could be walking down aisle 193 when all of a sudden you would come across a restaurant in the middle of the 892 varieties of apricot jam. And with true German efficiency, there would be trolley bays painted on the ground for parallel parking your trolley while you went inside for *Wurst* and *Sauerkraut*. Being the absolute rebel that I am, I parked my trolley across a line and, even worse, didn't parallel park. Sitting inside eating my *Wurst*, I have to admit I was a tad nervous but a little exhilarated at my blatant and dangerous flirtation with German high crime. Would I get a ticket, be dragged out by the police or simply taken outside and shot? Luckily for me a nice law-abiding German citizen wheeled my trolley into its proper, law-abiding parallel position.

When we finally got clear of the place, we'd use a combination of physics and sheer brute force to try and fit six trolley-loads of shopping into an already full bus. Then we'd be off, with the passengers munching on something like *Wammerl mit Schnittlauch* flavoured chips. I didn't have the heart to tell them it meant 'pig' stomach with chives'.

On one trip I had two real yobbos aboard who had already caused me lots of angst. They had got very drunk and very lost in Amsterdam. It was the first night of the trip and we waited almost two hours in the bus park for them to turn up. The buggers finally turned up at ten the next morning (remember the canal bikes incident?). Anyway, they were both almost wetting their pants at the prospect of buying cheap German beer (and lots of it) at the hypermarket, and bolted straight inside to the enormous beer section as soon as we arrived. They returned to the bus with two huge cartons of bottled beer and were over the moon that each bottle had only cost the equivalent of about 70 cents. Not long after we arrived at our campsite in Switzerland later that same day I walked over to the lads, who were already well into the beers. Now I love German beer, unquestionably the best in the world I think, and I consider myself a quasi-connoisseur, but I hadn't ever seen the brand of beer the lads were drinking. 'Can I have a look at one of those?' I asked. When I read the label, it is no exaggeration to say that I fell on the floor with laughter. The two beer-drinking yobbos had just bought 48 large bottles of *non-alcoholic* beer.

Leaving Karlsruhe, we'd soon be back on the autobahn heading south, and within minutes we'd be on the outskirts of the Black Forest. I find the comings and goings on Europe's motorways fascinating, with cars and trucks from every corner of the Continent at times seeming to outnumber local cars. Each car would have their country ID sticker on the back of the car (by law, on German roads, every car and truck must have one) and Chris, a driver, and I would take pleasure, albeit a rather sad one, in racking our brains trying to figure out where FL or SF cars came from (FL is not for Finland, it's Liechtenstein, while SF is Finland: go figure). Or, even harder, trying to figure out what state or city they came from. In countries such as Germany, Italy and Switzerland the first two or three letters on the licence plate denote the area they come from.

'That's Hanover,' Chris would say.

'No, I think you're wrong. It's Hamburg.'

We were very easily amused.

Truckloads (not to mention ferryloads) of trucks criss-cross the continent every day. You would see a Finnish truck laden with, well, whatever Finnish people make, in the middle of Spain; or a Turkish truck rushing an urgent delivery of fezzes to Holland. Whenever we saw, say, a Norwegian truck in Italy, either Chris or I would say, without fail, 'Fuck, they've come a long way!'

One afternoon, in the middle of a long drive down the autobahn through the Black Forest, a group of girls at the back of the bus attracted the attention of an uncommonly handsome young German truck driver. He would drive right up to the back of the bus, with only metres separating them, and the girls would smile, giggle and wave a lot. They made a sign on a piece of paper which simply read, 'HELLO, HOW ARE YOU?', at which he smiled and raised his thumb to indicate that he was in good health. One of the girls approached me at the front of the bus and said, 'Brian, you speak German, can you write out a sign for us?'

'Yeah, sure, what do you want me to say?' She thought about it for a second and said, 'Ohh, something like, "We think you're pretty cute. Do you think we are?"' I considered for a moment while I figured out the translation, then wrote neatly in German, 'WE HAVE BEAUTIFUL BREASTS, YOU MAY KISS THEM IF YOU LIKE'. She took this to the back of the bus, held it up to the window and our handsome truck driver moved within centimetres of our bus to read the sign, burst into laughter, raised his thumb again and nodded his head vigorously in agreement.

The girls thought this was a hoot and asked me for another. The next one read (in German of course), 'MY VAGINA IS WET AS I THINK ABOUT YOU'. Our handsome truck driver's eyes lit up and he immediately swerved all over the road, forgetting for a second that he was actually driving a twenty-tonne truck. A few hours later the girls were squealing with disgust when I told them what I had actually written.

I love languages and tried, with the emphasis on tried, to speak a bit in each country we visited. German was the only language I had actually studied, and I have to admit I used to have quite a chuckle at some of the words I discovered. For example: *Flugzeug* means aeroplane, but the literal translation is 'flying thing'. I can just picture two wacky German scientists early this century:

'So, vot shall ve call zis sing?'

'Vell, it flies.'

'*Ja.*'

'*Und* it's vell, a thing.'

'*Ja.*'

'Vell, it's a...flying thing.'

'Perfect!'

But wait, there's more. A *Feuerzeug* is a cigarette lighter, but literally means 'fire thing'. The word for toy, *Speilzeug*, means 'play thing'. A tool is a 'work thing' (*Werkzeug*). Even better, however, is my favourite, the *Luftkissenfahrzeug*—

the hovercraft. Believe it or not, the literal meaning of that catchy name is 'air-cushion travelling thing'.

What is even funnier is that I once watched an Elvis Presley film dubbed in German. I was transfixed. It was bizarre. He spoke in German, but with a real southern drawl. The songs were in English, though. The Beatles on the other hand sang in German (early on in their career they recorded a couple of songs aimed solely at the German market) but they didn't quite have the same appeal: '*Du Lieb Dich, Ja, Ja, Ja...*' Oh, those wacky Germans.

The major city and capital of the Black Forest is Freibourg which, like many other German cities during the Second World War, was blanketed with bombs. But the remarkable thing about Freibourg is that it was bombed by the Germans. In 1940, the *Luftwaffe* completed quite a successful bombing raid on a city they thought was in France. Now, fair enough, Freibourg is only about twenty kilometres away from the French border and it may have been cloudy, but there's a rather large river called the Rhine dividing the two countries.

My one and only visit to Freibourg was also a disaster.

I was leading a charter (that is, a trip where one group charters the whole bus and sets their own itinerary, going where they like for as long as they like) with a group of rather obnoxious Americans who wanted to visit at least 127 cities in three weeks. I couldn't believe head office would even contemplate agreeing to such a preposterous marathon.

The Americans had planned a flying visit to Strasbourg in France, but I told them we would have to do two border crossings and fight our way through the lunchtime traffic of what is quite a big city. So I suggested Freibourg instead. Now I hadn't been there before, but it was just off the motorway and, according to my guidebook, you could climb the stairs to the top of the town's *Münster* (cathedral) and be 'rewarded with incredible panoramic views of the Black Forest'. Our driver dropped us off in front of the cathedral and agreed to pick us up 45 minutes later. Everything seemed to be running perfectly, but when we walked around the cathedral looking for an entrance we couldn't find any way in. I apologised profusely to the passengers, explaining that there was no suggestion in the guide that it could be closed, so it must be under repair or something. Across the road was a sign for the *Altstadt* (old town) and, having just read that 'Freibourg is one of the loveliest historic towns in Germany, particularly the medieval splendour of the *Altstadt*', I suggested they take a quick look around. I too wanted to see the 'original and compelling medieval atmosphere', so I bolted off ahead of the group. Walking through the narrow cobblestone streets, I suddenly stumbled into a brightly lit square and there, standing in front of me, was Freibourg's most famous landmark, the 700-year-old and 120-metre-high spire of the town's *Münster*. Oh, shit! I'd taken them to the wrong one. I just stood there, my mouth agape. Looking at my face, passers-by probably thought that I'd just shat in my pants. I stood and stared, wearing an agonised expression, for some time.

By the time I got back to the bus it was too late. I was hoping in vain that no-one had seen the rather large and obvious *Münster*. Red-faced, I tried to explain: 'Hey, you knew I hadn't been here before. We drove in, saw that huge church and...and...' God, I was embarrassed. I finally knew how those German fighter pilots felt.

Half an hour past Freibourg we crossed the border into Switzerland and four days later we would return to Germany, straight into the heart of the Bavarian Alps. Full of fairytale castles and picture-book villages with 'Oh, aren't they cute!' wooden houses, this is the Germany of tourist office posters. On top of all that, there are lots of rosy-cheeked moustachioed Bavarians hopping around in leather lederhosen (which must give you terribly sweaty bollocks on a summer's day). And running through this idyllic scenery is the ever popular *Romantische Strasse* or Romantic Road. We would catch about the last 40 kilometres of this 420-kilometre route on our way to the roaming tourists' Holy Grail: Neuschwanstein Castle.

Inspired by the incredible success of the now famous *Romantische Strasse*, which carries over a million visitors a year, the German tourist board decided to transform a tourist-free patch in the middle of Germany into the Fairytale Road, featuring sites that starred in the tales of the Brothers Grimm. You can visit Little Red Riding Hood country, the woods of Hansel and Gretel, even Snow

White's castle. Tourists loved that one, too. So the German tourist board decided to make some more.

Now there's the *Wein Strasse* (Wine Road), the *Deutsche Alpen Strasse* (German Alpine Road), *Burgen Strasse* (Castle Road), *Edelstein Strasse* (Gem Road), *Fachwerk Strasse* (Timbered Building Road) and the *Ferien Strasse* (Holiday Road). Then, just when you thought they couldn't get any sillier, last year they opened up the *Spargel Spitzen Strasse* (Asparagus Road), showcasing the marvels of asparagus farming in north-eastern Germany. Next year marks the launch of the *Luftkissenfahrzeug Strasse*, which will take you on a spine-tingling journey from hovercraft to hovercraft along Germany's Atlantic coast. Actually, I made those last two up, but I wouldn't be at all surprised to see them in a German tourist board brochure in the near future.

Just about every coach tour known to man (well, those that do Europe, anyway) includes a visit to Neuschwanstein Castle and, by the look of the coach park, most of them can be found there at the same time. I counted 47 coaches one day, which is close to 2000 people from coaches alone tramping around mad King Ludwig's castle. And mad he was. Mad as a hatter. He came close to bankrupting his family (who had ruled Bavaria and banked the profits for over 700 years) with his building frenzy, which peaked at Neuschwanstein, a monument to his teen idol, Wagner. (It's a bit like Prince William building a huge castle and monument to Britney Spears.) It took seventeen years to build, and most days Loony Ludwig sat in his home below watching every brick being laid through his telescope. Ludwig would sit down to dinner with busts of Louis XIV and Marie Antoinette (they even had their own place settings). The dining table was built over a trap door so it could be lowered and reappear laden with food, just to make sure he didn't have to see anyone. Ironically, the gigantic folly that almost bankrupted a state now makes shitloads of deutschmarks for the Bavarian government.

On a few occasions I joined the masses for the long, steep climb to Neuschwanstein, and it is impressive; but, to be honest, five or six times is enough. On my other ten or so visits, I'd try to find something to do besides hanging around tacky souvenir shops full of personalised floral fridge magnets, with the only names left seeming always to be Adolf, Hermann and Eva, or spending half a week's wages on a *Wurst*. It was on one of my aimless strolls that I stumbled upon an immense and pristine lake, where I noticed rowboats for hire.

Trying my 'I'm a tour leader, how about a free boat?' trick worked (I once got into some monument in Thailand by flashing my tour leader card, even though my trips didn't go within 10 000 kilometres of the place). Soon Chris, the driver, and I—after rowing around in circles for fifteen minutes arguing over whose fault it was that we couldn't go straight—headed out into the middle of the emerald-green and perfectly still lake. When we finally stopped smashing our oars uncontrollably into the water and actually looked around for a minute, we realised we were surrounded by the most stunning vista. From where we floated we could see only two other rowboats, and even they were far enough away to look like toys. On one side of the lake were sheer rocky cliffs and on the other, rising dramatically from the lake, was a mass of green pines. Poking out from the very top, bathed in sunshine, was Neuschwanstein. It was perfectly splendid and impressively silent (which was particularly nice since Chris was the one who drove with the continuous *BEEEEEEEEEEEP*). You could easily forget the tour buses, the fat Americans, the camera-happy Japanese, our own beer-swilling brood and the hordes of Germans in check pants. We sat there, not talking, just taking in the view. Breathing clean, crisp air, with the warm sun on our backs. At times like this I'd think to myself, God, I love this job.

Glancing at my watch, I suddenly realised it had taken us 40 minutes to get to where we were, and the bus was due to depart in ten. There went rule no. 12, which states: *Punctuality. As a tour leader there is NO EXCUSE for being late.*

I would hassle, beg and even threaten the passengers to get them back to the bus on time, and I'd chastise those who were late. Yet here we were, stuck in the middle of a lake, with no chance in hell of making it back to the bus, even if we were members of the Olympic rowing team. By the time we reached the shore we were an absolute mess, covered in sweat and water from our flailing oars. We sprinted back along the dirt trail to the bus park and, puffing and panting, we stepped onto our bus twenty minutes late, to the inevitable barrage of abuse. Every time a passenger was late back to the bus for the rest of the trip I could only sit in silence. The most I could do was casually look at my watch and frown a lot.

The Bavarians consider themselves Bavarian first and German second. The blue and white flag of their former Wittelbach monarchs, of whom Loony Ludwig was the second last, is everywhere. Most cars will not only have their (D) sticker for Germany (Deutschland, as our checkpanted friends call it), but a (BAY) for Bayern (German for Bavaria). In fact Bavaria didn't become part of Germany until 1871.

Here's an astonishing fact for you. The mighty German nation is yet to celebrate its first hundred years. Australia, which achieved federation in 1901, has been a nation longer. Germany was a nation from 1871 to 1945, and then from 1990, when the Wall came down, to now. In the seventeenth century, the area that is now Germany was made up of over 350 *separate* ruling states, each with its own army and government.

But enough of that. Let's talk about beer.

The one and a half million citizens of München or Munich, the capital of Bavaria, relish beer almost as much as my passengers did. A local Munchkin could base his or her whole day around beer (and some probably do: I would). To start the day, it's beer for breakfast. You can see businessmen at the bars in train stations knocking back a *Weizenbier* (wheat beer) before they hit the office where, if they like, they can down a few more, since beer is recognised in Bavaria as food (liquid bread). By law you could, if you fancied, polish off a couple of Spätenbräus over the accounts. For those who don't work, there's always the 'Beer Faculty' at Munich University. They probably learn about the science of beer-making and stuff, but I'd rather stick to my romanticised version of three years spent sitting around getting pissed off your head, eating *Wurst* and dancing to the 'Birdie Song'.

After work, it's off to one of Munich's 400 beer halls or Europe's largest beer garden, the Biergarten Chinesischer Turm, where you could sample one of the 5000 varieties of German beer from over 1300 breweries. And on the way home you could always buy a beer from a drink machine —with Löwenbräus sitting among Cokes and Fantas— on the side of the road, or just drop into McDonald's for a McBeer.

If that's not enough, you could wait for the biggest and most indulgent beer festival in the world: the Oktoberfest. What started in 1810 as an engagement party for the Bavarian Crown Prince Ludwig (not the loopy one) and Princess Therese Von Sachsen-Holdburghausen (try saying that after a few Hackenbraus) proved so popular—almost the entire population of Munich attended—that they thought they'd do it again the next year. Today, over 150 years later, you too can drink copious amounts of beer, sing *Olé! Olé! Olé! Olé!* and throw up.

Obviously, our first night in Munich had to be spent at a beer hall. The Mathäser Bier Stübl, the world's largest, has seating for just over 5000 people. The place is basically a huge barn full of lots of checked pants. Smack in the middle is a large rotunda with the oompah band all in lederhosen, pissed off their heads, playing that oh-so-bloody-cheery polka music.

Some of our groups in the past had caused so much havoc in raping and pillaging the beer hall that our company was not welcome there. So when I booked our table, it would be under a pseudonym. I took great delight in coming up with bogus tour names. We'd arrive at our long trestle tables to find the handwritten cards saying something like 'Reserved for SCROTUM TOURS'. The Germans had no idea and the passengers would find it ever so amusing. On one occasion I called us simply Vomit Tours—after an above-average incidence of alcohol-induced chucking on the trip—and arrived to find six large cards on the tables neatly marked 'WOMIT TOURS' (the Germans pronounce W as V).

I would have prearranged the passengers' food and drinks order before we arrived, so when the Frau, who looked like a cross between Arnold Schwarzenegger and the Queen Mother, arrived I'd reel off 'Thirty-two *Mass Bier* (a *Mass* is a whole litre), eight *halbes Mass* (half a litre for the wusses), two Cokes and a lemonade (if Bavarians had control of their own borders, they probably wouldn't let non-drinkers in), 28 chicken and chips, fourteen *Wurst* with chips, and one mixed salad' (there's always one mixed salad, just like there's always one vegetarian on a trip). Our robust and usually grumpy Frau would return clutching all 32 *Mass Biers* and a few plates of chicken and chips as well.

Even the passengers who'd been extremely quiet and shy throughout the trip up to then would soon find themselves standing on the chairs with their pants down by their ankles singing that famous German folk song 'Take Me Home, Country Roads' by the end of the evening. And it would be looking as if Womit Tours might not be welcome back at the Mathäser again. But that's alright. Next time I'd visit I'd be with, say, BONKING TOURS.

The unfortunate side of all this, of course, was that I would have to get 40-odd loud, out of control and very pissed people back to the bus—a particularly challenging proposition when, in most cases, I was a bit how's-your-father as well. It was like a tipsy collie rounding up sheep. One moment I would have them all together, then one would stray off to the toilet or back to the dance floor to dance with the pretty German girl he'd just met (if he was sober, he'd realise she looked like a female version of Sergeant Schulz). Then I'd have to try and get them all in the bus. That is, of course, if the bus was there. One time we returned to find it gone. The bus—I'm talking about a huge bus here—had been towed away. Coach Captain Kevin Kelvin had parked it illegally, so he had to go off and retrieve it. In typical Kevin style he simply shrugged, smiled and said, 'Oh well.' When he couldn't find a spot to park earlier, he'd parked in a 'no parking' zone near the entrance to the beer hall. Coach Captain Kevin Kelvin was hungry and there was no way he was going to miss his pork knuckles and chips.

Finally all aboard, the passengers would scream and sing on the 30-minute journey back to Camping Platz Thalkirchen, then spew out of the bus (some literally) and run amok through the campsite.

In probably half the campsites we stayed in, the crew would be given a caravan, hut or room to sleep in. After spending most of your life on the road in tents, this was pure luxury. The last thing I wanted to do after checking into reception, going to the shop to order bread, and fielding questions about the intricacies of the laundry, phones and, more importantly, where to buy beer, was to put up a tent and blow up a lilo. Quite often I'd just sleep in the empty luggage bins under the bus. Late one night I was comfortably tucked up into my real bed in my caravan, just about to doze off into blissful slumber, when I heard a few of my passengers walking by outside making an awful racket. A very large security guard—I could tell how large he was just by his voice—came over and said, 'Can you pleaz be quiet und now go to bet?' To which one of my most delightful passengers charmingly replied: 'Fuck off, you Nazi *cunt*!' I lay in bed rehearsing my responses to the interrogation that now seemed inevitable: 'No, sir, I've never seen him before in my life.' The security guard, who probably looked like a cross between Arnold Schwarzenegger and Arnold Schwarzenegger, stayed surprisingly calm (he must have got called a Nazi cunt quite often) and asked, 'OK, who iz your tour leater?' The same passenger replied, 'I am, I am!' Oh shit, it looked like I would have to get out of bed before World War Three started. But Arnie just said, 'Come on now, get to bet pleaz,' and, in a fit of uncommon commonsense, my passengers slunk back to their tents.

During Oktoberfest, Camping Platz Thalkirchen was the scene of nothing more or less than full-scale, no-holds-barred debauchery. The whole campsite would be full, predominantly of Aussies and Kiwis. The Kiwis always seemed to easily outnumber the Aussies. For a country of just over three million people about as far away from Munich as you could possibly get (besides the South Pole), the size of its Oktoberfest squad was very impressive. From my observation, most of the population seem to relish the senseless destruction of brain cells, and would willingly travel to the other side of the world to participate.

Touring Kiwis are easy to spot. Just before they leave the fair shores of 'New Zullund', they are given a pair of black tracksuit pants with three white stripes, a green Steinlager T-shirt and a pair of 'Jandals' (thongs or flip-flops). I believe it's their national costume.

Munich Oktoberfest could easily be renamed 'Munich beer-induced bonking fest'. The amount of coupling that went on was incredible, with passengers and crew alike going at it in shower blocks, in tents, under trees, against trees, in trees and in the bus. Rule no. 5 of the crew manual stated: *Crew must not engage in sexual activity on board the bus with passengers or fellow employees.*

You'd be pretty lucky to find any crew member who hadn't broken that rule. Coach Captain Kevin Kelvin broke it almost daily.

There's something in the air at Oktoberfest—well, besides all the beer and schnapps—that makes people do the strangest things. Six million people visit Oktoberfest every year. Most of them get pissed off their heads and dance to 'Roll Out the Barrel'. It's frightening.

I remember seeing a young Kiwi fellow from my bus, out of his national costume and his head, standing in the middle of the campsite, naked. Sticking out of the eye of his penis was a lit cigarette. He was just standing, or rather rocking, there. What the hell was he doing? The New Zealand version of the cigar lady's act, perhaps?

Two of my passengers had been to Oktoberfest the year before—some go year after year until they have no brain cells left at all. They had been travelling on unlimited Eurail tickets and, when they couldn't find accommodation in Munich, they took rooms in Innsbruck, Austria, less than two hours away. They would commute each morning to the beerfest grounds, and back again to Innsbruck at night.

Have you ever caught a train home and, in your tiredness or just plain drunkenness, fallen asleep, missed your stop and woken up five stations later? Well, these guys did better than that. Having got pissed out of his brain and lost his mate, one of them had jumped on the train, fallen asleep, and not only missed his stop, but missed the whole bloody *country*. He'd left Germany, slept straight through

Austria and woken up in Italy. He opened his bloodshot eyes to find a conductor waffling to him in Italian. But things got even more bizarre. He stumbled off the train and there, fifty metres up the platform sitting on a bench, was his drunken mate. He'd done exactly the same thing.

I could never understand all the Aussies and Kiwis going to the Hofbrauhaus Hall at Oktoberfest. It's totally full of Aussies and Kiwis. It's a German beerfest, for God's sake! If you're interested only in getting blind with your own kind, you can just go to the one-day cricket at the MCG. In Munich, it's much more of a laugh hanging out with the wacky Germans. Except when you almost get killed...

My own brush with sudden death happened at the Häckenbrau Hall. I was there with a bunch of other tour leaders and drivers and I'd had a couple of beers—OK, a bucketload of beers—and had got up to stand on the long, bench-style seats (as you do). I then promptly fell backwards onto a table occupied by the East German weightlifting team, knocking over three beers in the process. One of the lifters, who looked like he ate nothing but steroids, grunted at me and ordered me to buy them lots of beers. I didn't want any trouble and, more importantly, I didn't want to die, so I bought them three beers each, three whole chickens and gave them my sister's address and said, 'She's yours.'

Oktoberfest was a sort of moral no-man's-land where all the normal rules were suspended, and we crew members, like the locals, preferred taking advantage of all the loose behaviour to taking offence.

With so many buses in the campsite, tour leaders could make themselves quite a bit of extra beer money by pimping. If a crew member from another bus bonked one of my passengers, they had to pay me one pound's rental (in local currency, of course) for the use of one of my passengers. This, of course, could work the other way: quite often another tour leader would say to me, 'Brian, you owe me one pound. Your driver bonked one of my punters last night.' I spent piles of cash supporting Coach Captain Kevin Kelvin's lustful exploits.

Sometimes, though, a driver would find himself a constant companion for the whole trip, who would be affectionately known as his DAF. As well as the make of coach we used, this was an acronym for the endearing term Driver's Available Fuck. I have a good friend who was a driver and now proudly tells everyone that he married his DAF (and I don't mean the bus).

A tour's first morning in Munich, after the fun and frivolity of the Mathäser beer hall the night before, would begin with a long wait in the shower queue. Feeling horribly hungover I would stand next to smelly foreigners—who I was sure smelt worse than me, but probably smelt the same—and wonder, sometimes aloud, what the fuck people were doing in there. You see, to take a shower, you had to buy a shower token from reception. The tokens gave you only a certain amount of time, which was always a little less hot water than you'd need to wash yourself properly. I was always paranoid about ending up with a head covered with shampoo and only ice-cold water to rinse it off with. Mind you, if you wanted a 'Thomas the Tank', it was definitely a two-token shower. Well, that's what I was *told*, anyway.

The owners of Thalkirchen had an odd sense of humour. Engraved in big bold letters across the token was the word GAS. In my tasteful way, I'd tell passengers these were left over from the Second World War. Sometimes I think being a tour leader warped me beyond repair.

Our first stop for the morning would be the Dachau Concentration Camp: Germany's first, opened only 45 days after Adolf Hitler came to power in 1933.

If the showers didn't sober people up, this soon would.

One time, while I was standing inside the compound explaining to the group the various things they could do and see, a very pale and severely hungover young lad put his hand to his mouth, took a few wobbly steps across to the nearest thing to lean on, and threw up. I don't think I have ever been so embarrassed. He'd just thrown up all over a large monument to all the Jews killed in the war. It's very hard not to feel that you are personally responsible for your passengers. Whenever they did something stupid or irresponsible I always felt embarrassed, like a parent who couldn't control his children. Sadly, I didn't have the luxury of being able to give them a good whack across the back of the legs. And boy, did I feel like doing it sometimes.

While the passengers trudged around Dachau, the crew would be next door at the Krone Hypermarket, home to possibly the world's best grilled chickens. We'd buy about a dozen whole chickens—'YES, I want twelve, TWELVE chickens!!'—for the passengers' lunch at our next stop, the complex built for the 1972 Olympics. Coach Captain Kevin Kelvin could devour a whole chicken in less than five minutes and still have another serve when we stopped for lunch. One time, being a bit tight on food kitty money, I told Kevin he couldn't have a whole chicken to himself. He seemed to take it alright until the drive to the Olympic stadium. I was halfway through my spiel about Shane Gould and Mark Spitz's achievements in the pool when Coach Captain Kevin Kelvin opened his side window and screamed out at the top of his lungs to a car stopped in front of him, 'Outta the way, you *fucking* German *arsehole* or I'll kill you!!' I don't think that was really in the spirit of rule no. 15: *Show a positive attitude towards local people.*

On another occasion, while driving into the Olympic stadium, I spotted a billboard for a U2 concert on the seventeenth. 'Hey, that's today! U2's playing tonight,' I said to Chris, my driver. 'Do you wanna go?'

'Yeah, if we can.'

'Why not? I'll try to get some tickets.'

It was perfect. I got tickets for myself, Chris and my cook, and even better, that night was a free night for my passengers, so they could run amok without me. We caught the train to the stadium, singing 'Where The Streets Have No Name' loudly and badly all the way in. But when we arrived at the station for the Olympic Stadium, it all seemed a little bit quiet. Still in high spirits, though, and now singing 'Pride (In The Name Of Love)', we walked upstairs out of the station, only to find the outside of the Olympic Stadium totally deserted. 'What the hell?' I said. 'What's happening?' I was now totally confused. Then I looked at my tickets. Yep, the date was right, the seventeenth—only it was the seventeenth of *July*. Today was the seventeenth of *June*. My passengers of course found it very amusing and for the rest of the trip kept asking, with large cheeky grins on their faces, for U2 to be played on the bus.

After lunch I'd troop the now weary bunch into Munich town for a walking tour. I would show them Munich's great treasures, including the Deutsches Museum, the largest and most impressive museum of science and technology in the world and home to the first automobile, an 1886 Benz. I would recommend the Alte Pinakotek, the largest and most important gallery in Germany, with works by Rembrandt, Rubens, Botticelli, Raphael and Leonardo; or if they preferred modern art, the Neue Pinakotek's wonderful collection of Van Goghs, Monets, Manets and Gaugins.

Without a moment's hesitation, most of the group would head straight to...the Hofbräuhaus for the afternoon, and proceed to pour copious amounts of beer down their throats. I went there once and was chatting to an unusually young and very attractive Fräulein serving beer who told me that in her whole shift that day she had not spoken to one German customer. The whole place was chock-full of tourists.

Back to the galleries briefly. In the twentieth century, the Nazis definitely take the cake in the art theft stakes. Goering, who thought himself a bit of an expert, and Hitler, the ex-art student (who must have thought to himself, 'I can't paint very well so, fuck it, I'll invade Poland'), were planning to build the world's largest art gallery. Krakow, Paris, Florence, Ghent, Amsterdam and many other smaller towns were robbed blind. Trainloads of stolen booty poured into the Reich, which is why their museums have such fine collections (a bit of a waste really, as most of the tourists are in the beer halls).

Personally I love Munich. It's one of my favourite cities. The Germans like it, too. In a survey a couple of years ago the German folk were asked which German city they would most like to live in. The vast majority chose Munich. For a start, it has the best beer in the world. It was the Bavarians who started the German purity law (Rheinheitsgebot) in 1516. That law dictates that only water, hops, barley and yeast can be used in the making of their fine brews. I help them out there as much as possible. I'm always tasting their beer—as much as I can drink—just to make sure that every beer is pure.

Munich has the cleanliness and organisation of a German city and the *joie de vivre* you'd find in Italy or France. While we're on the subject of cleanliness, you just have to have a look at Munich's U-bahn (underground train service). It's spotless. You could eat your dinner off the platform. (I haven't actually seen that done, but I have seen a passenger *empty* his dinner *onto* the platform.) The train service is free—at least, it's an honesty system, which for someone as dishonest as me makes it free. I made the mistake of telling one lot of passengers that I'd never bought a ticket and had never spotted an inspector in my travels. So of course two passengers came back at the end of the day with 50 deutschmark fines for not having a ticket. They weren't very happy with me, I can tell you. Imagine trying to do the honesty system thing on, say, the London Underground. They would be lucky to turn over £6.55 for the whole day.

I've got an old school friend, a director of TV commercials, who now lives in Munich. He had no idea I'd scored a job as a tour leader. In fact, he didn't even know I was in Europe. I was planning to call him while in Munich on my training trip, but I was running around like a headless chook trying to gather information as part of a practical exam. I had only three hours to find post offices, toilets, banks, train stations, telephones and consulates, and find out when they opened and closed, how much it cost, who was on first and what was on second. However, as I was scrambling down Kaufinger Strasse trying to find out what time the Uruguayan Embassy opens on a Saturday, who should I bump into but the only person I knew in a city of one and a half million people, my friend Matt.

On each subsequent trip I would have a night off in

Munich and Matt would take me to different beer halls, where we'd eat *Wurst* and drink ourselves pretty well senseless. On one occasion he couldn't come out at night so we met for lunch the day before at the Viktualien markt, an open-air food market smack in the middle of town. In among all the *Wursts* and cheeses are long tables under chestnut trees, full of chubby, check-panted Germans knocking back a beer or seven.

Anyway, six hours and five litres or so of beer later, our lunch finally ended and I had to meet 42 sober passengers in Marian Platz to take them to the Mathäser beer hall. I was a blithering wreck. As soon as we hit the beer hall, I was already on the table singing and dancing to 'The Hokey Pokey' and trying to pick up the Frau who looked like Sergeant Schultz. The passengers hadn't even taken their first sip. I think it was a good night. Well, that's what I was told, anyway.

Yet another one of my favourite places to wander in Munich is Englischer Gartens. You only need to walk a few hundred metres into Germany's largest park, past a cluster of thick trees and into a large open clearing to find yourself totally surrounded by stark-bollock-naked Germans. They just love to get their kit off and will swagger around with their willies and titties swinging all over the shop. On one stinking hot summer day, I took a couple of passengers with whom I'd become quite matey to have a wee look and grab a beer at the Chinesischer Turm Biergarten. As we began our second litre of beer, I suggested we strip off and join the nudey Germans.

So, with large steins of beer in hand, all three of us took our old fellas for a walk. I kept thinking just how grand it would be if a bunch of my female passengers walked towards us. As we left our clothes behind—and any chance of covering ourselves—we sauntered aimlessly through the park with our willies a-wiggling. After walking for ten minutes I noticed a lot of people with their clothes on. Looking around, I saw that no-one else had their clothes off—we'd walked out of the nude area into a normal part of the park. We were totally surrounded by nice and respectable families walking their dogs.

On our way back, I spotted the man-made river that runs through the park. A channel just a few metres wide runs off the Izer River and flows straight through the middle of the nude section. Discarding our steins—we could have got hung, drawn and quartered for that or, even worse, made to listen to lots of polka music—we oohhed and aahhed as we jumped into the ice-cold water that flows straight from the Bavarian Alps, and slowly floated downstream. It was a splendid idea. On the banks of the river all the nudies were sunbaking, and as we slowly drifted by we had ourselves a good look. The spreadeagled fräuleins didn't seem to care who was looking, and we didn't mind either.

I couldn't understand why other fellows weren't doing the same as us until we stepped out of the icy cold water. Then it became abundantly clear. My dick had disappeared into my body. It was no bigger than a jelly bean. Luckily for me, my friends had the same problem. As we sheepishly shuffled back to our clothes, I was hoping more than ever that we didn't bump into any of our female passengers. There would go any chance of picking up for the rest of the trip: 'Stay away from him, he's got the most incredibly small penis.'

Leaving Munich behind, with our bellies full of beer and *Wurst*, it would only be a short drive down the auto-bahn to Austria, where we could drink more beer and eat more *Wurst*. But first it was back to Switzerland for yet more beer and, as a nice change from *Wurst*, cheese, cheese and more cheese.

CHOCOHOLICS CHEESEOHOLICS & COWBELL CLUBS

Wank.

Now are the Swiss taking the piss, or what? We would scarcely be inside the country when we'd come to a huge green and white sign pointing to the town of Wank. And that's just one of the many delightful names for towns in Switzerland. There's Cunter, Lustdorf, Schatt, Schupfart, Buttishol, and of course you can't miss Mount Titlis. And I swear I'm not making any of them up. These are the same people who, when you sit down for lunch, have the daily special—which is usually three courses chosen by the chef—marked in big, bold letters on the menu as

Tageshit. Now I don't know about you, but that would turn me off anything the chef had to offer, however delectable.

The first couple of hours in Switzerland were spent on motorways, that sort of no-man's-land where you could easily be in Germany, France or Italy. It's not until we turned off the autobahn and began to make our way towards Thunersee, and spotted the odd so-chocolate-box-picture-perfect-it-looks-like-it's-made-for-tourists wooden house and some cows with those bloody noisy cowbells, that you'd really notice you were in Switzerland. Then, all of a sudden, we'd come around a sweeping bend and drive straight into a Toblerone commercial. The Swiss Alps. They truly are an astounding sight, with the shimmering grey and white peaks against the brightest, deepest-blue alpine sky. I never got tired of looking at those snow-topped giants.

As we began our ascent into the Bernese Oberland on one trip, an American girl sitting by the window said to her boyfriend, who was asleep after a rather big night at Herman the German's, 'Chad, you have to look at this view.' Without opening his eyes, he groggily replied, 'Take a photo of it, and I'll look at it when we get home.'

The Hong Kong Chinese, on the other hand, who don't seem to like the sun on their faces, will close *all* the curtains in the bus and look at a photo of the Alps in their guide books. I'd say to them, 'You're missing the most stunning scenery in the world, why don't you open the curtains?' They'd pull the curtains back for about two seconds, glance out, close them again and go back to looking at a photo of the Alps in their guide books.

We'd eventually wind our way up into the heart of the Alps and into the glacier-cut Lauterbrunnen Valley. Now I've travelled to many a beauty spot in both hemispheres, but the vista up the Lauterbrunnen Valley that looks towards the mighty Eiger, Mönch and Jungfrau peaks is the most breathtakingly beautiful I've ever seen. You could close your eyes, point your camera anywhere, click away, and end up with a perfect postcard shot. The village of Lauterbrunnen is hemmed in by towering cliffs on either side, and wispy threads of spray cascade hundreds of feet down onto the valley floor. All up, 72 waterfalls pour into this, the greenest of green valleys. It's like stepping into a jigsaw puzzle—you know, the one everyone had as a kid, with that hard-to-believe-it's-so-beautiful Swiss scene. Well, this *is* that scene.

The highest and most well-known waterfall in the valley is the Staubach Falls, which splashes down just across the narrow valley from the campsite. I would tell the passengers that, at six o'clock on the dot every night, the Swiss turn off the waterfall to save water. An hour or so later there would be over a dozen passengers standing outside, looking at their watches, waiting for it to be turned off. At one minute past six they'd ask, 'What's happening? How come it's still going?'

'I don't know, that's really odd,' I'd say. 'The Swiss are always on time.' Some people will believe anything. You probably believed it, too. Come on, admit it.

The town of Lauterbrunnen is like Main Street, USA in Disneyland. It's spotless. It's swept *hourly*, and the locals actually *use* those doggie poo bins, which have neat little piles of plastic bags attached to the side. There's no graffiti and no rubbish; at the petrol station there's not one drop of oil on the concrete. It's like no-one lives there at all, and the place never seems to change. I found an old postcard from the early sixties and the village looked exactly the same. If someone wants to build a new house, they don't just have to follow strict guidelines on its appearance and the materials used in its construction. Using long, thin pieces of wood, they actually have to construct a framework to the exact dimensions of the house on the spot where the real thing will (sorry, *may*) eventually stand. There the dummy will stay for a month or so while the rest of the village decides whether the planned dream home will block their views, or simply whether they really feel like having a new house in their village or not.

Before arriving at camp, I'd ring the site manager, Heidi—it seems everybody in the Swiss mountains calls their first girl Heidi—from the border. When we arrived, we'd find two crates of Rügenbrau beer (or three crates if I was with Coach Captain Kevin Kelvin) lying in the ice-cold stream next to the main road.

And not one beer would be stolen.

Mind you, that's hardly surprising. The Swiss mountain folk are an honest bunch. During the two winters I spent living in Lauterbrunnen, we'd never lock the door to our little house. At times there would be over 10 000

Swiss francs in cash just sitting on our kitchen table and we still didn't lock the door. In fact, I honestly don't know if we even had a key. One afternoon I was stupid enough to leave my thousand-dollar pair of skis leaning up against a wall at the train station. It only occurred to me the next morning that I had left them there. I was sure they'd be gone. Nevertheless, I trudged slowly down to the station and there, up against the wall exactly where I had left them, were my skis. If I'd done this in Australia, they'd already have been in the pawn shop.

The shops in Lauterbrunnen (like those of most Swiss towns) all close for an hour or so for lunch. The Swiss folk just shut the door and go home for their big midday meal of cheese and stuff, leaving their valuable wares out on the street. The co-op supermarket would leave laundry detergents, big bottles of Coke and whatever else right on the footpath. If they did that in Australia, the whole lot would last a few minutes—or maybe only seconds—before everything was loaded up in the back of Davo's ute.

What makes all this honesty so very hard for tourists to fathom is that so many things in Switzerland are so mind-bogglingly expensive. It's only the real necessities of life that are cheap: beer and chocolate.

The Swiss make a rather fine drop of beer and you can buy big bottles of the stuff for a lot less than in Australia or England. But the real temptation to overindulge is the chocolate.

The Swiss gave the world milk chocolate. In 1875 Daniel Peters mixed Henri Nestlé's condensed milk with chocolate and discovered an even more popular export than cuckoo clocks. All the pioneers of Swiss chocolate-making have familiar names: Phillipe Suchard, Henri Nestlé, Jean Tobler and Rodolphe Lindt. But while a fair bit of their product reaches our shelves, the Swiss themselves are the biggest chocolate eaters in the world. Not that it's terribly surprising that they get through 11.3 kilograms of the stuff per person per year. Swiss chocolate is totally addictive. I never used to eat that much chocolate until I lived in Switzerland. Soon I was salivating as Easter approached at the thought of metre-high bunnies made of Lindt chocolate. Ever since, I've seized every chance I get to shovel mountains of the stuff down my throat. I'm just lucky I haven't turned into a big fat bastard covered in pimples. Yet.

Unfortunately, other things were not so cheap. I once made the monumental mistake of dropping two rolls of film at the tiny photography shop in Lauterbrunnen. I had to mortgage my parents' house just to pick up one lot of photos. If I ever win the lottery, I'll go back for the second lot.

Never, *never* ask for a second set of prints.

In a great little bar in Wengen (the village above Lauterbrunnen) one night, one of my passengers walked up to me looking pale and shocked. He told me the small glass of bourbon and Coke he was holding ever so tightly in his hand had just cost him sixteen Australian dollars. The poor sod made it last two hours in a brave but doomed attempt to get his money's worth.

Another time, hiking above Grindelwald in the neighbouring valley, we'd been tramping for a couple of hours up steep and dangerous mountain paths when, in the middle of nowhere, we came upon a small shed. A stocky, bearded Swiss man stepped out and asked us for three francs (about three dollars) each to continue our hike.

No wonder they're not interested in shoplifting.

Chris Von Allmen, who owns the campsite, married his best friend's sister. She turned out, handily enough, to be another Von Allmen. This is nothing strange in Lauterbrunnen. Take a quick walk down the main street and you'll find the butcher is Hans Von Allmen, the vis-à-vis supermarket is run by Urs Von Allmen, the Silberhorn Hotel is owned by Chris Von Allmen—a different Chris Von Allmen. Once I rang 'enquiries' in Switzerland from Australia trying to find Chris-from-the-camping-ground's phone number and was told there were no fewer than six Chris Von Allmens in this town of just over seven hundred people. The neighbouring campsite is owned by Fritz Von Allmen, and it goes on and on. It's like Tasmania gone mad. Not that I think a lot of interbreeding goes on, but it is, you have to admit, just a little suss.

Up in the village of Mürren (which is full of folk named Feuz), I walked one day into a cosy restaurant/bar called the Stäger Stübli and soon discovered it was the favourite hangout of the local farmers and railway workers. Inside, sitting around large tables, was a bunch of what looked like slightly imperfect clones. They all had large foreheads, wispy moustaches and beady brown eyes set too close together; and they all wore identical black woollen ski hats with pom-poms. I was just waiting for someone to strike up a banjo.

But perhaps the most frightening thing of all is that all these chaps have very large guns at home. How would I know? Because every Swiss man has a gun at home, and the Swiss army can muster 680 000 odd people (and I mean that quite literally) in less than 48 hours. For a country that's been neutral for over 400 years, they're a paranoid lot. Every bridge and tunnel into the country is loaded with explosives so they can be blown up to block entry by land. The motorways are inset with giant metal plates that can pop up to stop oncoming tanks. They even paint their runways the same way as motorways to confuse any air attacks. And all that to protect a few cows and cheese factories.

People will tell you the Swiss are a dull and serious bunch but, to be fair, when you get to know them they really are quite jolly and friendly. To be accepted as one of them, though, is a different matter to breaking the ice in the local bar. Barbara, an ex-New Yorker, married Henri Von Allmen (funny that) and had been living in Lauterbrunnen for thirty years. She told me she still didn't feel accepted by the locals.

When a foreigner living in Switzerland applies to become a Swiss citizen, a government private detective will follow them around for a few weeks to check out where they live, work and play. If they pass that test, the village or area where they live will then vote on whether they deserve to be Swiss. There are thousands of foreigners who have been living and working in Switzerland for decades and have still not been accepted as Swiss citizens. Probably not boring enough yet.

Switzerland doesn't have the monopoly on supposedly boring people, though. One of the 'joys' of tour leading was that I had to socialise with everyone on the bus. That could mean sitting in a bar with someone called Ian, talking about quantity surveying and stamp collecting for two hours and trying to act interested, when all I wanted to do was have a few beers and try to become a close friend of the cute Danish girl I'd seen on the dance floor earlier in the night. Seriously, it was important to spend time with the 'quiet' passengers. Some shy loner could go the entire trip and hardly have a conversation with any of the other passengers. Yes, some were painfully boring, but I made some good friends as well, quite often inviting them to join me for lunch—it did get a bit tiresome at times, trying to talk drivers into coming into town with me.

Up until I became a tour leader I couldn't think of a worse way to see Europe than on a tour. But now I can see how good they are for a range of different people. There's the shy person who would really have a lot of trouble meeting other people if they travelled by themself. The naïve traveller—there seems to be lots of these—who thinks people from Switzerland are Swedish, for example. There are the people who can only take up to four weeks' holiday at a time and really, there's no better way to see a lot of Europe. And finally, of course, there are the people who just want to party and pick up a bonk or seven and don't really care where they are.

It wasn't only the passengers who didn't mind the odd ale: the local mountain folk drank almost as much as some of the guys at the back of the bus (but not quite as much as Coach Captain Kevin Kelvin). The locals start work early and stop at ten o'clock for a 'coffee' (which we all know means beer). Then it's home for plates of cheese and chocolate and beer for lunch, and at four they down tools to meet the lads for a few more down at the local Stübli. I'm amazed. With their dietary and drinking habits, you'd expect a bunch of sloths who die young. Instead, the Swiss have the longest life span in all of Europe. I met this old geezer who had only started skiing five years before. He was *83*! At the ripe old age of 78, he thought, What the fuck? I'll take up skiing. Christ, I'll be lucky to make it to the letterbox at 83, if I live that long. It must be the mountain air; I can't think of another reason.

The first thing we'd do when we arrived at camp was set up the cook tent. Somewhere among the 42 people's backpacks, twenty tents and 42 air mattresses (and all the hash they brought from Amsterdam) packed in the bins under the bus, there was room for a large cook tent. Along with, I might add, three trestle tables, 40 fold-out stools, three huge gas burners, two large wooden boxes and crates and crates of beer.

One of the many things I learned during my time as a tour leader is that there's no word for cook tent in Cantonese. In fact, there are quite a few English words that don't have a corresponding Cantonese word. When Hong Kong Chinese chartered a bus, they brought along their own interpreter/tour leader. I would do my spiel first in English then Tour Leader No. 2 would get up on the microphone and say something like, '*Jing jang low yow ying* cook-a-tent *jing low jang ling* walk-king-tour *low ling jow yang* pack-ed lunch *lang ling jow jing* free-time.' It's a little bit like the Danes, really. They don't have any really meaty Danish swear words apparently, so they'll go, '*Flop de flur hi hi de* fucking *de blur de flop* shit *flop de* fucking *flur.*'

The cook tent was the domain of the cook and he or she knew exactly where every pot and kernel of corn was and would shoo any stragglers out of their beloved cook tent. However, they couldn't watch over it in the wee hours of the morning and it would often be used for late-night liaisons because the passengers couldn't really take their newly acquired friends back to a shared tent. Every morning as I took my toast off the trestle table, I couldn't help thinking about bare bums bouncing on top of it.

A trip to Lauterbrunnen would not be complete without the spectacular journey to the Jungfraujoch on the highest and most expensive railway in Europe. And *faaaaaarck*, was it expensive! Not only expensive to build, but expensive to ride on. It's alright for the hordes of Japanese that swamp this part of Switzerland, because the train fare was about the same price as a can of Coke in Japan. For travellers of other nationalities, it was roughly equivalent to their first mortgage. Even the Daily Special—you had to catch the five past seven train in the morning—was close to one hundred dollars. Try telling the average bus passenger that's a good deal. Their minds just kept repeating: 'Thirty beers or train ticket? Thirty beers or train ticket? Thirty beers or train ticket?'

I must concede that I am something of a miserable bastard when I have to get up really early. And five-thirty, to me, is really early. One morning my alarm went off and I grunted and swore as usual, left my nice warm bed in my nice warm cabin and stumbled in the dark to the showers. I did the toilet thing, shaving thing, got dressed, then walked back into my cabin, glanced at the clock and saw the time. It was 3.20. The driver from another bus who had reset my alarm thought this was funny. This guy's nickname, by the way, was 'Wrong Way Rowan' because on his first ever trip he took a right turn instead of a left as he left the bus yard on the outskirts of London, and went on his way to Edinburgh instead of Dover.

Meanwhile, back in Lauterbrunnen, I'd walk the passengers through town to the tinker-toy-train station to catch the 7.05 tinker-toy-train. And I *mean* the 7.05. Werner Von Allmen, the toy-train station master, would come out of the station at 7.04. He'd look at the clock, wait till the second hand was two seconds away from the twelve and blow his tinker-toy-whistle for the train to pull out at exactly 7.05. One day the train was three minutes and twelve seconds late. The driver must have either lost his job and been sent to do eighteen-hour shifts down the mines or, as I suspected, committed suicide. It would not have been something he could simply live with.

The buses are the same. Herman the German, or his identical twin, would sit waiting in the bus outside the train station just staring at the digital clock, counting the blinking of the little dots so he could pull out at *exactly* five minutes past the hour. For the locals, it's a job for life. Herman Von Allmen would drive this bus ten kilometres up and down, and up and down, and up and down the valley for the rest of his life.

Everyone has a job. To be honest, though, I'm not sure what some of them actually do. Take those fellows I'd seen in the Stäger Stübli in Mürren, for example. I'd see them standing by the railway tracks in big orange coats. And that's it. They'd just stand there. I never actually saw them do anything. You might say that sounds quite like a certain class of labourer all over the world, but the thing is that these blokes earn the equivalent of a CEO's wage in Australia for their particular brand of just standing around.

Here's an astonishing fact. Around 25 years ago, in the whole of Switzerland the total number of people officially unemployed was 92.

On the train, Ulrich Von Allmen would walk through, wearing what looked like a secondhand Gestapo uniform, punching everyone's tickets. He too would be doing this till he was at least 65. Since the statistics showed little chance of him dropping dead any earlier, he'd probably still be doing it when he was 98, if he wasn't skiing, of course.

These same cog-railway trains are used in winter to transport the skiers up to the ski-runs. I can tell you it's a lot more pleasant sitting on a soft chair in a lovely warm carriage than having a T-bar up your arse in a blizzard. And warm is putting it mildly—stifling bloody hot might be a better description—and when you open a window to get some fresh air, the local Swiss folk will mumble some incoherent babble, get up and close the window. You can hardly breathe. The train is usually packed full of people with cheese and beer from the night before streaming and steaming out of their pores. I have a theory, though. Us city folk take a trip to the country for fresh air, to escape the stale, humid, putrid air of the towns. Well, I think the Swiss mountain folk must get sick of all that fresh mountain air and look forward to sitting in the train with a bit of stale and humid putridity for a change.

The cute little wooden houses and the seemingly backward Swiss mountain folk in their check shirts are very deceiving. Inside those cute little wooden houses, you'll find the latest technology. Even the humble ski-lift passes are deceiving. What looks like a rather plain, if just a little thick, ski pass is embedded with some sort of microchip thing (I'm sorry, this is about as technical as I can get). Which means you can keep your ticket inside your jacket. When you pass the turnstile in the lift queue, it beeps, a green light comes on, an LED screen says 'Gute Fahrt' (said the nun to the vicar), and the turnstile opens to let you through. Wow, it's amazing what a bunch of Von Allmens can come up with when they put their remarkably similar heads together.

Let me tell you how safety conscious the Swiss are. The cables that hold the cable cars and chair lifts are X-rayed every year at a cost, just in the Jungfrau ski region alone, of over a million dollars. They are X-rayed for the slightest flaw, and if there is one, they'll take the cables down and sell them to the Italians. When the Italians have had them for a couple of years, they'll sell them to the Bulgarians or Romanians. Finally, when they're very near the end of their lives, that lot will sell them to the Moroccans. So if you're ever in the High Atlas Mountains and you think, Gee, it's a lovely day for a spot of skiing, just think about those cables and the much-less-remote-than-in-Switzerland chance that you'll die horribly in a ski-lift accident.

Accidents would be the last thing on our minds as the incredibly punctual, safe and expensive train slowly wound its way up out of Lauterbrunnen Valley, past the car-less village of Wengen, to the end of the line at Kleine Scheidegg. The views on this leg of the journey were the most breathtaking, with cameras going off at machine-gun pace.

Kleine Scheidegg, at just over 2000 metres, is a tiny cluster of hotels and restaurants around the main station. This is where you'd find the hotel Clint Eastwood stayed in before tackling the north face of the Eiger in *The Eiger Sanction*. The Bahnhof restaurant served wonderful, if rather expensive, food. One day, after years of frustrated salivation, I thought, What the hell, I'll have the lobster and steak. Seafood in the Alps? Don't knock it: the lobster may not have been local, but it was just divine. Even as I read the bill, and faced the prospect of sending a small amount of cash there every week for the rest of my life, I thought it was well worth it.

Expensive food is hardly unusual in Switzerland, but security problems are. Another time I was sitting outside the Bahnhof, a passenger had just sat down to his large (and expensive) bowl of spaghetti when he decided he fancied some pepper. He left his seat and within seconds a group of five black Alpine crows (Swiss seagulls, as we called them) jumped on his food and began tossing the spaghetti up in the air and onto the ground. In less than twenty seconds they'd cleared his plate. I tried to stop them, but I was laughing too much.

Because I know basic German, I would try to figure out what place names meant in English, and if I didn't know the word I could always look it up in my trusty German–English dictionary. *Lauterbrunnen* means 'pure springs', *Schützenbach* (our camping ground) means 'protected brook'. But to be honest, I'm not quite sure what *Wank* and *Cunter* mean. I couldn't find them anywhere in my dictionary so I guess they must mean, well, 'wank' and 'cunter'.

With Kleine Scheidegg, I knew *kleine* was 'small' and *Egg* was Swiss–German for corner; however, I had no idea what *Scheid* or *Scheide* meant. So out came the trusty dictionary, and there under *Scheide* was…'vagina'. Right, so the train stops at 'Small Vagina Corner', which had me wondering where the small vagina was located. Then I remembered that on the other side of the valley there's a *Grosse Scheidegg* which is, of course, Large Vagina Corner. I made a mental note to go over there one day and look for large vaginas.

Schwzertütch, or Swiss-German, is barely comprehensible to a German person. The Swiss speak a language they can't write, and read a language they don't speak. I was sitting with a German fellow in a bar once and he was trying to eavesdrop on a couple of Von Allmens talking behind us. He turned to me after listening to them for a few minutes and said, 'I can't understand a single word they say. In fact, I think they're just making it up.'

There would be a twenty-minute wait at Small Vagina Corner before we changed trains for the final leg up to the Jungfraujoch. And that's where I came across one of the most enterprising entrepreneurs I've ever met. This Swiss fellow from Grindelwald (which meant he wasn't a Von Allmen) would travel up to Kleine Scheidegg each morning with his huge St Bernard wearing a so-bloody-cute-no-dog-could-possibly-really-wear-one-of-them whisky barrel around its neck. As the hordes of Japanese waited to change trains, he'd take what seemed like hundreds of photos of the tiny Japanese folk hugging the big, drooling dog with the snow-capped mountains in the background. He'd then rush down to Grindelwald, process the shots, and be back at Kleine Scheidegg for the return of the Japanese from their trip up to the Jungfraujoch. At about twenty dollars for a smallish photo, the Japanese would gobble them up—to them the price was the equivalent of buying a postage stamp—and our Swiss entrepreneur would make an absolute killing. I figured he'd sell, maybe, a hundred photos a day, which would have added up to 2000 dollars a day, 10 000 dollars a week and around 500 000 dollars a year. Gee, that's almost as much as those fellows with the orange jackets standing by the railway lines earn. And I bet that poor dog slept in a cheap kennel outside and got fed no-name brand dog food.

The final leg of the journey on the Jungfraubahn—*Jungfrau*, by the way, means 'virgin'—would climb almost one and a half thousand metres through seven kilometres of tunnels built right into the north face of the Eiger, and took sixteen years to complete back in 1912.

Here's a bizarre but absolutely true tale for you. A few years back an Italian climber died scaling the Eiger and was left swinging on his rope only metres above the thick glass windows built into the face of the mountain as a viewing stop on the Jungfraubahn. He stayed there, swinging about, for three years. No-one could reach him. The poor bugger froze solid to the cliff face in winter and just hung about in the summer. With a pair of binoculars you could just watch him swinging about.

The steep climb and gradually thinning air—there is one-third less oxygen on the Jungfraujoch than at sea level—would take its toll on the passengers, particularly if they'd been giving the Rügenbraus a bit of a nudge the night before. One girl, who was slowly getting greener and greener, finally succumbed and threw up, with horrendous accompanying noises, right into her neatly packed plastic lunchbag. Her breakfast went all over her ham sandwiches, Mars Bar and fruit juice, much to the amusement of my passengers and the absolute horror of the Japanese.

Just out of Kleine Scheidegg, the train would pass right by a collection of pens filled with huskies and Alaskan malamutes spreadeagled on the concrete, basking in the sunshine. These canine work horses were used to pull sleds of Japanese tourists up on the Aletsch Glacier (Europe's largest) on the Jungfraujoch.

During winter, the dogs would either be snuggled up in their heated kennels or lazing about outside in the warm alpine sun. In the winter when I worked there as a ski guide, I would take my group to see the dogs—it's actually in the middle of quite a difficult black run, so only experienced skiers got a chance to see them—and we'd stop for a pat. They are very beautiful dogs. One day, wearing my *brand new* one hundred dollar Reutsch gloves, I put my hand into the cage to pat a sweet-looking dog with the friendliest eyes. Suddenly it went for my hand and tore my glove off. Another dog tried to grab it and, in the ensuing game of keeping off, it was torn into a hundred neat little pieces. I was left with one extremely useless glove and my group falling off their skis with laughter. Whenever I visited the dogs after that, I'd just throw heavy snowballs (preferably made of hard ice) at any dog that looked even vaguely similar to the little shit that ate my glove.

As you step out of the station complex at the Jungfraujoch into the snow, you are hit by the blindingly intense white light, the noticeably thin air, and the fact that it's damn cold. I'd tell the passengers to bring a jacket, but no, the know-alls would all think, Well, it was 28 degrees Celsius yesterday in the valley, I'll be right. The temperature up on the Jungfraujoch would be hovering around the −5 degrees Celsius mark, even in mid-summer.

Personally, I always felt sorry for (and, even though it wasn't my fault, a little guilty about) the passengers who spent five days of beer money to arrive at a complete whiteout. When that happened, you couldn't see two feet in front of you and, if you even tried to step outside, you'd be blown to Belgium.

But on a clear day the Jungfraujoch earns every superlative the visitors can throw at it. Standing at 3454 metres, the panorama of peaks is unforgettable. You can even see the Black Forest—a bit like the Münster in Freibourg, I believe!

Fritz Von Allmen operated a little ski-run on the glacier and, even though it was only 50 or so metres long and relatively flat, one could ski on it even in the middle of summer. On my first trip up to the Jungfraujoch, I sold the idea to the passengers and got fourteen willing participants. For twenty francs you got skis, boots and poles, and an hour falling down the hill. And, of course, as tour leader I got a freebie. I left before the group, to set everything up. I trudged through the snow to Fritz, introduced myself, and told him I had fourteen people who were going to ski. He gave me free skis, slipped me a twenty franc note, and told me to buy myself a few drinks that night (or one bourbon and Coke).

I skied up and down, and up and down, and up and down for about 40 minutes and not one passenger had turned up to ski. Fritz walked over to me and asked, 'Vhere are all your peoples?' I pointed in a vaguely downhill direction and said, 'There's one, and…arrr…another couple there. Oh, there's probably about seven or eight of them.' They were obviously not my passengers: the check pants gave them away at a glance. They were all Germans.

I skied for about another twenty minutes, with not one single passenger turning up. As I returned my skis, Fritz said rather coldly, 'Maybe next time you bring zum passengers along.' I skulked off with Fritz's twenty francs still in my pocket. He wouldn't miss it. The Swiss probably use twenty franc notes to line the bottom of their budgerigars' cages.

One of the advertised 'highlights' of the visit to the Jungfraujoch was the ice palace. I would recommend a visit to my passengers not for the actual ice palace, which was not that impressive, but to watch the Japanese tourists. Just watching the Japanese women trying to walk on the ice in unsuitable high-heeled shoes was an absolute scream. The women would be flailing around on the ice, screaming their heads off, while their husbands would stand out of reach and casually video the whole thing.

Most of the passengers would be dead to the world on the slow, chugging journey back down the mountain. As part of our 'special fare' we had to catch a train no later than midday. I was too terrified to even contemplate taking a later one; it would probably mean a five-year jail sentence.

One particularly glorious, early spring day, six of my passengers decided to walk from Kleine Scheidegg to Wengen. There was still a little bit of snow on the ground, and it seemed like a marvellous idea. While the rest of us waited for twenty minutes at Kleine Scheidegg, they began the long trek down. Fifteen minutes into our train journey, we came around a bend and a huge snowball came through the window—we could have the windows open on this leg as there were no Swiss passengers on the train—and hit me fair and square in the back of the head. Standing outside, with a gigantic pile of perfectly formed snowballs and big grins on their faces, were my guys. But we didn't cop the full force of the attack: the Japanese in the carriage next to us did. In between mouthfuls of snow, I was choking with laughter as the poor Japanese totally freaked out, trying to close the windows under a barrage of snowballs. But the sad thing is that this was the sole reason why my passengers wanted to walk down. Not for the fresh mountain air or the stunning views, but to throw snowballs at the train.

The Swiss love to walk, and there are a phenomenal 50 000 kilometres of walking tracks in Switzerland. That's like walking around the world. Twice. And each and every walking track is painstakingly marked with bright yellow signs. They will have the distance, 12.35 kilometres, and the time it takes an average person to walk it, 1 hour 17 minutes. I timed a walk one day and it was minute perfect, which meant I must be an average person. I believe the average Swiss person has sex for thirteen minutes and 22 seconds, and the only reason it takes so long is that they check their watch every minute to make sure they don't go over.

The afternoon was usually spent just lazing about doing sod all. One afternoon I was standing chatting to Chris and Henry Von Allmen in the grounds of the campsite when suddenly Henry shouted, 'Look!' From the top of the sheer cliff above Lauterbrunnen, two people had parasailed off and were just beginning their long glide down when one of the parasails collapsed into itself. It was totally surreal. The man started to scream. It was the scream of someone who was about to die. It echoed around the narrow valley and he literally just fell out of the sky, hitting the cliff face on the way to the valley floor. I'd never seen someone die before. We all just stood there until Chris softly said, '*Er ist tot*'. ('He is dead.') The other parasailer had to slowly descend to the ground, and to his now dead friend. I can't even imagine how he'd be feeling on the way down. No passengers saw it, but even they were genuinely shocked by the fact that I'd seen it. (When I think about it now, it was probably that train driver who was three minutes and twelve seconds late.)

The passengers would spend their afternoon visiting Trümmelbach Falls—a waterfall that pounds through a subterranean gorge inside the mountain—or shopping for souvenirs and the prerequisite purchase on any trip to Switzerland: a Swiss Army knife. Lauterbrunnen had a well-stocked knife shop run by the lovely Regula—isn't it a bit odd to name your daughter after your toilet visiting habits? According to Victorinox, makers of the original Swiss Army knife, there are over 100 million authentic Swiss Army knives in circulation around the world. Victorinox itself produces over 4 million a year and has over 100 different models. There's a version for just about every occupation imaginable. There's the Waiter, Hunter, Alpineer, Angler, Ranger, Camper, Scientist, Golfer, Mountaineer, Handyman, Farmer, Electrician, Explorer, Climber, Hiker and even the Picnicker. I believe you can also get one called the Mime Artist (which has nothing in it at all).

Another popular souvenir from Switzerland is the cowbell. You can buy one of these in any shape or size to take home and…and…put in the back of your closet. One passenger returned from his afternoon shopping with four rather large cowbells.

'Tim, how much did they cost you?' I asked.

'Nothing!'

'What do you mean, nothing?'

'I got them from the cows.'

Christ, he was lucky he wasn't shot. He'd jumped the fence into Farmer Von Allmen's field, run up to a herd of cows and just unclipped the cowbells from around their big fat necks.

Our 'national meal' that evening would be a cheese fondue. The Swiss just love their cheese and a traditional Swiss fondue is just that: cheese. A huge pot of bubbling Grüyere and Emmenthal cheese, mixed with white wine, kirsch (cherry schnapps) and garlic, would be served up with a basket full of stale bread bits. And that's it. That's the whole meal. Our back-seat passengers would find that a bit too much—'Where's the fucking meat?'—so we'd have fondue for a starter followed by schnitzel with chips for the main dish.

I recently went back to Switzerland with my wife. (I might add here that my wife and I got together after my life on the road. And yes, she knew what we got up to. She too was a tour leader.) She and I were invited to dinner at three different family homes on consecutive nights (strangely enough, none of them belonging to a Von Allmen). The first night we were served fondue, and just fondue. The second night was raclette, which is nothing more than huge slabs of cheese melted over boiled potatoes. The third night we were asked whether we wanted fondue or raclette, and we told them we'd just had both. We were both feeling pretty cheesed out. So we turned up and were served Alpen Macaroni, which is pasta tubes absolutely smothered with guess what? Damn cheese!

Vegetarians, on the other hand, are another story. The Swiss just don't understand them. Once I saw this happen: a girl asked if she could have a vegetarian meal and was brought out a salad with huge bacon bits in it. She said, 'I asked for a vegetarian meal.' The waiter just stared at her, dumbfounded. 'It iz, zat iz a salat.' They hadn't quite grasped the concept of vegetarianism yet.

On one trip I had just one vegetarian out of 42 people and Heidi, my poor cook, had to prepare a separate dish for this girl every night. You can imagine Heidi's delight when, about two weeks into the trip, I told her I'd spotted the vegetarian in McDonald's scoffing down a Quarter Pounder with cheese. The next night Heidi dished up a meal with meat in it and she said, 'I don't eat meat.' Coach Captain Kevin Kelvin leant over and whispered in my ear, 'I'll give her some bloody meat.' Being a tour leader, you would have to be oh-so-nice to people who in normal life you wouldn't even give the time of day to.

It's roughly a ten-kilometre drive down the valley to the tiny hamlet of Stechelberg and the fondue restaurant we patronised. One evening there were two busloads of people heading down, so the two drivers decided one of them could have a drink. They tossed a coin and 72 of us crammed ourselves into one bus. Coach Captain Kevin Kelvin lost the toss and grudgingly drove us down the valley.

The Stechelberg hotel was a quiet, family-run place where the locals met to play cards or just sat mumbling to themselves and staring into space. As you can imagine, they would be quite startled by 72 noisy foreigners taking over the restaurant. We would be shown to our seats by Rolf Von Allmen, a gigantic man with a ridiculously long and bushy moustache who, when he spoke, sounded like Mickey Mouse with a Swiss accent.

There is an old Swiss tradition that if you drop your piece of bread into the fondue, you have to buy a round of drinks. However, I made up my own tradition, which I thought was more fun. (And, anyway, just imagine someone having to buy a round of 72 drinks in Switzerland: 'Zat vill be 968 dollars, pleaz.') My tradition was that if you dropped a cube of bread into the fondue pot, you had to kiss the person on the left. I once had a group with twenty girls and two guys. Only one person dropped their bread that night. It was one of the guys. Sitting on his left was the other fellow and, without any hesitation, he grabbed him and stuck his tongue right into his mouth. The girls were horrified.

All night—and I believe they did this to get us to leave early—the restaurant would play yodelling music. Now, I always thought this was just for the tourists, along with fondues and the alpenhorn. As it turns out, none of it is.

As you've just learnt, the locals live on fondue. Alpenhorns? Each village has its own alpenhorn club and it's so popular there's a five-year wait to join. And then there's that bloody yodelling music. One morning I was catching a ride into town with Henry Von Allmen, who had a cassette playing full-on yodel-eh-hee-who music on his car stereo. I asked straight out, 'Henry, do you actually like listening to this shit?' He just smiled and nodded. And every time I went in Henry's car, he'd have a different—well, as different as bunches of people going yodel-eh-hee-who can get—tape on. I would turn it up to full volume, yodel along at the top of my lungs and then burst into uncontrollable laughter for five minutes.

I think Henry thought I was a bit loopy. Mind you,

I had nothing in the loopy stakes compared to the local cowbell club. What they do is ring cowbells. When you join the club, you start with a small bell and as you get better(?) at it, you are promoted to larger bells. The largest of them all is just monolithic. It must have come from one of those growth-hormone-fed cows in Holland. Anyway, this fellow has to hold it in front of his chest and use his knees to make it ring. A group of about fifteen of these fellows then walks in a neat line making the most horrific noise you could ever hear. Klunk de klunk de klunk de klunk. And Henry thought *I* was loopy.

After our 240 000 calorie meal of cheese, half a loaf of bread, a whole baby cow schnitzel and five kilos of chips each, most of the group would tackle a Stechelberg coffee. This was an Alice in Wonderland-sized cup filled with coffee and five different schnapps. Swiss schnapps, by the way, also doubles as lighter fluid and paint stripper. With 72 drunk people crowded into one bus and singing loudly along to Australia's unofficial national anthem—Cold Chisel's 'Khe Sanh'—it was a noisy journey back to the campsite. By the way, Coach Captain Kevin Kelvin, who had lost the toss and had to drive, skolled three quick beers as soon as we arrived at the restaurant so he didn't have to drive back after all. Cheeky sod.

Every so often, after our fondue meal, I'd walk whoever was interested, or still standing, up to the one and only disco in town, the Horner Bar. And boy, was that a happening place. The disco would have no more than twenty people in it, even on a Saturday night. There would be a dozen or so Von Allmens sitting at the bar, who would never have stepped on the dance floor in their life, except maybe accidentally stumbling across it on the way to the loo. Up on the dance floor, dancing to 'I Put My Blue Jeans On' by David Dundas or some eighties shite that made you want to kick the speakers in, would be two or three couples. The lads would be dressed in those drip-dry grey nylon slacks—not pants, but slacks—and matching grey slip-on leather shoes with that very useful chain across the top, and a body shirt. The girls would be wearing incredibly tight acid-wash jeans and dangerously high white stilettos. Their dancing would be a cross between milking a cow and stomping on ants, a form ideally suited to the next number, another great speaker-kicking classic, Kenny Loggins' 'Footloose'.

One of my guys would inevitably walk up to Herbert Von Allmen, the DJ, and ask for a Cold Chisel song.

There was another disco in town, but that belonged to another tour group. I'd just tell my passengers to sneak in and pretend they were on one of their tours. The 'Bomb Shelter', as it was and still is called, was always full of pissed people trying to get a bonk.

One day, while skiing in the winter, I was sharing a chairlift with another ski guide from Oakhall Tours, who used the same chalet that the 18-to-30s tour used in the summer. Oakhall Tours were an English Christian group, and the ski guide soon began selling God to me. He was preaching and ranting away about how Jesus was going to save me. (Maybe he could make me a better skier?) And horror of horrors, there was no means of escape, apart from jumping to my death from a great height. After ten minutes the thought did cross my mind that if I landed right, I might only break a leg or two.

I then had great delight in telling him that the room they held their (no doubt riveting) Bible readings in was used as a disco in the summer, when it was always full of sweaty, drunk and oversexed young people throwing up and fondling each other's buttocks in the corners. Meanwhile, upstairs, their perfectly made bunks would be rocking across the room, propelled by bonking eighteen-year-olds. He shut up after that.

On a decker, we would sometimes do a 'rolling start' at six in the morning. On one cold morning the bus wouldn't start. This would happen now and again because the shits would leave all the lights on for most of the night and drain the battery. So I had eight rather groggy lads, dressed only in their jocks and shoes, running up the main street trying to push-start the bus. It actually only took a few metres of pushing to get it going, but it made quite a sight as the bus spluttered up the hill with eight semi-naked men running as fast as they could to jump in the back door as it drew away. The conservative Swiss folk might have thought we were a bit strange, but at least we didn't have a cowbell club.

Push-starts were often pretty comical. The night before another one, someone had emptied the dishwashing water straight out the back door onto the ground, even though I expressly told them not to. The temperature dropped below zero that night and, of course, the slops froze solid. The next morning we had to try and push start the bus standing on what was essentially a dirty grey ice-skating rink.

Next stop: Luzern, and the world's biggest watch shop. But first we had to tackle the Brunig Pass. At just over a thousand metres, it wasn't actually the height but the steepness that the old deckers had a problem with. They would chug noisily up the mountain pass, sputtering and growling, with the driver wrestling the steering wheel all the way. Then we would descend in first gear as the driver kept his brake usage to an absolute minimum to stop the brakes overheating, seizing up and sending the bus careering off the road and down a sheer cliff face to our untimely deaths. When we reached the bottom, the acrid stench of burning brake pads was all but overpowering.

One fine, sunny afternoon, while waiting at the bus park in Nice (in France, as I'm sure you know), side-by-side with a second decker, Coach Captain Kevin Kelvin was checking and re-adjusting his brakes. This would need to be done every ten days, and the Nice bus park was always one of the major brake-checking spots.

Kevin, who was wearing his overalls and was covered with grease, asked the other driver, who was just relaxing in a deck chair at the front of his bus in his freshly washed shirt, 'Hey, aren't you doin' your brakes?'

The other bloke casually replied, 'No, I try to avoid using them.'

'What?'

'Yeah, well, it means I don't have to adjust the brakes at all for the whole trip.'

So this mad bastard was driving his bus 5000 kilometres around Europe without using his brakes. Thank God I wasn't on his bus.

Luzern sits on the mirror-like Vier Waldstättersee (Four Forest Cantons Lake), which is criss-crossed by chugging paddle steamers and flanked by two mountain giants, Rigi and Pilatus, and the less-than-ample Mt Titlis. Luzern's best-known landmark is the wooden Kapellbrücke (chapel bridge), built in 1333. Sadly, within weeks of its 660th birthday it burnt down. The ever-efficient Swiss had it rebuilt in a couple of days and tourists were none the wiser. It looked identical to the 1333 model, cobwebs and all.

But that was not what we came to Luzern to see. Our main port of call was Bucherer's, the world's biggest watch shop. Five floors filled with thousands of watches on show and for sale.

The Swiss are a smart bunch. The watchmaking industry was nearly destroyed because the leaders of Switzerland's main watchmaking companies were smugly convinced that Swiss timepieces were the best in the world and always would be. They failed to notice that their venerable little cog-wheeling watches had been overtaken by the quartz watches produced by the less complacent and very uncheesy Japanese. Stung into action, the Swiss put their heads together and came up with the Swatch. Within a few short years of its conception, the Swatch had recovered all their lost market share and then some. Today, Switzerland exports 96 per cent of watches made in the country.

And that mention of commercial canniness leads me to a small confession.

Just as waitresses at fleapits rely on tips to supplement their meagre earnings, so we tour leaders relied on commissions. Whenever passengers we had taken to a shop or demonstration bought something, we received a commission. Generally, of course, the shops were not only of a high standard but also good value. Not only that (said he, in desperate self-defence), but the commission came off the shop's profit, not out of the passengers' pockets.

In typical Swiss fashion, we'd get something like 7.23 per cent commission. When the calculations had been worked out, the watch shop could be quite profitable for me and the rest of the crew. I'd quite often walk out with 300 Swiss francs (around $300) or so.

I'd be walking around the store with the passengers and one would ask, 'What do you think of this watch, Brian?'

'Oh, that's gorgeous,' I'd say.

'Shall I get it?'

'Might as well get one each for the whole family. How many brothers did you say you had?'

But the graft, as they say, is always greener on the other side. What would make me envious were the tour buses filled with rich, fat Americans from Boise, Idaho or, even better, money-spending-mad Japanese. I was talking to one tour leader who walked out with just over $4000, which means his group had spent over $60 000 on watches in just over an hour. With just one co-operative passenger's purchase of a $10 000 Rolex, a deserving (and grossly underpaid, remember) tour leader could make $700. There was one watch there for $24 000. That's over $1000 in commission. I tried to talk my passengers into buying one, but strangely no-one seemed interested.

I would see those same tour leaders, with the rich Americans or Japanese, in the tiny country of Liechtenstein, adding thousands to their already swelling Swiss bank accounts.

Bastards!

Talking about loads of money, I bumped into 'Wrong Way Rowan' one evening coming out of the Luzern Casino with a huge wad of cash in his hand. After I had abused the hell out of him for setting my alarm to 3.00 am, I discovered he was a bit of a casino addict. Monte Carlo, Luzern, Cannes, Innsbruck, he frequented them all. Made himself shitloads of money, and I believe he now owns Luxembourg. The bastard still wouldn't buy me a beer, though.

Liechtenstein is a joke. Nothing more than a glorified toilet stop. We would stop at the bus park—a very nice one, I might add, with lovely toilets and soft toilet paper—and the passengers would wander the main street of the capital,

Vaduz, looking at stuff they could never afford in the shop windows. Not too many were after false teeth: Liechtenstein is the world's largest manufacturer of false teeth.

The Grand Duchy of Liechtenstein was founded in 1719 and is the last remaining piece of the once huge and powerful Holy Roman Empire. It's a tax haven for fat businessmen in brown suits and commission-rich tour leaders.

On trips that ran in the opposite direction we would enter Liechtenstein from Austria. The Swiss border is actually at the Austrian/Liechtenstein border. As it would be the passengers' first time in what I described as the technologically advanced country of Switzerland, I would tell them that the Swiss had the most sophisticated border procedure in the world. I would say the bridge we were about to cross, at the Liechtenstein/Swiss border, had 30 high-resolution digital video cameras mounted on both sides. 'As we drive slowly through,' I would solemnly explain, 'all you have to do is hold your passport up against the window, with your picture page open and your face next to it. The cameras will zoom in, take a shot and register your entry into the country.'

The bus would slow right down as we approached the bridge and the passengers would all have their passports out, squashed up against the windows with their faces right next to them. We would cross a very plain and simple bridge, and I would barely make it to the other side before I'd burst into wetting-my-pants-type laughter. There were obviously no cameras and, in fact, there wasn't even a real border. Just a sign to say we were now in Switzerland.

SHOWERHEADS STRUDEL
& SIXTEEN GOING ON SEVENTEEN

Through the bus stereo would come the syrupy sweet voice of Julie Andrews as she made the hills come alive with, 'The Sound Of Music'. Moments later she'd be drowned out by, 'Turn that *fuckin'* crap off!' There'd be a chorus of groans and a smattering of profanities from all corners of the bus. However, by the time Maria, Gretl, Marta, Leisl, Brigitta, Kurt, Louisa and Frederich broke into 'The Lonely Goatherd', most of the bus would be singing merrily along as we drove the short distance from the German/Austrian border to Sound of Musicburg, or Mozartburg, or, as the locals prefer to call it, Salzburg.

I would always endeavour to play some sort of music appropriate to each country as we drove in. In Italy, I'd play Dean Martin singing 'That's Amore'. In Spain it would be the Gypsy Kings. OK, they are actually French, but hey, they sing in Spanish, play a dozen acoustic guitars all at once and clap a lot. Instant coffee commercials made Edith Piaf an instantly recognisable choice for France, and in Germany I'd play a delightful tape entitled *German Beer Drinking Favourites*. This collection of favourites sounded wonderful when you were rolling drunk, but in the clear, sober light of day it was enough to drive you to drink.

I never could find any comparable music for Holland. I just couldn't think of anything. What music do they have? Do they just bang wooden clogs together? After all the spacecakes, is Neil Young as close as they get to national music? The only thing I could think of was that fine Dutch group Golden Earring, with their toe-tapping classic 'Radar Love'. But with English lyrics and no mention of poffertjes or space cakes, it didn't sound very Dutch.

A couple of years back the Salzburgers implemented what I dubbed 'the anti-tourist law'. It's not that they were anti-tourist as such. On the contrary, if there were no tourists, Salzburg would have crumbled apart and slid into the Salzach River years ago. It's just that they didn't like tourists who didn't spend money. They were sick of tourists turning up by the busloads, clogging up the narrow and already crowded streets of the Aldstadt (old town) all day and not spending one single *Groschen*.

Buses even more ancient than our deckers, predominantly from Eastern Europe, would turn up billowing huge clouds of black, thick smoke. The Polish buses for example would have food piled halfway up the windows, including large smelly sausages that had somehow managed to survive two weeks of glaring sun. The low-rent tourists would troop off their buses in the centre of Salzburg, walk around the streets munching smelly sausages for a few hours then piss off.

Chatting one night to a cute nineteen-year-old Polish girl in the disco at our campsite in Venice, I asked her why she wasn't drinking. She was sitting with a couple of friends by the bar (you could tell they were Poles because they all wore shell suits) and getting up now and again for a dance. She told me how much she earned in Polish zlotys. At the then current exchange rate, I figured out a beer would cost her the equivalent of about 80 Australian dollars!

Being the gentleman that I am, I bought her a couple of beers, but sadly she ran off to bed before I could show her my smelly sausage.

Now, what is it about Poles and shell suits? Every Polish person out of Poland seems to wear those horrible, outrageously brightly coloured, wafer-thin, shiny shell suits. Apparently, and I believe this to be true, when a Pole leaves Poland, they are given a shell suit and a string of smelly sausages at the border. I met a Polish couple back home who had been living in Australia for six years, and they both had horrible shell suits on. I asked, when I first met them, 'Are you from Poland?'

'Yes,' they replied enthusiastically, 'how could you tell?'

'Your accent,' I replied.

'Ah, you are very clever.'

But perhaps the most bizarre thing of all was what happened when Poles and showerheads met. This totally baffled me. When the Poles arrived at a campsite, they *stole* the showerheads. Was there a shortage of showerheads in Poland? Or was it like collecting matchboxes or something? And why didn't they at least wait until they were ready to leave? I would go for a shower and find nothing but a stump that poured water out in one long, impossible-to-wash-yourself-under stream. I can just imagine going to the Zlockow's family home in Warsaw and having the very proud owner show me his impressive collection of showerheads from all over Europe, beautifully presented in a large glass case. 'Thiss vun's my fawourite, I got it from the wery nice cumpsite in Parris. Oh yass, it took me twenty minutes to get thiss vun orff.'

So, anyway, this was how the grumpy Salzburgers implemented their 'anti-tourist law'. They set up huge bus parks ten kilometres or so from the centre of town where you would have to park your bus and pay 30 schillings per person (about four dollars or 1 320 000 Polish zlotys) for a shuttle bus into town. Of course, most of the Poles and other Eastern Europeans couldn't afford it, the fee being about three years' wages, so it made the grumpy Salzburgers very happy. Only people with money would now enter Salzburg.

The funny thing is, the only business in Salzburg that made money out of my groups was McDonald's.

We would have barely two hours in Salzburg. By the time we'd allowed for the parking and shuttle-bus lark, we'd be lucky to have one hour left. But after a couple of frustrating trips, Coach Captain Kevin Kelvin solved that. 'Fuck it,' he announced, 'we'll just drive in.' The new bus rules were heavily policed, so we nervously scanned every corner as we drove right through to the centre of town. I was expecting to hear sirens at any second. Being the only bus besides the shuttles, we stood out like a...well, like a Pole not wearing a shell suit.

Kevin, who I was screaming at by this stage, dropped us off smack in the middle of the central shuttle-bus station and drove off in fits of hysterical laughter. Making sure no tourist police were following me, I began our walking tour at a cracking pace, ducking down side lanes and back out again until we finally reached the relative safety of the crowded Mozartplatz.

Salzburg was founded way back in 798 but didn't join Austria until a thousand years later when, in 1816, the Holy Roman Empire finally collapsed. The Aldstadt is full of gloriously grand baroque buildings, mighty fortresses and divine (well, they would be, wouldn't they) churches. However, my walking tour went something like this:

Mozartplatz
Mozart: Statue of Mozart erected in 1842
The Sound of Music: Maria and the kids (dressed in curtains!) ran around the statue singing 'Do-Re-Mi'.
Residenzplatz
Mozart: Mozart played here as a child in the conference room
The Sound of Music: Nazi headquarters
Residenz Fountain
Mozart: Wrote *Eine Kleine Nachtmusik* while he sat on the edge of the fountain (don't panic, musicologists—I made that one up)
The Sound of Music: Julie Andrews sang, 'I Have Confidence', while she ran around it, splashing water everywhere
Dom (Salzburg Cathedral)
Mozart: Christened here and resident organist 1779 to 1781
Sound of Music: Interior wedding scenes (when the dashing captain married Maria)
St Peter's Abbey and Cemetery
Mozart: Mozart's sister, Nannerl, buried here
The Sound of Music: This is where the Nazi-loving Rolf blew the whistle on his girlfriend Leisl and the rest of the Von Trapp family

And so it would go on. 'This house belonged to Mozart's mother's best friend's cat, and if you look carefully while Julie Andrews is singing the third verse of "Sixteen Going On Seventeen" you can see that same cat up a tree at the right of the screen', etc, etc.

The locals must have been well over *The Sound of Music*. The film was actually a flop in Austria when it was released in 1965. On my first visit to Salzburg as a back-packer, about fifteen of us from the hostel spent a beer-swilling evening at the Augustiner Bräu Stübl, the finest beer hall I've had the pleasure to visit, I might add. Run by monks (who looked like they'd sampled quite a few ales themselves), the dark underground cavern was a hoot. Even the oompah music was good—well, as good as oompah music can get. Staggering out at some time in the morning, we then waltzed back to the hostel through the quiet inner suburbs of Salzburg, belting out 'Do-Re-Mi' and 'These Are A Few Of My Favourite Things' at the top of our well-sozzled lungs. This, I imagine, must happen on most nights of every summer.

Tourists can be horribly crass.

I once took a four-week Korean charter that my driver and I dubbed 'The Korean Food Frenzy', seeing that all they did, all day, non-stop, was eat. I would tell them dinner was at seven o'clock, and they would be queuing at the cook tent at 6.30. When they eventually got their food, they'd shovel it frantically down as they headed straight back to the end of the queue to be first in line for seconds.

Anyway, when I played my *The Sound of Music* tape coming into Austria, they had no idea what the songs were, even though the film was hugely successful in Korea. It turns out that the Korean Censorship Board, or whatever they're called, found the film a shade overlong, so they cut out *all* the songs. It was shown with no music whatsoever, but they still called it *The Sound of Music*.

I have to confess, and I'm putting my credibility on the line here, I'm a *The Sound of Music* fan. And no, I don't watch Doris Day or gladiator movies. I love the naff songs and I actually find Julie Andrews quite cute. During the film I'll find myself trying to get a peek at her pert breasts beneath the puff blouses, tweed jackets, evening dresses and even those damned curtains.

Yes, I know, I'm sick.

The *real* Von Trapps (they did exist) were nothing like the sweet, clear-skinned, slim and ever-smiling Von Trapps in the film. Maria Von Trapp looked more like a German beer hall frau than Julie Andrews. She had another four or five kids to the captain in real life, and the real Von Trapp family singers toured all over Europe for a couple of years before they escaped over the Alps (in the film they walked; in real life they caught a train). They eventually went to the States, toured all over the country, ended up opening the Von Trapp Family Singing School in Vermont and made absolutely shitloads of money. True.

The passengers, too, would be Julie Andrewed and Mozarted out by the end of the walking tour, and would rush off to that celebrated Austrian institution McDonald's for some local fare. Which, I have to admit, I recommended—but for one reason only: the toilets. You can't find toilets anywhere in Europe, and when you do track them down, they either have no toilet paper (or no toilet for that matter, being just a hole in the ground) or they charge you a few dollars for a leak and you get the fat toilet attendant lady—they're always fat—watching your every move. McDonald's will never trouble the judges at any culinary awards but by golly they have nice toilets.

An American guy I had on a trip, who looked like he lived on McDonald's, and probably did because he was American, showed me his meticulously drawn chart: 'The Big Macometer'. In every country we visited he bought a Big Mac and converted the price to American dollars. This way, he told me, he could figure out the most expensive (and cheapest) countries in Europe.

In my free hour I would quite often catch the *Aufzug* (lift) that's built right into the cliff face of the Mönchsberg to Café Winkler for *Kafé und Küchen* (coffee and cake). The Mönchsberg is a huge rock that rises almost vertically for over a hundred metres above Salzburg. From the café's terrace, set right on the cliff's edge and dotted with pristine white tables and umbrellas, the view was nothing less than spectacular. Even in peak season, on a perfect summer's day, you'd be pretty much guaranteed a seat with a view (the exorbitant prices probably scared most people away). I would be greeted by a smartly dressed waiter and escorted to my seat. From there I could look straight down the deep valley and over the baroque splendour of Salzburg, nestled in the greenest of green valleys, with the Salzach River—bright silver in the sun—snaking through the middle. I just loved it there, even if I had to spend half of the trip's funds to buy a nice cup of tea (Why is it, by the way, a 'nice' cup of tea?). The prices are not too bad, really; considering the service, the view, and the best Schwarzwälder Kirchtorte (black forest cake) I've ever tasted.

While we're on cakes, boy, do the Austrians love their *Kafé und Küchen*. Funnily, the Germans' nickname for the Austrians is 'cake eaters'. (The French, on the other hand, call the Brits 'roast beef'.) The Austrians not only love their *Kafé und Küchen*, they love food, full stop. They are known to have six meals a day. Breakfast (*Frühstück*) is rolls, jam and coffee, followed at ten o'clock by morning tea (*Gabelfrühstück*), which consists of more bread, meat and cheese. Lunch (*Mittagessen*) is a big affair and the main meal of the day, followed by *Kafé und Küchen*—two of Austria's greatest claims to fame.

When the Turks laid siege to Vienna back in 1683, a small army of 80 000 Austrians managed to scare off the 250 000 strong Turkish force who, in their haste to retreat, left behind many large bags of coffee beans. The Austrians tried eating them, playing marbles with them, baking them in a pie and even shoving them up each other's noses before they discovered you could just add hot water and end up with a pretty decent drink (with quite a kick). It was the Austrians who introduced coffee to Europe and eventually the rest of the world. Austrians are also world-renowned for their pastries. It was the Austrians who introduced the croissant, the bagel and apple strudel to the world.

After *Kafé und Küchen* they roll on to dinner (*Abendessen*), followed by a late night supper and, finally, 'just one wafer-thin chocolate'. No wonder you tend to spot the odd fat bastard rolling around the hills of Austria.

It still amazes me to think that Austria, at one stage in history, was the most powerful nation on earth. As Charles V, Emperor of Austria and the Holy Roman Empire, once boasted in the sixteenth century: 'The sun never sets on the Habsburg Empire.' Beginning in 1273, the Habsburgs ruled Austria for almost 700 years. At the empire's peak they also controlled Hungary, Czechoslovakia, most of Italy, Belgium, Poland, Romania, Spain, Holland and lands in South America and Asia. During Austria's Golden Age, Queen Maria Theresa not only ruled her vast kingdom successfully, but managed to pop out *sixteen* kids along the way (that's 144 months, or just over twelve years, of pregnancy). Before the First World War, the Austrian empire had a population of 53 million people and covered 261 000 square kilometres. Five short years later a mere 6 million people were left with just 32 000 square kilometres to their names. Being on the losing side is never a good thing.

I would tell the passengers to meet in Mozartplatz at *exactly* two o'clock, because Coach Captain Kevin Kelvin would have to pull up quickly while we all jumped in. I'd arrive at Mozartplatz fifteen minutes or so early and there they all would be, sitting around Mozart's statue eating *ein Grossen* Big Mac *mit* fries. Despite the many sights of Salzburg competing for their attention, most of our highly imaginative passengers would head straight to McDonald's then straight back to Mozartplatz to wait for the bus.

To the strains of Wolfgang Amadeus Mozart (who, by the way, wrote 'Twinkle, Twinkle, Little Star' at the age of six) on the bus stereo, we'd begin our drive through the Austrian Alps. Just out of Salzburg we would pop back into Germany to take an eleven-kilometre short cut that cut over 50 kilometres off the total trip. The only drawback, of course, was the two extra German/Austrian border crossings and all those bloody annoying stamps.

Approaching the border one time at Bad Reichenhall, there didn't seem to be any guards manning the border. We drove up slowly but noisily in the decker, and still no-one came out of the little office. Coach Captain Kevin Kelvin asked me what I thought we should do, but made up his own mind before I had time to answer. 'Fuck it,' he said as he planted his foot and sped right through the border in a cloud of black smoke. The passengers were all squealing with laughter but there, standing on the road behind us in a grey uniform and jackboots, was the German border guard. Waving a very large rifle. I spent the next eleven kilometres expecting, as we came around each bend, to find a whole Panzer division blocking the road, with men shouting 'Raus! Raus! Schnell! Schnell!' like they always do in war movies (strangely enough, those movie stormtroopers tend to speak English with a dodgy German accent and only break into German when they're excited and yell Raus! and Schnell! a lot). I was sure they'd capture us, kill us all and bury the double-decker bus in the woods. I screamed at Kevin, 'You know he would have called the other border and they'll be waiting for us?' to which he confidently replied, 'We'll just fuckin' drive straight through.' Oh good, so Kevin thought he was Steve McQueen.

As we approached the border again, a guard with an uncanny resemblance to Boris Becker came out to greet us. Now, my German is good enough to understand border guards asking, 'How many passengers?', 'Where are you going?', 'Where have you come from?' and 'Are you free this evening, sweetie pie?', but I could only make out a few words of this guard's entire five-minute lecture. If I heard what I think I heard, there was something being said about labour camps and being strung up by piano wire. Finally, after we got our 27 stamps, they let us go.

The Germans, for some reason or other, seem to have something against South Africans. The first time a border guard asked me, without even glancing at the passports, if I had any South Africans aboard, I said yes. He then proceeded to go through all the passports, search every inch of the bus and interrogate the two poor South Africans under hot lights for about twelve hours. So the next time I had South Africans aboard, I answered the same enquiry with a confident no. He handed me back my bag of passports and waved us through the border. I have to say, though, I was just a little nervous that we would be stopped in the middle of an autobahn by the German army for a spot South African check. Having disposed of the dreaded Selth Effrikan infiltrators, they would be bound to shoot me as well for smuggling them into Germany without getting their visas stamped.

Leaving the German/Austrian border behind, in the blink of an eye we would be smack in the heart of the Tyrol, considered the cradle of alpine skiing. It was here in 1907 that Hannes Schneider refined the Scandinavian skiing technique to what is now known as the Alberg method—he added the 'bend zee kneez' bit—and taught all over the world. Skiing is Austria's national sport, equal with thigh-slapping. Only 50 years ago there were all of eighteen ski lifts in the entire country. Today, there are close to 4000 ski lifts and over 20 000 kilometres of downhill skiing.

Our two nights in Austria would be spent at Club Habitat, 'A 400-year-old chalet nestled in the village of Kirchberg and surrounded by some of the most spectacular scenery in Europe. A paradise for the young and lively, where the adventure doesn't stop and the nights are just as exciting as your days.' This is what the brochure told the passengers, but the main reason they looked forward to Club Habitat was that it meant not having to put up their tents and eat their meals sitting on little camp stools in front of the cook tent, which at times could be bloody unpleasant.

On one occasion, we *attempted* to set up camp in Avignon, France, in horrendous gale force winds. There was cursing and screaming all round as the passengers tried to hammer their pegs into the rock-hard ground while trying to stop their tents being blown into the Rhône River.

I awoke in the morning (I'm not silly, I slept on the bus) to find ten people asleep on air mattresses in the cook tent. Their tents had blown down around them in the middle of the night and, in the pitch-black darkness with hurricane-force winds blowing, they had given up the struggle to put them up again. As we tried to get the cook tent down an hour or so later, the whole thing—and I do mean the whole cook tent—blew away. It just lifted up and, staying in perfect shape, flew over a couple of cars and a low wall and onto the road outside the campsite. Luckily there was no traffic. Can you imagine driving along when all of a sudden a UFT the size of your average one-car garage comes in for a landing on the road in front of you?

On another occasion we had to put up the tents in ten centimetres of thick, sloppy mud. Our cook was preparing tacos for dinner, sloshing around the cook tent in gum-boots. Another time we awoke in the morning to find freshly fallen snow on the ground around us, turning each tent into a nylon-walled deep freeze. But my greatest joy was putting up twenty-odd tents in the middle of mon-soonal rains. Everything, and I mean *everything*, was wet. This made it extremely difficult to enforce Rule no. 9: *Ensure no wet clothes are hung inside the bus.*

One tour leader I know set off on a 28-day trip and had 23 days of torrential rain. 'Just to the left everyone, through the mist, is the Eiffel tower...*I think!*'

Club Hab, as it's affectionately known, is old.

It's got squeaky floorboards, squeaky beds, squeaky

stairs and squeaky doors, but it's certainly not squeaky clean. It's got possibly the world's most debauched bar. I'll tell you why in a second.

The passengers would lug their bags up to their compact rooms, drool over the real beds for a minute, then make their way downstairs to the bar, which also served as the dining room. Our Austrian national meal that evening would be meatloaf(!). I was always too terrified to ask which particular meat this was a loaf of. It was probably best I didn't know.

While waiting for dinner, most people would be checking out the framed photos of the bar in full swing that cover the wall. And in full swing it certainly was. Most of the photos show large groups of girls standing in neat lines at the bar with their 'tits out for the lads'. In fact, nearly every photo features either girls' breasts, men in jocks, Coach Captain Kevin Kelvin without jocks or people skolling ludicrous fluorescent-coloured drinks. Some of the group would think, Cooooool! Tonight should be fun, but most would think: That's disgusting. By two o'clock in the morning, these same people would be dancing to 'Nutbush City Limits' in their underwear. I shouldn't talk. I've done it. I had thought to myself, I'll have a reasonably quiet night tonight, only to find myself whooping it up, singing Cold Chisel songs in my jocks at three in the morning.

The bar itself is nothing special. It's tiny, with a low ceiling and huge wooden supports stuck smack in the middle of the dance floor. However, there are three main culprits responsible for giving it a touch of the Jekyll and Hydes.

The first one is a fuck. Well, five fucks actually. A somewhat dubious Turkish schnapps called *Fuck* (it probably gained something in the translation) is served up in five identical shot glasses set in a neat row along the bar. You then form a fist with your drinking hand, grab the first glass by extending your thumb and little finger, and down the whole ghastly concoction in one. Straight away it's on to the next glass, with thumb and second finger, and so on. The fifth and final is picked up by the teeth, without any hands, and you then simply throw your head back. When this remarkable feat is completed, the barman hands you a certificate that reads: 'I had five fucks at Club Habitat.' Just the sort of thing to show your grandma when you get home.

The second culprit is a *Flügel* ('to fly'). This is a deadly mix of vodka and Red Bull. For years Red Bull was banned in every country in the world except Austria. It's one of those energy drinks, with about ten times the kick of Coca-Cola. Mixed with vodka it is deadly. But probably even more deadly for the barman than the drinker. The *Flügel* is served in a wine glass with a large piece of ice in it, and the tradition is that after you've skolled your drink, you flick the large piece of ice at the barman as hard as you can, preferably aiming for his head. With ten or so people downing a *Flügel* at the same time, the poor barman faces an absolute blitzkrieg of ice.

The third culprit is the most bizarre of all. It's called a

'Nipple Suction', and if that name alone conjures up horrible images, well, let me assure you that it's a whole lot worse than that. An iridescent blue drink—to this day, I have no idea what it is—is poured into a wine glass, set on fire by the barman, and placed carefully on (usually) a man's chest over his nipple. As the little chemistry you remember from school has already led you to expect, the oxygen is sucked in by the flame, the flame goes out and... you're left standing there looking rather silly because there's a glass of strange blue stuff stuck to your chest. The skin around the nipple is sucked into the glass. Even now it makes me squirm to just think about it. The recipient of all the attention then jumps up and down, dances and jiggles about while the glass remains firmly stuck. He finally pulls it off, making a noise similar to that of a wet plunger being pulled off a kitchen bench, and skolls the blue firewater. What stopped me from ever doing this horrid little party trick were the terrible looking red welts it left on the poor guy's chest. The marks on some of my passengers eventually scabbed up. Erghhh! Personally, I much preferred a nice simple drop of Austrian beer. That only left you with a sore head.

Seeing girls do it was even more entertaining. Because of the abundance of loose, soft flesh—well, on most girls anyway—the glass would basically be...full of tit. It truly is a weird and wonderful sight to behold. More amusing still, I once saw a guy try it on his testicles. This was not a pretty sight. He ended up with singed, smelly pubes, a rather red face, and even redder bollocks.

Naturally, by the time the evening wore on, and the effects of *Fucks*, *Flügels* and Nipple Suctions took over, strange things would begin to happen. Here are just a few I witnessed.

Just outside the entrance to the chalet was a low, wide brick wall with a fast-flowing river on the other side. Late one balmy evening, two of my passengers were going for it on top of this brick wall—a small, shy fellow from Hong Kong and a rather inebriated Australian girl. The guy was making a continuous loud groaning noise and this soon woke the people sleeping on the first floor. A girl called out loudly from her window, 'Hey, can you keep the bloody noise down?' to which the young, drunk Aussie girl replied, without stopping for a second, 'Leave him alone... it's his first time.'

At least in my role as tour leader I was doing my best to obey Rule no. 8: *Encourage all nationalities to mix.*

One of my guys who'd disappeared upstairs with one of the chalet girls came back to the bar half an hour later with a big smile on his face. He had something on his chin and around his mouth. 'What's that?' I enquired. He wiped a bit off with his finger, looked at it, and casually replied, 'Blood.'

'Blood! From where?'

He looked at me and smiled. 'It's the Dolmio grin.'

I thought about it for a second, then burst out: 'You're joking!'

But he wasn't.

Another tour leader, who, by the way, asked specifically

not to be named, was in Club Hab at the same time as me and had drunk herself silly. At six in the morning, Julie Thompson (whoops, sorry) couldn't find her room in her drunken stupor and collapsed upstairs in the loft. At nine o'clock, departure time, with the bus full of people ready to go, she was nowhere to be seen. At about ten o'clock her driver finally found her, fast asleep and still dressed as a punk from the 'P Party' the night before. She jumped straight on the bus to the loud cheers of her passengers and, an hour or so later, performed the complicated and nasty German border procedure dressed in torn fishnet stockings, a mini-skirt, a T-shirt full of holes and safety pins, with purple spiky hair, dark, sinister make-up and, to top it all off, black jackboots. Astonishingly, she got through. More amazing still, she did her whole walking tour of Munich dressed like that. Another fine example of Bavarian tolerance.

Needless to say, there would be a bunch of incredibly sore heads in the morning and more photos undoubtedly destined for the wall. Half the group would just lounge around the chalet all day nursing hangovers, while the energetic ones would go hiking, bike riding, horse riding, boating or swimming in the warm waters of the Schwarzsee.

I always spent the preceding days looking forward to a hike. Not only for the exercise, fresh air and scenery, but also for the lovely peace and quiet. One of my favourite little expeditions was to catch the chairlift (OK, I cheat a bit on the hike thing) up the Gaisberg, wander aimlessly up into the hills, find a spot in the sun and read or simply doze off. One perfect afternoon I was traipsing up a steep field of tall grass and wildflowers in the middle of nowhere when I came across a 35mm Instamatic camera lying in the grass. I thought to myself, Wow, that's alright, I'll keep that. About ten shots had already been taken, and over the next week I finished off the roll of film. Back in London, I had the shots processed. What should the first ten photos be but shots of women's tits and men in their jocks in the Club Hab bar. Not my group, I might add, just one of the hundreds who inevitably end up in their underwear.

That same evening, it would all happen again. *Fucks*, *Flügels*, Nipple Suctions, people in their underwear, Cold Chisel songs and more *Fucks* (which generally led to more of the latter of the horizontal kind).

The next morning I'd wake up (with yet another sore head) to Club Hab's biggest surprise. The bar bill for Coach Captain Kevin Kelvin. Because Kevin had a rest day in Kirchberg, on his first night he would try to drink three times his body weight in alcohol. Most of the time he succeeded. I would then spend most of the trip trying to hide the bar bill somewhere in the accounts.

Finally escaping Club Hab, we would drive through ski resort after ski resort to the town (well, four houses and a pub) of Imst on the Inn River for a spot of white-water rafting. Most people would leap at the chance, but I always had a hard time convincing the New Zealanders to do it. 'What grade ruver uz ut?' they'd ask. 'Oh, about grade three or four.' (I had no idea what this actually meant, but it's what the rafting guides told me.) 'Ohh, uz *thet* all? In Nu Zulund we raft on grade sux or siven.' (I eventually found out that grade seven is the equivalent of rafting over the Niagara Falls.)

The New Zealanders would often come up with these unflattering comparisons. On a small cruise ship through the spectacular Geiranger fjords in Norway I'd get, 'Oh gee, the fjords are *heaps* more bitter un Mulford Sound.' Driving through the awe-inspiring Swiss Alps, 'Oh yeah, but the Southern Elps in Nu Zulund are *shutloads* bitter.' Even as we approached the Eiffel Tower, some Kiwi came out with, 'Gee, the old fire station tower un Waikika-moocow is more *umpressive* then thet!'

One thing I wouldn't pass on to the passengers about the rafting was the fact that the fast-moving Inn River was *pure* snow-melt. That meant it wasn't just freezing, it was 'oh, fucking hell, I only have seconds to live' cold. We donned full wetsuits, booties, spray jackets, life jackets and helmets, and as we were being dropped off fifteen kilo-metres upstream we were told to jump into the water to *acclimatise* ourselves. After jumping in and losing a few layers of skin, which froze and fell off, most of the group would try to negotiate a last-minute change of schedule involving no further rafting from that moment on—only to find that they couldn't move their lips. Their mouths were set in a frozen grimace. The rafting trip itself would inevitably involve a few more plunges into the 'I'll never be able to have children now' icy water.

Early one morning I decided not to go rafting so

I could hang around the rafting camp to see what the people who didn't go rafting did with their time. OK, that's a lie. Because it was early spring, with a whole winter's worth of snow in the river, I was fully expecting to see the rafts returning to camp unguided, just floating downstream laden with exceptionally large ice blocks. What I did find out was what those New Zealanders who didn't think the river was exciting enough did to entertain themselves. On this day at least. Two of them got themselves horribly, stinking drunk, donned one of the large yellow protective helmets each, stood twenty metres apart, then ran at each other and rammed their heads together to see who would fall over first. This kept them thoroughly amused for about half an hour, till they both finally collapsed with massive brain damage—well, more massive brain damage than they already had.

Leaving Imst, it was only a relatively short drive to the Brenner Pass and into Italy.

Here's an amazing fact. During our whole stay in Austria, most passengers wouldn't actually meet or even speak to any Austrians except for the adolescent and spotty—being spotty is a prerequisite—Austrian boy or girl behind the counter of McDonald's in Salzburg.

We drove straight into Salzburg, where I took a walking tour, then usually they went straight back onto the bus. On to Club Hab, which was owned by a New Zealander and where the manager, bar staff and chalet maids were all Aussies and Kiwis. Feel Free Rafting was owned by a

Brit, and the rafting guides, shop and restaurant staff were all Brits as well. Some passengers would spend three days in Austria and not utter a single word to someone who was actually born in the country besides, 'A Big Mac, large fries and a Coke please', followed by, 'No. Did I ask for an apple strudel?'

ROMANS
RED GARTER
& ROOSTERS' TESTICLES

'Dolce fa niente.'

That's what I love about Italy. That well-known Italian saying simply means 'it's sweet to do nothing', and as the seventh most powerful industrial nation on earth (and former rulers of a vast empire stretching from Northern England to North Africa), the Italians seem to be bloody good at doing the absolute minimum required to stay a world power. I should have been Italian. I not only admire the adage that 'it's sweet to do nothing', I also believe I'm quite good at putting it into practice. Former workmates all over the world can confirm that I have 'doing nothing' down to a fine art.

But that's not the only reason why I love Italy. For a start, there's the food. From all those delightful little antipasto bits and pieces and over 600 varieties of pasta (I'd be lucky to name ten), to pizza, risotto and minestrone, and gelati, tartufo or tiramasu (even if you don't have any room left, you can always find some space to fit these in). I'd eat pasta every night if I could, but as my wife says to me whenever I serve up pasta yet again, 'Honey, don't you think it would be nice to have something different for a change?'

This should, of course, all be washed down with a lovely drop of Italian wine. First casked in 500 BC, there are literally thousands of varieties from the world's largest wine producer to sample. Yes, the world's biggest. France, for years the leader, is now second.

There's more exquisite art and architecture in Italy than you can poke a stick of grissini at. Walk down any *via* in Milano, Torino, Palermo, Positano, Orvieto, Catanzano, Arrezzo, Pesaro—in short, any one of the 23 567 towns in Italy that end in 'o'—and you are surrounded by incredible art and architecture.

Then there are Italian women.

Mamma mia.

With those long, tanned, slender legs; that shiny, dark hair; that beautiful skin; those big, dark eyes and...and... I'd better stop. I'm getting all unnecessary just thinking about them.

If you asked the passengers at the end of a trip what their favourite country was, nine out of ten would say Italy. However, it wasn't until we left the Alpine landscape of Northern Italy, and the immaculate wooden chalets (this area was part of Austria until 1918) changed to farmhouses with crumbling terracotta roofs and peeling plaster walls— with, of course, people sitting around doing nothing—that the passengers would even realise we were in Italy.

The passengers' first real taste of Italy would inevitably be the Services. These are giant petrol-stations-cum-mini-cities just off the autostrada. Every three hours we would have a toilet stop. In some countries where services were few and far between, that meant finding a strategically placed bush by the side of the road and sending twenty girls to squat behind it. Your average guy, of course, will proudly piss anywhere.

The largest of these services chains in Italy is Agip, and these mini-cities in the middle of nowhere are always absolutely chocker with people. Half of Italy must be in these places at any one time. At a petrol station back home, you're lucky to get a five-day-old pie and you'd struggle to find anything edible containing less than 25 000 kilojoules. At Agip, they have a well-stocked supermarket with a dazzling array of fresh breads, a hundred varieties of sliced ham and a phenomenal collection of smelly cheeses and fine wines. It also has the most comprehensive but excruciatingly hard to use takeaway food section on earth. Many surgical procedures would be less complicated than getting the hot snack of your choice. First you walk over to the long glass display cabinet full of different panini and foccacia, all clearly labelled. You decide what you want, remember the name (it's a lot easier if you're, say, Italian), walk twenty metres to the cashier, stand in the queue, buy a ticket, go back to the glass cabinet and hand it over to the signore, who will toast or simply hand over your selected item. It's that simple.

I must be even simpler. The first time I tried it I walked up to the glass cabinet and, after trying to figure out what the hell everything was, selected the *foccacia con cotoletta pollo*, which was (I believe) slices of chicken in toasted bread. I then kept repeating the name (or tried to) in my head as I joined the back of the horrendously long queue. The man in front must have thought I was a loon as I mumbled some incomprehensible Italian words to myself over and over again. Finally, getting to the front of the queue, I blurted out, in what I thought was beautiful Italian, my foccacia order. Given my ticket, I sauntered back to the glass cabinet and watched in amazement as the signore casually reached towards my chosen item, then, almost teasingly, picked up a totally different snack four delicacies along. This one was called something like *foccacia con Lollobrigida*. Come on, my pronunciation can't have been *that* bad. To make matters worse, it was a vegetarian foccacia. Only once in at least 30 visits to Agip have I got what I actually wanted.

Quite often I would be approached by well-dodgy-looking characters in the car park, trying to sell me something they'd just stolen from my bus or hot electrical goods. Terry, one of my drivers, was once approached by a little man, with beady eyes and more gold chains than the Pope, selling video cameras. He took one out of its box and showed him, beady eyes constantly darting about. 'Thisa good camera fora you. Youa buy in a shop-ah for eight hundret tousand lire [about A$800], buta fora you, my frient, tree hundret tousand lire.' Terry checked over the camera, while this dodgy little man kept pushing him. 'Youa have to take nowa, if youa want it.' Terry wasn't stupid, he knew it was probably hot, but it was a bloody good deal so he handed over the cash. The little man gave him a new box, opened it to show the camera inside and said, 'Youa take now ina the bus and youa hider this tilla later, OK?' He pocketed his cash and, with a loud jingling of gold chains, slunk off to his large mansion in the hills.

A couple of hours later, after pulling into our camp-site, Terry was smugly bragging about his ever-so-clever purchase and took out his new video camera for a play. He opened the box, tore away the plastic wrapping and pulled out a perfectly crafted video camera. Made entirely of wood.

It was cut exactly to the shape of a video camera, with all the dials and bits included—rather cleverly, it has to be said—on stickers. He'd just paid three hundred dollars for a monumentally useless sculpture.

Laugh? I nearly wet myself!

Another time, when all the passengers had finally returned to their seats after the toilet stop, Chris, our driver, suddenly decided *he* now wanted to go to the toilet. When he ran inside, I jumped into the driver's seat and announced, 'I'm driving!' To the hooting and encouragement of the passengers, I started her up. Having no idea that I'd never driven anything larger than a stationwagon before, they egged me on further. So I put it into what I guessed, and hoped, was first gear, slowly let out the clutch and rather tentatively drove 50 metres around to the other side of the building. When Chris reappeared, his bus was nowhere to be seen. 'Shit,' he said out loud to himself, 'where the fuck is it?' He then ran around for five minutes in sheer panic before finally spotting the bus around the corner. When he stormed aboard to shrieks of laughter, I whispered to him, 'I've never driven a bus before.' He just shook his head in disbelief, put it into what he *knew* was first gear, and drove off.

At around this stage of a trip, quite a few passengers would have coupled off. Some might have played the field a bit before choosing their life partner—well, life-of-the-trip partner, anyway. The newly coupled would then spend most of their time looking for somewhere to bonk (and never mind the scenery). On the deckers, a night rarely went by without the whole bus rocking away. The bonkers seemed totally oblivious to the fact that there were another 22 people sharing a space not much larger than your average family bathroom. When two or three couples were having a good go at it and jigging about, it was like trying to sleep through a major earthquake.

On the drive to Venice one time, a girl went upstairs looking for something or other and spotted, at the back of the bus, a couple doing the business. She also saw her sleeping bag lying on top of them and charged up, pulled it off them and squealed in disgust, 'Ohh, it's got spunk on it!' Without losing his timing for a second, the guy casually replied, 'It can't of, I haven't finished yet.' The innocent bystander rushed downstairs to tell us all, so five people went upstairs and took photos of the copulating couple. Something else to show grandma, perhaps?

This sort of behaviour is nothing new, according to Thomas Nugent's 1749 book, *The Grand Tour*. He said of that famous Venetian, Casanova: 'He shared a young woman with five or six others, who made love to her one after the other until her cheeks were flushed with joy.' Casanova was also then having an affair with, of all people, a nun. 'She was a deliciously sensual creature,' he said, 'who enjoyed the bodies of women as well of those of men, and gave as much excitement as any girl I have known.' I don't think even my passengers would stoop that low. (Or do I mean aim that high?) But then again, there were no nunneries on our itinerary.

We didn't stay in Venice itself. There's not enough room among all the canals and gondolas for a campsite, so we stayed on the mainland, just south of the industrial town of Mestre. In fact, out of the twenty million tourists who visit Venice each day—sorry, every year—less than half actually stay in Venice. Most are camera-wielding, gondola-riding, straw-hat-buying day trippers. Nor, come to that, do the Venetians seem to stay in Venice. In the last 40 years, the population has dropped from around 170 000 to about 80 000. Most have moved to the industrial centres of Mestre and Marghera. And there, in the stagnant and polluted waters of the lagoons that surround the chemical-belching factories, horribly mutant and lethal mozzies breed.

These monsters are the size of a small family pet, and every night they make a pilgrimage to Camping Fusina for their daily feed. Lying in my cabin at night thinking I was safe, having mastered the art of opening the door, entering and closing it again in less than two seconds, I would be ready to doze off when, above my head, I'd hear what sounded like a large radio-controlled Cessna. There was no point at all in pulling the sheet over your head because these buggers could bite through anything. I would, of course, warn the passengers about the mutant mozzies and most would buy extra-extra-strong insect repellent at the hypermarket. But it never worked. These chemically dependent horrors loved the stuff. It probably even attracted them. And it didn't seem to matter what you wore, the buggers would still get you. In the stifling Venetian summer heat, denim jeans were both bloody uncomfortable and totally useless as protection. The mozzies just bit right through them. Even if you wore a NASA-issued space suit, I still think the supermozzies would somehow get to your blood.

I was told that if you drink lots of alcohol, the mozzies

won't bite you. Apparently, so the story went, they can smell it in your blood and they don't like it. Now I don't know if this was true or not, but I did my very best to get pissed every night I was in Venice. Just in case.

One girl who had drunk a couple of flagons of wine didn't quite make it back to her tent late one balmy evening. She fell asleep on an air mattress outside, wearing only a mini-skirt and singlet top. In the morning she was completely covered in these horrid looking huge red bumps. The poor girl could hardly walk. It must have been the wine that attracted the mozzies, so it's just lucky I stuck to beer and sambucas.

Inside the entrance of the local Panorama hypermarket was a long glass bain-marie filled with roast chickens, roast pork and spare ribs. Towards the end were what looked vaguely like tiny roast chickens marked as *uccelletti*. I'm pretty sure if I looked that up in an Italian dictionary I'd find 'mosquitoes'. I stared at them for a minute and walked away shaking my head, convinced that the extra-large mozzies were roasted up and eaten by the locals with a nice side dish of polenta and maybe a rocket and shaved parmesan salad.

With Italy so well known for its glorious, glorious food, the passengers would look forward to the first of their two Italian 'national meals'. According to the brochure, on their first night in Italy they would be treated to an 'Italian BBQ'. The only Italian thing about this barbecue was that the barbecue itself was set up in Italy. The meal consisted of BBQ chicken, salad and the barbecued ribs of an unknown animal. As I think back to buying meat in the midst of all those chemical factories, I have a terrible suspicion that they had found a way to breed 80-kilo mozzies with large and tasty ribs.

Sitting in the dining-room-cum-bar-cum-disco-cum-mozzie-central-feeding-centre, we always seemed to time eating our 'Italian BBQ' and drinking our ridiculously cheap but surprisingly palatable wine to coincide with the nightly eight o'clock screening of 'Tutti-Frutti' on the gi-normous video screen. While people were tucking into their mozzie ribs and salad, this Italian 'talent show', with a host who looked unsettlingly like the beady-eyed and gold-encrusted fellow who was selling video cameras, would take normal looking housewives and make them, well…strip off. To the accompaniment of rather awful Europopmusik, the signoria would take their kit off to reveal all, apart from what the tiniest of G-strings could conceal. A panel of judges, including someone who looked suspiciously like Bernard King (well, have you seen him in Australia recently?), would waffle away for five minutes. I haven't the slightest idea what they were going on about for so long. There must be a limit on how many ways they could say 'nice tits!' The winner was invariably the one who got her kit off the quickest and spent the rest of the allotted time just jiggling her boobs at the camera and smiling a lot. The female passengers would be disgusted while the boys, naturally, moved closer and soon forgot about their mosquito ribs.

On most trips I would take two of the passengers who had 'got together' on the tour and marry them off. I would organise a mock wedding and even a mock hens/bucks party. Once I was marrying this dashing English chap to a lovely New Zealand girl. The night before, as usual, the lads settled into the small bar area for the bucks party while the girls sat in the adjoining disco area for their hens night.

Both parties proceeded to get legless and, in true pre-wedding tradition, both the best man and the bridesmaid had organised a stripper. Each person on the bus played out a character for the wedding. There were the best man and bridesmaids, two sets of parents, an alcoholic uncle (this role was never hard to cast), a jealous ex-girlfriend, photographers, and me playing the role of the priest.

One shy girl from my bus performed a strip to the strains of 'You Can Leave Your Hat On' that would have put the cigar or candle lady to shame—right down to her rather skimpy underwear, exposing what one of the lads eloquently described as 'Nice mozzie bites!' The girls, on the other hand, had recruited a bronzed, handsome but rather drunk Aussie fellow from another bus for their show. He stripped off, rubbed himself up and down the bride-to-be, then took her back to his tent. The groom-to-be, strangely enough, didn't seem to mind that much.

The wedding itself was a lavish affair. The bride and the bridesmaids had made a stunning wedding dress from garbags and toilet paper, while the men decided to wear nothing but long T-shirts with no underwear. (Don't ask me why. Please, don't ask.) I pulled out a few of the seats from the bus and made pews leading up to the altar—the front door of the bus—where I stood, dressed in my priest's outfit. Well, top half anyway. I, too, was told not to wear any underclothing. Anything to keep the punters happy.

The groom waited nervously in front of me dressed in a clean white T-shirt, bow tie and nothing else. The blushing bride arrived and, as the congregation hushed, I began my long sermon in rather badly pronounced Italian. I was actually reading from the instruction manual for a fridge my driver had bought earlier that day. What sounded like a romantic Latino sermon actually meant 'do not place the fridge next to any heating systems' and 'to defrost, simply turn upside down and wipe out with a damp cloth'.

We all then moved to the disco to share the wedding reception with another five busloads of people. Mind you, I must admit I was a little worried about the T-shirt thing. If a mutant mozzie got a feed out of my John Thomas, it would end up looking like something that belonged to John Merrick.

Later that same evening, I was standing by the dance floor eyeing off girls (as you do) when Coach Captain Kevin Kelvin approached me and said, 'Hey Brian, you won't believe this. I've just walked over to that table over there, and a girl asked me what was under my shirt. She lifted it up, grabbed my dick and started sucking it.' I looked at him in total disbelief. 'Kevin, I think you've gone to the toilet, fallen asleep and had a dream.'

'No, really!'

'Yeah sure, Kevin.'

Just then this lovely, sweet girl walked over to where we were standing on the edge of the crowded dance floor and, to the cheers of her friends, lifted up Kevin's shirt and, right next to me and pretty damn close to a few hundred other people, started having a good go at his John Thomas. My mouth opened almost as wide as hers.

Without fail, on any given night in the Fusina bar, you would find Loris. Loris was a small, fiftyish Italian with a lovely head of silvery-grey hair. He was always dressed impeccably, and he was always pissed off his head.

Even though his English was virtually non-existent, he was great to hang around with because he was loaded—with money I mean, even though he was also loaded in the other sense—and bought you sambucas all night. (For me this was for medicinal purposes only, to prevent mozzie bites.) Anything standing nearby that resembled a pretty girl would also be plied with sambucas.

Now this is the frightening thing. Loris owned and operated part of the floodgate network into Venice. One evening, after it had been bucketing down with almost monsoonal rain all day, Loris got an emergency call at the bar to open up the gates. He couldn't find any of his staff (well, he was so pissed he could hardly pick up a telephone), so he talked one of the coach drivers into driving him there in Loris's own car. The driver, who'd had a few sambucas himself, really shouldn't have been driving, but he seemed relatively sober compared to the blithering Loris.

When they arrived at the small control centre, Loris

stumbled in, leant against the wall and stared hazily at the control panel.

'You…pusha button,' he mumbled.

'Which button?'

'You *musta* pusha da button!'

'Which one? This one? This one?'

'Uh-uh,' says Loris with half-closed eyes.

Eventually, the driver just pushed *a* lever, any lever. Magically, the gates opened. The driver returned to the bar to a hero's welcome and was pronounced 'the man who saved Venice'. A few months later the campsite printed its own play money for crew to use at the bar (we were given 30 000 lire of this to use as bar money). One of the notes carried the head of 'The Driver Who Saved Venice'.

When we reached Venice on our training trip, the trainers organised to have our drinks spiked. Vodka was slipped into our beer and we were given countless free sambucas. You see, they wanted to see us drunk. They wanted to see how we reacted and how much control we retained because, let's face it, they knew this was bound to happen at some stage of every trip. One trainee driver ended up dancing on a table in his jocks, totally covered with beer, dribbling all over himself and hollering along to the music loudly and out of tune.

He got a job.

At some point during the story so far you may have thought to yourself, Gee, Brian must drink a *lot*! Some other tour leaders—well, most tour leaders—would manage to get pissed at least every second night for years on end. I just couldn't do it. Instead, I became quite an expert at pretending to drink. I could nurse one beer for two hours. It would soon be flat, warm and horrible (a bit like English beer, really), which would help me just take tiny sips while my passengers got drunk around me. Some time before midnight, when they were all pissed, I'd sneak off to bed. I really don't know how the other tour leaders did it. I was always knackered, and I only got pissed every *fourth* night.

The next morning, in bright, warm sunshine, I would walk my passengers the short distance to the Fusina boat jetty for our bumpy ride into Venice. The girls would ogle and drool over the young, handsome Italian boatmen. Even the lads whose job seemed to involve nothing more than simply untying the rope from the pier, then just standing at the back of the boat looking cool, were dressed in the latest Armani, Versace and Zegna. Most of their wages must have gone on looking good, but that seemed to be par for the *corso*: in domestic sales alone, Italians spend over $10 billion a year on fashion. Their average of $3000 a year per person spent on clothes is three times that of Australia. (But then again, a pair of thongs, a singlet and a pair of footy shorts don't cost that much.)

Italians find the outrageously coloured and badly matched outfits of some of the tourists (read Americans) painful to the eye. Italians will judge people on their appearance. In Venice we used to come across what I dubbed the Fashion Police. They would walk up to people with shirts or shoes off and ask them to put them back on. It's the least they could do. They were just sorry they couldn't make us all shop at Armani. God knows what they thought of Aussies in those singlets, thongs and footy shorts.

The Italians have a saying, *fare bella figura*, which means 'looking good' or 'making a good impression'. In one Italian town they took 'looking good' just a little too far. In 1982, in a beachside town in Calabria in the south, the mayor banned topless women bathers—*unless* they were young and attractive. It worked for a while, until the inevitable disputes arose over drawing the line between attractive and unattractive. So they banned it completely. They would rather have no topless bathing at all than have a few heifers with no taste or shame getting their tits out on the beach.

I must confess that I felt very self-conscious standing next to these perfectly groomed Italian men, so I would do my utmost to dress up when I went into any Italian city. I'd don my best pants, and I even bought a beautiful long-sleeved silk shirt in Florence to wear only in Italy. I'd polish up the expensive shoes I'd bought in Paris, take my small black leather designer backpack—which was cool in Italy, but according to my friends back home in Australia, made me look like a raving queen—and walk the streets pretending I was Italian and cool. I never really got away with it, though. I just wasn't cool enough and, more importantly, I looked nothing like the incredibly handsome

Venetian men. I did, however, stand out from my T-shirt, boardshort and thongs-wearing passengers.

After a big night of sambucas, there would be many a green face on the bumpy and stuffy 30-minute boat journey into Venice. We would dock in a nondescript part of Venice on the southern side of Dorsoduro, and I'd walk the group through a labyrinth of narrow, shaded alleys, across canals and past mask shops, glassware shops, straw hat shops and miniature brass gondola shops, all set among wondrous churches and palaces. The 'oohhs' and 'aahhs' would be replaced with one big 'ohhhhh!' when we stepped through a narrow archway and, in a sudden change of light that dazed you for a second, found ourselves standing in brilliant sunlight in the Piazza San Marco. Even packed with a zillion tourists, I think it's still one of the most glorious squares in the world, or as Napoleon called it, 'the finest living room in Europe'.

Designed primarily by Jacopo Sansovino in the sixteenth century, the piazza includes the glittering Byzantine splendour of the Basilica San Marco, the magnificent Doge's Palace, the thousand-year-old campanile, and at least two million rats with wings. Yes, bloody pigeons. In the Middle Ages, they were Venice's major source of meat, which I guess would at least have helped keep the population down. Now vendors sold packets of pigeon food for a thousand lire so visitors with absolutely no idea could feed the lice-infested pests. Only recently they started adding an anti-fertility drug to the feed—even the Venetians were sick of having their city and monuments shat all over and having to spend millions trying to clean it up. I did my bit, though. I ordered pigeon now and again in a restaurant, even though I didn't like it that much. If it helped to keep the population down, I was content to grin and bear it.

At dusk, when the pigeons had gone to crap somewhere else, the straw-hat-wearing day trippers had left, people were in their hotels or having dinner, and the narrow streets and squares were relatively empty, Venice really was the most beautiful city in the world.

I'd only do a relatively short guided tour of Venice as apparently it was against the law to take a guided tour without being an 'official' Venice guide. So we were told by the office, anyway. I would then tell our passengers that if we were pulled up by the police, they should explain that I was just an eccentric friend rambling on about Venice. Yeah, right! I just happened to be travelling with 43 of my closest friends...

At the end of my walking tour and as part of the cultural dynamic of the trip, I would take the passengers to a glass-blowing demonstration at Murano Glass, just off St Mark's Square. Glassmaking has been practised in Europe since ancient times, but it wasn't until the thirteenth century that transparent glass was first produced, on the island of Murano, just off Venice. They managed to keep their method secret for over 50 years, then, once someone had leaked the magic formula, it spread all over Europe in under twelve months. This was soon followed by the invention of the spectacles (1260), glass windows for houses and test tubes. The mirror was invented and first manufactured in Murano, which makes sense, considering that the Italians spend most of their time trying to look good.

Outside Murano Glass it would be a sweltering 35 degrees, and the glass-blowers in our demonstration must have been melting themselves in no less than 45 degrees. But they still managed to look very cool and stay impeccably dressed, without a crease or mark on them. These glass-blowers gave the passengers very stylish and highly polished demonstrations of making the most god-ugly, bright-blue vases with useless orange swirly bits around the top. They may have invented glass as we know it, but most of the huge showroom was full of crap. To their utter disbelief, the passengers would be shown bright-red flowered decanters with matching(?) yellow, green, mauve and orange glasses that would cost, wait for it, over two hundred dollars. God knows someone must buy this crap, or the hundreds of shops like this in Venice wouldn't exist. Please tell me there aren't that many 65 year-old ladies with absolutely no taste at all visiting Venice. Ahh, but then again, there *are* over 250 million Americans.

The ever so suave gentleman who owned the glass shop was called Marco. He was a lovely man. When I would return later in the day to pick up my commission, knowing that not one single passenger would have bought anything but having to get a stamp to prove I went there for the office, Marco would hand me an envelope with at least 20 000 lire in it, saying, 'Sorry, no-one boughta any-thing, but this izza for you.'

One of the greatest joys I got from the job, apart from meeting all those wonderful passengers, of course, was the food. I would regularly go to lunch by myself, sniffing out new, out-of-the-way restaurants. Having the advantage of access to local knowledge, I would ask one of our city con-tacts how I could get away from tourists and menus printed in six languages (or, even worse, the 'tourist menu': it doesn't seem to matter what country you're in, the local specialty is always chicken and chips) and eat where the locals hung out.

On one occasion Marco gave me the address of 'the besta restaurant in-ah Venice-ah', gave me his business card, and told me to tell the waiter that I was a good friend of-ah Marco. The problem then was one of addresses in Venice. The city is divided into six districts, known as *sestieri*, and within each *sestieri* there is one long series of street numbers. Some go as high as 6000. You can have number 124 on one side of the street and the house directly opposite might be 3942. Even the locals have no idea where the hell they're going; only the post office staff seem able to make sense of it all. But for some reason they're not telling anyone.

So after taking two hours to do my 'a fifteen-ah minute walk-ah', I found Marco's favourite restaurant. Set in a narrow alleyway away from the tourist hordes, it had a tiny, intimate courtyard with four small tables and large white umbrellas to block out the hot midday sun. When I showed the impeccably dressed waiter the card and informed him I was a friend of Marco, he brought out a litre carafe of wine and said, 'It's-ah on the house-ah.' Still feeling very how's-your-father from the previous night's sambuca abuse, I reluctantly accepted. The food was divine, if not a bit expensive for an underpaid tour leader, but I ended up sitting there for almost three hours trying to finish the wine so I wouldn't offend them.

One of the reasons for the expensive restaurant prices in Venice is that the cover prices are twice as high as anywhere else in Italy. I've ordered a simple 9000 lire plate of pasta in a restaurant and ended up paying over 20 000 lire for it. There is a charge for bread, water and grissini (even though I never eat any). Then there's the service charge, value-added tax and what I *think* was a donation to the owner's son's university fund.

After the glass-blowing demo, we would head straight into Il Merletto School of Lace, situated in a former church that was just off St Mark's Square. Our demonstration would be given by the deliciously gorgeous Rosa. She spoke very slowly, in the sexiest of Italian accents. 'I'm-ah going to-ah show you 'ow to make-ah the Bobbin Lace-ah.' She would then go off into some babble about different types of lace, tablecloths, pillows and girly stuff. Most of the girls seemed interested, while the guys just tried to get the front pews to see if they could look up her skirt.

I was hopelessly in love with her.

One afternoon, while standing in St Mark's Square surrounded by, funnily enough, pigeons, I glanced around to see if anyone was looking and swung my leg out at a group of pigeons putting out a particularly annoying brand of cooing. I collected one a beauty that would have done Ronaldo proud: a delightful 30-metre shot straight through the middle of two columns. Then, out of the corner of my eye, I saw the beautiful Rosa standing no more than five metres away. I thought, Rats, there goes any chance of marrying her, having beautifully dressed children and eating delicious pastas for the rest of my life. But she smiled at me and said in that sexy Italian accent, 'I've always-ah wanted to-ah do that.' I could have married her right then on the spot.

With the afternoon free, I always took great joy in telling the passengers to get lost! And I meant it. The major sights of Venice are connected by a series of large yellow signs: Piazzale Roma to Ponte di Rialto to Piazza San Marco and so on. The sheep-like processions of wrinklies and Japanese cram into the already narrow streets and grind to a virtual standstill. All you have to do is move fractionally away from these streets and you'll find the real Venice. Even in peak season, in the course of my aimless wanderings I've happened upon a brightly lit and virtually deserted Campo with just one little black-clad Italian lady filling up a bottle from the lone water fountain in the centre. Prices drop dramatically as well. In the packed tourist streets, I've seen cans of Coke being sold for 2500 lire when only three streets away they're selling for 1000.

Speaking of which…Once upon a time I was in a tiny Egyptian village in the middle of the desert and my friend bought a can of Coke for about 50 cents from a drink vendor on the side of the road. Two minutes later a bus-load of American tourists pulled up and they were promptly charged two dollars a can. Ten minutes later the bus left and the price went back down to 50 cents. These, I imagine, are the same Americans who'd buy a set of revolting fluorescent-green wine glasses covered in purple and orange flowery bits for $500 in Venice.

Two passengers once took my advice of 'getting lost' a little too literally and somehow got themselves *completely* and *irretrievably* lost. God knows how, but they wandered around for five hours trying to get back to the dock and missed the last boat back to Fusina and ended up spend-ing a small fortune on a taxi from Piazzale Roma. They blamed the 'stupid' Italians for their street signage. Oh, and me of course. One of the burdens of life as a tour leader was that what ever bad thing happened to them, it was the tour leader's fault. No toilet paper in the camp-site toilet. My fault. Banks closing at three o'clock. Why, my fault. My favourite, however, was when an American passenger came up to me one morning in Luzern, Switzerland, and said in complete sincerity, 'Why did you bring us here? It's raining!'

Another passenger told me he was pissed off with the Italians because he desperately wanted to buy a slice of hot pizza when *every* shop had a sign announcing *Calda Pizza*. 'Why the fuck do the stupid wogs only sell cold pizza?' he screamed at me. He was even more pissed off when I told him *calda* is Italian for...hot.

Most of the other tour leaders would head straight back to camp after their walking tour, but I loved to just hang around Venice and find a restaurant or spend my time ambling happily down tranquil lanes, discovering some new hidden corner—and believing, perhaps a little naively, that I was the first foreigner to set foot into the more obscure squares. I could never understand the crew wanting to hang around the campsite all day. Why do the job? There is all the drinking and bonking of course, which can make one very tired, but even after a particularly big night I would still stay in town, even if it meant I had to have a wee nap for an hour or so. All over Europe, I had the best napping spots sussed. In Venice, I would make my way to Giardinetti Reali, on the waterfront just around the corner from Piazza San Marco. There I would lie on a wooden bench and, to the chatter of Italian children playing around me, doze off to sleep. It was wonderful to wake up and, for a split second, not know where I was, then realise I was in Venice, Munich, Paris or wherever.

One afternoon, I took the 45-minute boat journey on the *#12 Vaporetto* (the inter-island ferry service) to the island of Burano. Burano is just one of Venice's 118 islands. One of the others, San Michele, is a cemetery— the *whole* island—where most Venetians are buried. Well, buried for ten years, anyway. Then they're dug up (what's left of them) to make room for more Venetians, unless they have bucketloads of lire, in which case they can stay as long as they like. San Clemente is an island set aside for the mentally disturbed and ex-tour leaders. The island of Vignole is basically a huge vegie patch, supplying quite a bit of Venice's fruit and veg.

Burano is home to most of Venice's lace-making, and its tiny fishing village is full of brightly painted houses with ever-so-cute, perfectly matching, brightly painted boats bobbing in the canals in front of each house. Life there is still amazingly traditional: the men go off to fish while the women sit on their doorsteps 'making the Bobbin-ah lace-ah' and gossiping about…well, probably fish and lace, I imagine. Each woman specialises in one particular stitch, and each piece is passed from door to door in a very long production line to make the finished piece.

I just loved the place. I ambled around for a few hours, watching the fishermen bring in their catch, peeking into people's lounge rooms—incidentally, no matter what country you're in, if you look into people's lounge rooms in the middle of the afternoon they're watching soaps on TV—and sitting on benches gawking at beautiful Italian women (a pastime I became quite an expert at).

Back in London a few weeks later, I was browsing through a large book on Venice and discovered that Burano is where *spaghetti alla vongole* (spaghetti with baby clams) was first created. Now that just happens to be my favourite pasta dish, so I had to return to Burano and eat what I imagined would be the best *alla vongole* in the world.

So on my next trip, I talked Coach Captain Kevin Kelvin into coming to Burano with me. That in itself was no mean feat, because most drivers would much rather sit around the campsite and...just sit, really. However, it did cost me. Lunch and wine on me, and the promise of the most beautiful women in Venice on the streets of Burano. We walked straight into the small square at the heart of the village where there were about half a dozen bustling restaurants. I painstakingly checked out the menus, checked the clientele, checked for the right view, the right light, the right ambience and the right amount of beautiful Italian women. Finally, when Coach Captain Kevin Kelvin threatened to beat me to a pulp if I didn't choose a restaurant soon (once roused, drivers are a very impatient mob), we sat down in what looked to me like the best of the lot. I just wanted everything to be perfect for the ultimate *spaghetti alla vongole*.

I ordered a nice bottle of the local Soave white wine and some bruschetta to start. Coach Captain was happy now. He had alcohol, a seat and passing women to look at. I was buzzing with anticipation as the friendly waiter placed my steaming bowl of spaghetti in front of me.

But, alas, it was no better than ordinary. In fact, it was very how's-your-father. I was shattered. I tried to pretend it was wonderful, but I'd had much better *vongole* in a cheap dive of a restaurant right next to a *vaporetti* stop on Dorsoduro, frequented by the boat drivers of Venice. The *vongole* there was simply scrumptious and, in all the many Italian restaurants around the world where I've ordered and eaten *vongole*, no other version has ever matched the delicious taste of the simple dish that came from a cheap, dodgy café for boat drivers.

The morning after two nights of debauchery was always a slow and tedious affair. Trying to get groggy passengers to pack up their tents, shower, eat breakfast, and load up the bus was hard work, especially when I felt like shite as well. One swelteringly hot morning I joined the queue for the unisex showers, saw a cubicle with a vacant sign and walked in. I was taking a Hong Kong Chinese charter at the time and I walked straight in on a Chinese girl standing there totally in the nuddy. She screamed. I sort of laughed nervously, said sorry, and hastily shuffled out. But the problem was that she went straight to the other passengers and whispered into everyone's ear that she'd been attacked by this disgusting pervert in the shower. Consequently I was given dirty looks for the rest of the trip and only a couple of the guys bothered talking to me.

At the end of each trip all passengers have to fill out a detailed report on the trip and their glorious leader, giving scores for personality, organisational skills, general knowledge and 'fun skills'. The office takes these reports very seriously and any negative remarks are investigated.

On nearly all of my trips the reports were good, but my reports for that Chinese charter were absolute shockers, with 'poor' ticked in nearly every category. A couple of the guys on the tour gave me good reports, but the girls gave me a real bagging. 'He is a dirty old man.' 'He is a pervert.' 'He is vulgar.' 'He is unclean' (which was totally unfair: I was on my way to the shower, for God's sake). And: 'He is always trying to look at girls' (well, I suppose that one's true). All because I accidentally walked in on a girl in the shower who, I hasten to add, had not closed the door properly. Anyway, I was quite upset: I didn't even get a good look at her.

On yet another morning, with a shocking hangover, the old woollen tongue and a stale taste of sambucas and mozzie ribs in my mouth, I stumbled out of bed in my cabin to catch the last five minutes of breakfast. Only there was no cook in the cook tent, and his rostered helpers were cooking toast and preparing salads for the day's lunch. Bloody cooks. Can't they get up in time? Rule no. 15: *BE UP EARLY to wake cooks and passengers. It's not your holiday.*

It may not be *my* holiday but it sure ain't the cook's, either. I eventually found my cook in his caravan, dead to the world and snoring heartily with his mouth wide open. 'Hey Scott, get up! The passengers are making their own bloody salads,' I screamed. I left him grunting and groaning and joined the queue for a well-needed shower. Departure was at nine o'clock, and at five minutes past nine the tents, lilos, food, bins, bags and human bodies were all packed tightly into the bus ready to go. Yet there seemed to be something missing.

Terry, the driver.

While the passengers sat patiently in the bus, I scoured all 30 caravans looking for the elusive driver. I began walking between the caravans, softly calling out his name, but five minutes and 30 caravans later, I was banging on doors screaming, 'Terry! Terry!' I finally heard something that sounded like a dying bear and burst through a caravan door. He gave me a look through half-closed eyes as if to say, 'Who the hell are you?' I yelled, 'Terry, it's half past *fuckin'* nine. The passengers are already sitting in the bus.' He rubbed his eyes, ran his fingers through his hair, chucked on his shorts from the night before and stumbled out of the caravan. Within minutes he was sitting in the driver's seat reversing out of the camp, set for a five-hour drive.

Coach Captain Kevin Kelvin, on the other hand, would *always* wake up five minutes before departure, saunter downstairs (it was a decker) and get behind the wheel, where I would serve him up a one-litre German beer stein full of coffee, with six sugars. This, and chain-smoking three cigarettes, would keep him going for the long drive ahead. Kevin would wear nothing but the tiniest of footy shorts, whether, I might add, he was driving the bus or having dinner in a flash restaurant. I don't think he read rule no. 7: *Crew must always be of smart appearance on the road and maintain a high standard of dress.*

But then again, they were a rather smart pair of footy shorts.

Italian autostradas are teeming with toll booths. You're constantly stopping to fork out thousands of lire. On some stretches you can stop as many as six times in just a couple of hours. Our total bill for tolls in Italy was up around the

130 000 lire mark (about $130), which is pretty steep for only four days of autostrada driving.

I once noticed that Robbo, our driver, had slowed down to a snail's pace 40 metres or so before the toll booth. Then all of a sudden he put all our futures at risk by swerving across six lanes of dense traffic to one of ten toll booths. 'Robbo! What the hell are you doin'?' I screamed. He shrugged and said, 'Just going to the booth with the best-looking girl in it.' After ten years on the road, his Italian ran all the way to *ciao* and *grazie*, so when he got to the booth, he leant out of his window with a big smile and a wink and said, '*Ciao!*' in a strong Yorkshire accent. The toll-booth goddess reeled off some price in Italian and, having no idea what she'd said, he glanced at the price displayed above the window. He handed over the cash, smiled, winked again and said, '*Grazie, ciao!*' He then drove off with a smug look on his face, as if he'd just arranged to meet her for a romantic *tête-à-tête* somewhere in Rome. Robbo, who hailed from a small village in the Yorkshire Dales, was a hopeless, and I mean *hopeless*, romantic. He was sure he'd meet the girl of his dreams somewhere in Europe, marry her, and live happily ever after in a villa overlooking the Mediterranean.

We were about 50 kilometres out of Rome on another trip when a passenger came to see me with a very worried look on his face. He had a large wad of Italian lire in his hand. In a voice husky with panic he asked, 'Brian, I've still got all this Italian money. Is there anywhere I can spend it, before we get to Rome?'

Slightly confused, I said, 'What do you mean? You can spend it in Rome.'

'Ohh! Is Rome in Italy?'

'Umm...yes.'

'Oh, good,' he said with a beaming smile.

Relieved, he then plodded off to the back of the bus. I never did ask him what country he thought Rome was in. Romania maybe? I don't know. Frightening, really.

Seven Hills Camping in Rome, like Girasole Camping in Florence, is an absolute joy to visit. Each have been voted the best camping ground in Europe. They have the works: swimming pools, wonderful restaurants, nightclubs, Italian women, supermarkets, and even a zoo. And get this: when the kangaroo in Seven Hills zoo died (probably from too much rich food and pampering), they had a replacement in two weeks! Rome's main zoo had been waiting two years for one. Mafia connections, I suspect.

After we had set up camp and scoffed down our dinner, I would take the group into Rome for a walking tour in the relative coolness of the evening. I found the heat was so oppressive during the day that the passengers would walk around in a stupor, even more so than usual. It's a long walking tour and can take up to two and a half hours, allowing, of course, for the four absolutely mandatory gelati stops along the way. One can never eat too much Italian gelati.

Rome is a wonderful city to just wander around. The delights of Rome are intimate, not grandiose, with little piazzas with bubbling fountains hidden around *nearly* every corner and small coffee bars on every single one. There is one coffee bar for every 367 Romans.

I would start my walking tour at the Piazza Navona (great tartufo). The first great moment came as we walked out of the narrow Via Giustiniani into the open space of Piazza della Rotonda. There, standing in front of us, would be the magnificent 2000-year-old Pantheon. Even after the umpteenth time, I still stopped and looked in awe at this perfect Roman building. In ancient times it would have been an absolute marvel. The entire interior would have been encrusted with the rich gilt bronze and marble decorations that were later nicked by thieving emperors and greedy popes. Even today, walking through the massive front portico and seeing the dramatic opening in the centre of the huge dome (permanently open to the weather, be it blue skies or torrential rain) is simply breathtaking.

Around 27 BC, when work began on the Pantheon, Augustus Caesar had just become the first absolute ruler of the huge Roman Empire. Rome was universally recognised as *caput mundi* (the capital of the world) and life, especially for the rich, was just dandy.

A day in the life of a wealthy senator went something like this.

He would usually wake around dawn and slip on a toga and sandals while his slaves cleaned and prepared his house. For breakfast he'd have a slice of bread and cheese and a glass of water flavoured with a little wine, then he'd head out for a couple of hours of idle chit-chat with the other senators. A light lunch would be followed by a short rest, then it was time to hit one of the city's numerous baths. This was where men and women met to gossip, play games and wrestle(!). Most baths had separate areas for women and men, but some establishments permitted mixed bathing, and some of these were more like brothels. Our senator might in fact have visited any one of around 50 brothels in Rome, after they opened at three o'clock, before heading home for dinner. Meals were eaten at a leisurely pace, commonly taking up to five or six hours, and in some houses as many as ten. Dinner would include seven or more courses, which might include oysters, truffles, snails, sea urchins, boiled eggs and ham, lobsters, goose liver, eels, roasted veal, suckling pig, mullet, pheasant, peacocks and goose, asparagus, mushrooms, fruits and cakes. They might be entertained by naked Spanish dancing girls who pranced about between the guests as they lay reclining on huge cushions. Guests could, if they desired, stagger into a specially designed room (the vomitorium) to have a chuck and make room for more food and wine. And if you couldn't be shagged getting up to go to the loo, you could always call over a slave with a jug and fill it up. You could even get the slave to hold your willy.

After dinner, guests would just lay about talking and playing board games or they'd head back to the baths or over to the Circus Maximus for a spot of chariot racing.

Augustus himself would quite often go to his room and

have virgins brought up for deflowering. As one senator commented, 'They would go up in droves.'

Without the togas bit, it almost sounds like one of my tours.

Next, it was on to Piazza di Spagna for more gelatis and a toilet stop at the twentieth century's version of the Black Plague: McDonald's.

I'd then walk the group down the narrow Via di Stamperia and stop in front of a small but ornately deco- rated courtyard with a high, iron-barred fence blocking it off from the street. The walls inside were adorned with small but pretty fountains. There was another one mur- muring away in the centre of the courtyard, partly hidden in the gloom. I would turn to the passengers. 'What can I say, everyone? I'm really sorry, but the Trevi Fountain is closed for some reason. It's usually all lit up with bright lights and the fountains gush great plumes of water 30 metres in the air.' I would go on to tell them that the Fontana di Trevi was designed by Nicola Salvis in 1762 and apologise once again for its uncharacteristic closure. Then I'd march the group twenty metres further on, and into Piazza di Trevi. One by one they'd look to the right and catch sight of the blinding white and brilliant blue of Rome's largest and most famous fountain, the Trevi Fountain, built into the backside of a renaissance palace. The passengers' eyes would widen, their jaws would drop and they'd glare at me as I casually kept walking, pre- tending it wasn't there—until I couldn't keep a straight face any longer and doubled over with laughter. Maybe you had to be there.

The walking tour would then continue down the Via del Corso, past the monstrous Vittorio Emanuele monument and the Forum, and finish at the Colosseum.

Back in the good ol' days, Romans flocked to the Colosseum for many things, including good ol' gladiator contests. One event lasted 117 days, with over 9000 gladiators killed. I imagine that would be a bit like sitting through a five-day cricket Test (well, some of the players move about as often as dead bodies).

Circus acts were also popular at the Big C, with panthers pulling chariots, elephants writing in Latin with their trunks and bizarre fights to the death between exotic animal pairings, like rhinos and elephants, or buffalo and bears. On one day alone over 5000 animals were killed. So many animals were slaughtered, these contests are believed to have led to the extinction of entire species of African animals.

They also had exhibitions of fornication. Not unlike the back of my bus, really.

I would arrange for the driver to pick us up from the Colosseum at 10.30 pm, because he couldn't park anywhere near there and would have to do a quick drive-by pick-up. One evening it got past 10.30, and Robbo and the bus hadn't turned up. It got to eleven o'clock, then eleven-thirty, and still there was no sign of Robbo. As you can imagine, the passengers were getting restless and I was getting worried. Was he alright? Had he crashed the bus? Had he been dragged away by the police? Had he fallen in love with the Italian girl from the toll booth and moved to Naples? Finally, just near midnight, he turned up with glassy-looking eyes and said, 'Sorry, I fell asleep.' And boy, he must have been absolutely dead to the world, because while he lay in his peaceful slumber at the back of the bus, a band of gypsy kids snuck aboard through the open front door and ransacked the joint. Luckily, though, they only got away with a bit of food, some orange juice and some Cold Chisel tapes. Incidentally, if you're ever in Rome and you hear some gypsy kids singing 'Khe Sanh', can you thank them for me? Even though I still have terrible nightmares about Cold Chisel songs, the few days of relief they provided may have saved my sanity.

Back at the campsite after the walking tour, the passengers and crew alike would hit the 'Bunny Club Disco'. Male drivers and tour leaders would don their CFM (Come Fuck Me) shirts: our 'road crew' shirts, with which we hoped to impress the girls enough to pull a root. Now I am by no means a handsome man, but by golly, some of the drivers were dog-ugly and they still managed to pick up quite regularly. Some girls are simply much too easily impressed. Whenever a driver heard the question 'How do you ever get such a big bus around those little corners?' he knew he was odds-on.

The problem that faced some of the drivers was that when they eventually returned home to Australia or New Zealand, they would spend six months standing in bars with their CFM shirt on, wondering why no-one gave them even a passing glance. Then, depressed and bonkless, they would return to life on the road and get back to the discos in their beloved CFM shirts to explain how they get those big buses around those little corners...

At one stage, two of my passengers, who were a trifle drunk and had become rather amorous in the Bunny Club, snuck off in the wee hours of the morning looking for a place to bonk. They had taken a mattress and laid it under a large tree away from the tents and returning disco-goers. Hidden in the dark, they stripped off, did the business and fell into a drunken slumber. They woke up at seven o'clock the next morning, still naked and surrounded by about a dozen people, with many more walking by. They had placed the mattress only metres away from the shower block, and at least 60 people would have almost stepped on them on their way to have a morning shower. I never saw them, but I did see the photos. More snaps for grandma, I imagine.

Another evening, I was woken by a bloodcurdling scream from inside a girl's tent. Oh God, I thought, she's being raped or mugged—or, even worse, she's woken up sober and realised she's taken a dog-ugly driver back to her tent for sex. But no, it wasn't that bad. She was only sharing her tent with a large rat, which soon fled from the horrible, high-pitched screaming. Given that there are eleven rats for every person in Rome, she was lucky to find just one. The city has a legion of rat-catchers scouring the streets and sewers in nice matching uniforms. Back in Roman times, though, rats were quite useful. The ashes of rats' heads were mixed with valerian (a herb) and the mix-ture was gargled to get rid of bad breath. Also, the ancient version of Head & Shoulders dandruff shampoo, favoured by Cleopatra, was made from vinegar mixed with rat shit. I think I could have lived with dandruff and bad breath. Most of the drivers seemed to do alright with both.

The next morning would always be the most dangerous part of the trip. Driving into the city of Rome was terri-fying. Italian drivers are like Belgian drivers on speed. It never ceased to amaze me. When Italians stopped at traf-fic lights (I was amazed they stopped!), they would sit five cars abreast on a two-lane road, wait for the lights to turn green—unless there was no traffic going across the inter-section, when they'd just go as soon as they felt like it—and, in a suicidal dash, try to squeeze into two lanes. In a recent Europe-wide survey, Italy topped the list for the worst drivers and the most accidents. Which, if you've ever seen Italians driving, really isn't all that surprising.

The Italians consider the Vespa (Italian for wasp) more of a household appliance than an automobile, and their skill at scooting in and out of traffic would put even Michael Doohan to shame. Once, though, I was sitting by the front door of a decker when suddenly there was a huge crash, the doors burst open and a young Italian chap fell into my lap as his Vespa ploughed into the door of the bus. But he simply regained his balance and nonchalantly weaved back into the traffic as if nothing had happened at all.

For some passengers, the first stop on our first morning in Rome was a holy pilgrimage, while for others it was just a visit to a big-fuck-off-church. That stop, of course, was the vast square of St Peter's and the Vatican. Not permitted to do a spiel inside the church, I would address my little flock while we stood in the middle of Bernini's grand Piazza San Pietro, flanked by gigantic Doric columns topped with 140 statues of history's greatest saints. I would tell the group, 'We are standing in front of the largest and most important Catholic church in the world. It is the governing body for hundreds of millions of Catholics worldwide. Behind St Peter's is the Vatican, home of the Pope', etc.

On one trip I had three or four very religious girls on board. While I was giving my spiel in St Peter's Square they clutched rosary beads tightly in their hands, ready to take them inside to be blessed by the Pope or someone. I was in the middle of telling my little congregation about St Peter's being the most important Catholic church in the world when I was interrupted by Dave from Dandenong at the back of the group. 'Excuse me, Brian! Excuse me, Brian!'

'Yes, Dave,' I said.

He pointed up and enquired politely, 'Who are all those cunts?'

I paused for a second before replying. 'Well, Dave, those are 140 of the greatest saints in history.'

'Ohh, right,' he said, and went back to staring at girls walking through the square.

Dave from Dandenong dropped some classic lines that trip. After an afternoon in Barcelona, as all the passengers were returning to the bus, I was asking them one by one how their day went and what they had got up to. Dave was one of the last to return and, as he stepped aboard, I asked, 'So Dave, what did you do today?'

'Oh, I went up that Marco Polo cunt.'

I smiled. I didn't bother telling him that he'd actually climbed to the top of the 58-metre-high statue of Barcelona's adopted son, Christopher Columbus. I think the distinction might have been lost on him.

On another occasion, walking through a hot and steamy Venice, a passenger enquired innocently, 'Brian, what's that church called?' At which Dave snapped: 'Who gives a *fuck*, let's keep walking.'

After I'd finished my spiel, I sent the group off for free time. Quite a few headed into St Peter's one morning because the Pope was doing a sermon, or talking in tongues, or whatever popes do. I couldn't go in, though. I had much more important things to do. I had to go buy some chicken fillets.

I watched as the religious girls scurried inside, clutching their rosary beads even tighter since the distinguished Dave from Dandenong had labelled that crack team of saints chosen for the Vatican All-Stars as cunts.

In Via Andrea Doria, only 100 metres down twisting side streets from the never-ending queues for the Vatican museums, there's one of Rome's fabulous food markets. It never attracts too many tourists: zucchinis and salami don't make that good a souvenir. 'Here Mum, look what I got you from Rome.'

'Oh wow...a zucchini!'

I would usually be able to get by with my schoolboy Italian, which was just extensive enough to count and order, well, zucchinis and salami. But on one occasion, I sauntered up to the large chicken lady—that is, a large lady who sold chickens—and said, '*Lo voglio cinque petti di pollo, per favore.*' ('I want five kilos of chicken breasts, please.') She responded with about a three-minute barrage of Italian, of which I would have been lucky to catch three words. When she'd finished she stared at me, waiting for a response. So I confidently said, '*Si, molto bene.*' ('Yes, that's fine.') She then handed me a large plastic bag of what looked like chicken giblets.

Let's face it, it doesn't really help knowing only a few words of a language, when you can't understand any answer that isn't 'yes' or 'no'. Nine times out of ten, you end up just standing there dumbstruck. Once I was lost in a small Italian town I hadn't been to before and asked a man in near word-perfect Italian, '*Mi scusi, dove si trova la stazione?*' ('Excuse me, where is the train station?') He gestured off in a vague direction and jabbered on in Italian for about a minute. I smiled, said, '*Grazie*', and headed off in that vague direction for about twenty metres. Then I asked a little old lady the same question. Her answer was as incomprehensible as the man's. Eleven people, eleven questions and eleven un-understood directions later, I'd walked less than two blocks to finally arrive at the train station.

I would have had even more trouble back in 1871—this was when Italy reunited again for the first time since Roman times—because only three per cent of Italians spoke Italian. But then again, even if I knew how to ask for the train station in 73 different languages I'd still end up confused and wandering off in the wrong direction.

Whenever anything was bought from 'the food kitty', we had to get a receipt. In the Rome markets, that could mean the price scrawled with a crayon on a torn-off piece of cardboard, a discarded banana peel or even a piece of wood (I was once given a receipt scrawled on a thin piece of board). This would come in handy at the end of a trip—the receipts, that is, not the piece of wood—when, inevitably, the food kitty receipts wouldn't add up. I would just tear a corner off an old brown paper bag, scribble down a few prices with a crayon—I had one specially for this purpose—and then write neatly, in pen, on the back: *22/7. Fruit and veg. Rome markets.*

Meanwhile, as I was purchasing my chicken giblets, the religious girls were having a rather unholy experience inside St Peter's. Arriving late, they were stuck at the very back of the church, craning their necks to catch a glimpse of the Pope. Then one of them felt something against her leg. She looked behind her to find a dodgy looking Italian chap with his *cazzo* out, having himself a casual mid-morning wank. By God, did it freak the girls out. What with Dave's antics, the general debauchery on the bus and now a wanker inside the holiest of holy churches, I didn't know whether the girls would join a nunnery on their return home or sign up for a satanic cult.

The final day in the Eternal City was a full free day for the passengers and on most occasions I would head into the city to wander around and eat lots of Italian food. I would get hopelessly lost in the districts of Trastevere, Testaccio or the Villa Borghese and love every minute of it.

Getting unlost was part of our training. During our training trip, while driving through the outskirts of Rome, the tour leader trainer suddenly stopped the bus and threw us all out into the street in the middle of a God-knows-where-we-are part of Rome. She was testing us. She was testing our ability to show a bit of initiative and find the right bus connections back to camp. When all the other trainees had wandered off looking for buses, I grabbed one of the trainee drivers and said, 'I've got an idea.' We snuck around the corner and hailed a cab. In just over half an hour we were sitting at the bar just inside the entrance to the campsite, drinking pieronis in the warm sun and munching on delicious calzone.

About two hours later, the first couple of trainees turned up. I enquired politely which buses they took and from where. Then, five minutes later, the trainee driver and I strolled down to the bottom end of the campsite and the waiting trainer. She asked how we got to the campsite and

I confidently said, 'Oh, we caught the number 907 bus from Piazza del Risorgimento, then the 201 bus to here.'

'Very good,' she replied happily.

Now, that's what I call initiative.

In my constant quest for authentic local restaurants, I asked the absolute goddess at the campsite reception where I might find some good Italian tucker. She told me of a restaurant which sounded perfect, about seven kilometres away on the road into town.

'How are you going-ah to get-ah there?' she asked.

'Walk, then the bus,' I replied.

'Why don't-ah you take my-ah car?' as she threw the keys to Robbo, my driver.

'Gee, thanks,' we chorused.

'Would you like to join us?' Robbo asked, all glassy eyed.

'No, sorry, I have to-ah work.'

As we sauntered off to her car Robbo said, 'I think she likes me. Do you think I've got a chance?'

'Oh, for sure Robbo, she'll probably ask you to move in with her when we get back.'

Robbo's eyes lit up. 'D'ya reckon?'

Ristorante La Graticola, on Via Cassia, was the most Italian of all the Italian restaurants I'd ever had the pleasure to visit. There were no English menus, no English-speaking waiters and no badly painted pictures of the Colosseum. All the diners were Italian, and in front of them were authentic not-set-up-for-tourists check tablecloths. The food and wine lived up to my highest expectations as well.

The wine, made only kilometres away, was poured into plain bottles from a huge wooden cask. It was the best frascati I'd ever tasted. We feasted on local Roman dishes including a splendid *spaghetti alla carbonara*, probably Rome's most famous dish, and *coda alla vaccinara*, which the waiter informed us (well, I think he did) was a traditional Roman dish. It tasted divine, and it wasn't until I got back to camp and my Italian dictionary that I found out we'd just eaten braised oxtail with tomatoes, but, hey, it was delicious. We followed this with *saltimbocca alla romana* (veal with Parma ham, white wine and sage), which was so tender it simply melted in my mouth.

Bloated, but very content, we finally waddled out of the place over two hours later. And the very best thing about our new discovery was that the bill was a simple adding machine print-out. When I returned to camp I wrote neatly on the back: *23/7. Delicatessen. Rome.*

Thank you, Frank (our nickname for the food kitty).

On our last afternoon in Rome on one trip, I returned to camp to find a handful of my passengers ready to kill me. They were in the throes of trying to organise a full-blown mutiny. They'd gone to the Sistine Chapel that morning, only to find it was closed because the Pope was having a bit of a do there. According to the group of mutineers, it was my fault the Pope had chosen that day to have a knees-up. I showed them my list of public holidays observed by the Sistine Chapel. That day wasn't listed, but the passengers still thought I should have known. Apparently they thought I should ring the Pope whenever I hit town and ask if he was having any shindigs I should know about.

I told them I was terribly sorry, but there was sod all I could do about it. They then ordered me (and the rest of the group) to stay in Rome for another day so they could visit the Sistine Chapel. Two girls even went as far as to say that the only reason they did this whole 28-day tour was to visit Michelangelo's ceiling—yeah, right!—and started hurling abuse at me.

I said, 'Look, the only way I can change an itinerary is if every single person on the bus votes to stay in Rome for another day, but that means they'll lose a day in Florence. So I have to put it to a vote.' Scraps of paper were handed around and the passengers could vote YES for staying in Rome, NO for going to Florence or I DON'T CARE for either way. There was a Brownlow-night-like atmosphere as I opened each vote to count it. The final tally showed only six votes for staying in Rome, 26 votes for going with the flow and ten votes for going on. All hell broke loose. The people who wanted to go to Florence started screaming at the people who wanted to stay in Rome, who in turn started screaming at me. I just wanted to strangle the whole bloody lot of them. I was ready to give the Pope a real earful next time I bumped into him.

As far as I was concerned, I *had* to get away from them for a minute and I snuck off to the bar for a quiet drink. I couldn't believe how downright rude two of the girls were. One had even written, underneath her YES vote, 'Because Brian fucked up.' They honestly believed I should have known, and told them to visit the Sistine Chapel the day before. Bloody maggots (the crew's affectionate name for annoying passengers).

Anyway, I solved it. I rang the Pope and told him to get his arse down to the Sistine Chapel now and open it up. Only joking. I did, however, organise another bus to take the six maggots into the Vatican the next morning, *and* I found the train times to Florence *and* I gave them each a map of Florence *and* I marked where to meet the bus at 5.30. The two girls were miserable cows for the rest of the trip, bitching and moaning constantly, and ended up giving me shocking reports.

The funny thing is that about eighteen months later I bumped into one of them in Melbourne, and she came rushing up to me like a long-lost friend. She even hugged me. I had to restrain myself from telling her to fuck off.

South-east of Florence, set right in the heart of the Chianti district and just out of the village of Figline Voldarno, lies Camping Girasole. Of all the campsites I've visited in Europe, I think this one is by far the best. It has everything one's little heart could desire. There are two huge swimming pools; a mini-supermarket full of those delectable little tidbits that are served up in antipasto, like cheeses, hams, olives, sundried tomatoes and marinated seafood; and a wonderful restaurant with a wide, vine-covered terrace that (if you weren't too busy hoeing into the sumptuous food and wine) would give you a great opportunity to enjoy the magical views of rolling Tuscan hills. It's got a buzzing bar, a happening disco, shower blocks that are spotlessly clean, NEW washing machines that actually work and don't turn your clothes that sort of greeny-bluey-reddy-greyish colour. *And*, to top it all off, the staff are both friendly and helpful.

(P.S. Girasole, you can forward my commission via the publisher. Thank you.)

This campsite, like every other campsite in Europe, was constantly swarming with German tourists. Thousands of the buggers, all in campervans, listening to polka music and eating *Wurst*. I have a theory I'd like to share with you. After Germany's two failed attempts to take over Europe last century, I believe they have found another, even sneakier way to do it. Their plan is this. At the height of the European summer, when every campsite in Europe is absolutely chocker with German campervans, there will be half a dozen German soldiers hidden inside each van. At the appointed time, they and their group sergeant, heavily disguised as a fat German tourist in check pants, will burst out and, without too much problem, take over even the tiniest corners of the European continent.

Don't laugh.

When it eventually happens, remember that I was the one who first broke news of this devious plan.

After our relatively short, four-hour drive from Rome to Girasole, we would set up camp, have lunch and head straight into Florence for the walking tour. Parking alongside the other 942 coaches at Piazzale Michelangelo, I would march the group down to the River Arno, across the Ponte alle Grazie and into the heart of medieval Florence.

First stop would be a leather showroom where passengers would hold up, say, a gaudy purple leather jacket with long green tassles and say, 'Brian, what do you think?'

'How much is it?'

'Um, about $450.'

'Yeah, it's stunning. In fact, I'd buy two if I were you,' I'd say enthusiastically, while trying to figure out in my head exactly how much commission I'd get.

Just a short stroll would take us into the old civic centre of Florence, the Piazza della Signoria, where I'd give a long spiel on the piazza itself, the Palazzo Vecchio, the Loggia dei Lanzi and the many grand statues in the piazza. On one Hong Kong Chinese charter, I had only just begun my spiel when two people wandered off to take a photo. A few seconds later they were followed by a couple more. By the time I was halfway through my spiel, I was standing there literally talking to myself. *Every single one* of the 22 passengers had walked away. Now, my spiels weren't boring. Honestly. So I was well pissed off. In our next city, Venice, I marched them into St Marks Square and said, 'OK, this is Venice. Bye', and walked off. I hope they learned a valuable lesson.

During our training trip, each tour leader was given the role of 'tour leader of the day' and, under the watchful eye of the trainers, had to perform all the tasks a regular trip usually involved. The jobs included leading walking tours and shopping trips, making phone calls to

HQ, planning the day's itinerary, and generally organising anything and everything. You would get maybe two chances like this to prove yourself during the trip.

An Australian fellow called Brian (not me) was given his first opportunity to prove himself in Florence, and he did a highly commendable job of totally fucking it up. In Piazza della Signoria, at the beginning of the walking tour, he stood in front of the large statue of Neptune and started telling us all about Michelangelo's *David*, which stood no less than twenty metres away. He told us how the original stood here for 400 years until 1873, and was then moved to the Accademia. Poor Michelangelo must have been turning in his grave. He once said of Ammannati's *Neptune*, 'Ammannati, Ammannati! What lovely marble you have ruined!'

Brian then walked straight past *David* and through the long courtyard of the Uffizi Gallery, without even mentioning it. Well, I suppose the Uffizi only houses the most extensive and important collection of renaissance art in the entire world. He finally stopped on the bank of the Arno River, told us about the Ponte Vecchio and said, 'That's it, everyone, you now have free time.' Then he looked at the head trainer for approval.

'Um, what about the Duomo, Brian?' she enquired.

'The what?'

She was getting a little annoyed now. 'The Duomo. The large church that no building in Florence can be built higher than. The one you can't possibly miss.'

I'd have to say his chances of scoring a job were looking

rather shaky at this point. As a matter of fact, they were looking rather shaky on the *first* day. He missed the departure in London. I couldn't believe it. He made his own way to the campsite in Paris and turned up in a downpour, drenched to the skin and looking like Quasimodo. Not a good start, really.

The Medicis ruled Florence from 1437 and, for three and a half centuries, set the standard not only in art, but in medicine, science, engineering, astronomy, physics, politics, economics and, most important of all, gelati, which was first made in sixteenth-century Florence.

In a book I found in a London bookstore I came across the name of a gelateria in Florence that had been voted the best in Italy only the year before. On my next trip I would have to take my passengers there, I thought. But what I really meant was that, by hook or by crook, *I had to get there.*

Gelateria Vivoli is situated in Via dell'Isola delle Stinche, which is not only hard to say but also bloody hard to find. The first time I took a group there, or attempted to take a group there, I was trudging through the narrowest of alleys with a map in my hand, totally lost, with 40 people trundling behind me. As we circumnavigated the same block for the fourteenth time, I was really hoping the ice-cream was worth it. Finally I found it. And yes, it was worth it. The mandarin and sinfully rich meringue flavours I tried were just orgasmic.

Goodness knows, though, I've seen some incredibly

odd ice-cream flavours in Italy, including champagne, chestnut, ricotta, date, prickly pear, fig, rice, whisky, muesli, avocado and prosciutto. (Mmmmmmmm, ham-flavoured ice-cream!) I'll just stick to my mandarin and meringue, thank you.

I would finish my walking tour at the impossible-to-miss Duomo, which, by the way, was started way back in 1294 and wasn't finished till 1883. I think the Italians took the 'it's sweet to do nothing' thing a bit too far in that case.

The passengers would then have free time to go to the markets and pay $500 for a vinyl jacket that the proprietor would swear was anything but: 'You-ah smell. It's-ah good leather. You see, good-ah leather.' I would mostly just saunter around town and, to be totally frank, perve.

If you ask me, Florentine women are the most beautiful in Europe. In fact, at the end of each trip, I would compile a chart (I know, I know) with the top five cities for beautiful women. Florence finished on top nearly every time. After my final trip, I compiled the top five outright. This is, of course, only my own unqualified opinion, but this is how it ended up:

1. Florence
2. Copenhagen
3. Barcelona
4. Amsterdam
5. Paris.

So I don't sound like a sexist pig, I asked a couple of female tour leaders to agree on the top five cities for men. They came up with:

1. Rome
2. Stockholm
3. Venice
4. Barcelona
5. Florence.

In short, it seems unanimous: the Italians are the best-looking bunch in Europe.

On the journey back to camp later that afternoon, we would stop at the co-op supermarket in Figline Voldarno for a spot of food shopping. Earlier that day, as we drove into Florence and I was doing my history spiel, I would tell the group about a famous and much-sought-after Florentine delicacy: roosters' testicles. (This bit was true, by the way.) The passengers would squirm in their seats and screw up their faces at the thought of it.

When we reached the supermarket, I would buy a small plastic tub of these tiny periwinkle-type things (removed from their shells), take it back to the bus and hold it up to the passengers 'Here everyone, look. At considerable personal expense, I've bought some roosters' testicles for you to try.' I would then open the lid and wave the tub of 'testicles' in people's faces. They'd recoil as if it was a tub of my own testicles. 'Does anyone want to try one?' I'd ask.

'Ergghh! Nahhh! Fuck off!' would come from all corners of the bus. So I would take one out, put it in my mouth and begin to chew ever so slowly, going, 'Mmmmmmm', and generally carrying on as if it was Vivoli gelati. Most of the passengers seemed on the verge of being sick, but one or two would invariably bite the bullet—or testicle, as the case may be—and have a try. 'It tastes almost...fishy,' they'd say.

I never did tell them what was really in the plastic tub.

After returning to camp for a quick dinner, we would head back into town to visit an Italian nightclub. Only an olive stone's throw from Santa Croce, the Red Garter nightclub should perhaps have been renamed 'The Fair Dinkum Beauty Bonzer Dinki-di Down Under Bar'. The nightclub was filled every night with 18-to-30 trippers by the coachload. And because each bus had at least a 3:1 female to male ratio, the place would be teeming with rampaging, drunk girls. The Italian men outside would be down on their knees begging to get inside, offering their Vespas or even their beloved mothers to the doormen. Not only was the place jumping with Aussies and Kiwis, but every night Gordon, in his Akubra hat, would perform great and famous Italian classics like 'Eagle Rock' and 'Down Under'. Now don't get me wrong. I liked the place, and for one reason above all.

There was a fellow at the Red Garter whose sole responsibility was to make sure I always had a drink in my hand. That was it. That was his job. He looked after the dozen or so crew in the club and would bypass the queues at the bar to personally make us our desired cock-tails. I would be standing there with my pint glass of strawberry daiquiri (which was more daiquiri than straw-berry), having only taken a sip or two, and this fellow would be handing me another one. As you could well imagine, I tended to get a trifle drunk—well, pissed off my head actually—and would send him off for some exotic drink, hoping it would keep him delayed for an hour or so. But even if I asked for a kiwifruit, lychee, paw-paw and African artichoke daiquiri, he would return five minutes later. 'Here you go, Brian. I'm sorry it took so long.' Even as I left the Red Garter, my drinks host would hand me a large milkshake container, with accompanying straw, filled to the brim with an ungodly cocktail called a Zombie, or as it should be known, 'Brain-Numbing-Stomach-Churning-Shocking-Hangover-Inducing-Delight'. The next morning was never a good one for me.

Back to our training trip. The other Brian, who had started his stint as 'tour leader of the day' so disastrously, ended it with a rather big thud. As tour leader, his responsibility was to get the drunken group back to the bus, which was waiting around the corner at midnight (no easy task at the best of times), but Brian was nowhere to be seen. He had passed out under a table covered with banana-daiquiri-flavoured vomit. The next morning the trainers put him on a train back to London. Pity, really. I was quite looking forward to him telling us about the Eiffel Tower, also known as the *Mona Lisa*, and how it was designed by Leonardo da Vinci back in 1502.

Immediately after the downfall of the other Brian, we got into the bus and drove straight through to Venice. A four-week trip was condensed into three, so it involved a few night drives to fit everything in. I drew the short straw and had to keep the driver company between four and seven in the morning. After I was rudely awoken by one of the other trainees, I made my way to the front of the bus and asked the trainee driver (who, by the way, was the same chap who'd danced semi-naked on the bar in Venice), 'How you doin', alright?'

'Yeah, fine,' he replied happily. I then plonked myself down in a deckchair—this was a decker—and stared out into the night. It was only a couple of minutes later that I saw a huge sign on the side of the autostrada that read RIMINI 27 KMS. Now, my knowledge of Italian geography was good enough to figure out we were sort of off the track. In fact, the way we were going, we wouldn't get within a bull's roar of Venice. I stuck my head through the tiny window into the driver's cabin, and calmly said: 'Steve, you're going the wrong way.'

'Uggh, what?' he grunted.

'We're going south. We should be going north.'

'Oh, shit.'

Somehow we managed to arrive in Venice only two hours late, with the trainers none the wiser that we were behind schedule, let alone aware that we'd taken a side trip to the lovely seaside resort of Rimini.

Drivers and tour leaders had a combined set of rules, but we also had our own separate rules. Rule no. 3 for the drivers states: *You must not get lost.*

Yeah, like it's a rule a driver would break on purpose: 'Stuff it, I'll take this turn-off to see if I can get lost.'

One time, while trying to find the ferry terminal in

Patras, Greece, our driver Terry (this was the same driver I couldn't get out of bed in Venice and who liked spending lots of money on wooden video cameras) kept on insisting it was further down the road we were travelling on. 'Terry,' I said, 'this road seems a bit narrow. I'm sure the turn-off was back there.'

'No, no. This is the way!' was the grumpy reply.

'This road goes nowhere. We'd better turn back.'

In a huff he bellowed 'Fine!' and turned off the road to do a U-turn on, of all places, a sandy beach, and promptly got us well and truly bogged. We then spent the next hour trying to dig this huge coach out of the fine sand. Well, the passengers and I dug while Terry barked orders at a safe distance from the flying dirt. After an hour we'd only progressed about twenty centimetres. Then I had an idea. I remembered seeing, only a couple of kilometres back, two British-registered semis stopped on the side of the road, having a break for lunch. So I hiked back and asked one of the drivers ever so nicely if he could give us a bit of a tow. Five minutes later I rolled up as a passenger in this big fuck-off truck. 'This won't be enough,' the driver announced. 'I'll have to get the other semi.' So, with one semi pulling the other semi, which was in turn pulling the bus, we finally slid out of the sand and back onto the road.

'Maybe you'll listen to me next time,' I grumbled to Terry as we drove off.

'Fuck off!' he snapped.

'Moron!' I snapped back. 'You've really got *no* fuckin' idea, have you?'

There went rule no. 7: *Compliment one another (driver and tour leader) and do not highlight your offsider's faults in any way.*

We didn't get on at all that trip. It wasn't my fault. I'm a nice bloke. He was just a miserable git.

The final day in Florence was designated a free day and it was amazing how many passengers stayed in the confines of the campsite to take advantage of the resort-like facilities. Stuff the world's greatest art treasures when you can just lie by the pool and do nothing all day.

I would head into Florence in my almost obsessive quest for good food. Once, though, having had my fill of Italian food, I decided that what I really missed was Japanese. I eventually hunted down a Japanese restaurant in a back alley just near Santa Croce. Walking in was like stepping into any Japanese restaurant in Australia. It had the same stark furnishings, and a little Japanese lady in her kimono and wooden sandals waddled up, bowed and started waffling to me in...Italian. I was taken aback. I was expecting (perhaps, in retrospect, a little foolishly), 'G'day, 'ow ya going, ya wanna table for lunch?' She spoke no English, only Japanese and Italian. The menu listed Japanese dishes I recognised, like teppanyaki, but the names were followed by a long string of Italian words. They probably said, 'Made with Teppanyaki sauce, this special Florentine version is served with the bowel of a hog.' Mind you, it tasted quite nice. The restaurant was filled with Japanese students and Japanese tourists. The

Florentines, I imagined, would rather stick to their roosters' testicles.

On another occasion I decided that I not only wanted to dress like an Italian, I wanted to be cool like one as well. So I hired a Vespa. But my first attempt at hiring one didn't go too well. I headed for the south side of the river looking for a place that hired mopeds, and to my delight I found one only a short stroll from the Ponte Vecchio. I tried in vain for ten minutes to explain to a small Italian man that I wanted to hire a moped, but he just kept shrugging his shoulders, saying, 'Non capisco.' Suddenly I remembered there were some posters of Vespas near the entrance to the garage, with large prices next to them. So I dragged him outside and pointed to the poster. 'Ahhhh!' he said, and rushed inside with me scurrying behind him. He led me into another large room and, from the rack above, pulled down a large clear plastic wind protector for the front of the Vespa. 'Ahhhh,' I said. The place didn't rent Vespas at all. The poster out the front was advertising plastic windguards *for* Vespas. I shrugged, said, 'Non capisco', laughed and rushed out.

I did eventually find a Vespa and spent the day trying to look cool, but just ended up looking scared shitless as I tried to dodge suicidal Fiats, tried to keep my eyes on the road when gorgeous Italian girls in Vespas zoomed past me, and tried to dodge the 13 million other tourists who visit Florence every day.

Sadly, Florence is all a bit noisy and frenetic nowadays. It must have been an extraordinary place to be at the height of the Renaissance. Even when the Medicis' rule was in its death throes, they still managed to live in the absolute lap of luxury.

At the marriage of the Grand Duke Cosimo III to Marguerite Louise D'Orleans in 1661, the wedding party walked through town with *all* of the streets carpeted with rich Turkish rugs, houses on either side of the street hung with the most splendid tapestries and paintings, and massive awnings of crimson velvet draped over the street to shield the celebrities from the sun. Four thousand soldiers lined the streets, with 100 footmen and twenty pages for the bride. The wedding itself was a ridiculously lavish affair followed by an even more ridiculously large feast, including lots of roosters' testicles, no doubt.

All this was when the Medicis were supposed to be in a horrendous slump. I can't even imagine what a wedding was like when the Medicis were at their peak.

With the sun low on the horizon, and the rolling vineyard-covered hills and perfect lines of cypress trees all bathed in golden Tuscan light, we'd be cantering at full pelt along the narrowest of tracks, trying to keep up with Paolo, our horse-riding guide. Passing picture-postcard-perfect stone farmhouses, we'd be riding through the rows of aged chianti vines, looking across Tuscan hill after Tuscan hill. The one-hour horse-riding trek out of Girasole was simply wonderful. Paolo, who was as mad as a cut snake, only spoke a few words of English. His favourite sentence was, 'Hey, you-ah John-ah Wayne, banga bang.' Whenever he said it, you were expected to pretend to shoot him, then he'd fall backwards until he was hanging with only one foot in a stirrup and his head bobbing dangerously close to the ground.

Two Australian girls who were keen on going horse riding asked Paolo, with the help of five minutes of charades, whether he had any helmets. When Paolo finally figured out what they were after, he burst into uproarious laughter. You have to remember that this is the same country where you don't even have to wear a helmet on a motorcycle, let alone on a horse or (even stranger to most Europeans) a bicycle. In a lot of places in Europe, people who wear bicycle helmets are considered wankers or posers who think they're Olympic cyclists.

Paolo was very well practised in his other English phrase. So much so, in fact, that he sounded very much like Homer Simpson assessing a doughnut as he checked out girls' posteriors (as every good Italian man does) and said: 'Hmmm, nice bum!'

With a nice sore bum and chafed thighs, I'd join the passengers in Girasole's restaurant for our second Italian 'national meal'. A simple pasta for starters, the way pasta should be, would be followed by Hungarian goulash for main course. Naturally, I couldn't tell the passengers that we were about to eat something Hungarian for our Italian national meal, so I'd tell them it was called *stufato alla Toscana* or Tuscan stew and was a favourite dish of the Medicis in the fifteenth century. They seemed very impressed with that. It's amazing what I could get away with.

After dinner we would rock on downstairs to the Girasole disco, where I would watch the *true* Italian masters at work. No, not Michelangelo, Leonardo or Raphael. Paolo, Andrea and Mafisto. These were local Italian lads who had picking up women down to a fine art.

They were good.

I readily concede that I'm somewhat inept at sleazing onto women, so I would just stand at the bar with a beer in my hand and watch in awe as the lads performed their magic.

Each one had his own individual style which left telltale signs. When girls returned to the bus in the morning, I could figure out which lad they'd been with the night before. If a girl came back to the bus with wet hair, she'd invariably been with Paolo (not to be confused with Paolo the horse-riding guide), who seemed to favour the old bonk-in-the-shower routine in the morning.

He was good.

Andrea, on the other hand, would fall hopelessly in love with each girl and promise to write to them and visit them in Australia, New Zealand or any one of 63 other countries. At least that's what he'd tell them. Any girl who had been with Andrea would come rushing back to the bus and gush about his undying love. 'I think I'm in love,' she'd say. 'I just can't wait to see him again.'

He was good.

But in my eyes the master of all masters was Mafisto, who worked as the lifeguard at the Girasole pool and looked like a bigger, bronzer version of Jean-Claude van

Damme. Dressed impeccably, as they all were, and only speaking a smattering of English, he would simply stand next to a girl and smile a lot. But astonishingly, that's all he had to do. He'd pick up. Boy, it made me jealous. One evening I spent three hours chatting to this gorgeous English girl, buying her drinks and being a total gentleman, but when I went to the loo, I returned to find that *bastardo* Mafisto standing there with his arm around her and a big 'I'm taking her home tonight' smile on his face.

That was definitely the last time I ever did him a favour. A few weeks earlier he'd been trying to pick up a German girl and, with not a single word of shared language between them, had asked me how to say 'you are beautiful' in German. All things considered, I wasn't going to make him say, 'Would you like a look at my incredibly small penis?, or anything silly. After all, Mafisto could break my legs with his little finger. So I taught him to say 'you are gorgeous'. He repeated it to himself at least 30 times (he wasn't a smart man, but he knew what love is), then said it to the girl, who smiled and promptly left the disco with him. One of Mafisto's favourite and often used pick-up tricks was to invite girls to the pool—he had the key, of course—for a skinny dip. And God knows, it always seemed to work.

He was the best. In fact, he was even better than Coach Captain Kevin Kelvin.

I used to watch them for hours, trying to pick up this valuable skill, but my problem was that I didn't look as if

I'd just stepped off the set of a Fellini film. All I had was my CFM shirt.

Late one evening, after a less than successful evening in the disco (I don't know why I even contemplated competing with the Italian masters), I stumbled back to find our camp in absolute chaos.

The passengers were pulling tents apart as they racked their drunken brains trying to figure out why they couldn't get in. Earlier in the evening one of their fellow passengers had taken the top fly off each tent and put it back on the wrong way round. He or she had done this to twelve tents, which must have taken quite a while. I had to admit, though, it was pretty funny watching these drunk people trying to work out why they couldn't get into their tents.

On our way out of Florence and on to France, we would drop in at the world's leading source of miniature Leaning Tower of Pisas. You had to fight your way through about 300 metres of souvenir stalls on both sides of the narrow road before you stepped through an archway and onto the sprawling lawns of the vast Campo del Miracoli, featuring one of the most recognised landmarks on earth. Like the Duomo and the Baptistry, the tower itself is an almost freakishly beautiful building, but I would spend most of my time wandering around the souvenir stalls. I've never seen so much crap in one place at one time in my life. But I loved it. I would pick up a Leaning Tower of Pisa toilet brush or a Leaning Tower of Pisa nasal hair remover and chuckle to myself. These were the people who put 'tacky' into tacky souvenirs. The array of useless crap on each stall astounded me. Who actually bought this junk?

One Chinese girl returned to the bus with, wait for it, a 60-centimetre-high ceramic Leaning Tower of Pisa in a fetching shade of bright purple and totally covered with little gold sparkly bits. Best of all, though, this frighteningly ostentatious sculpture was a lamp. There was a small globe on the fifth floor, and the cord came out of the base. It was fantastically horrible. But looking back now, I honestly wish I'd bought *two*. For matching bedside lamps. Sometimes souvenirs go so far beyond naff that they actually become cool.

I'm not quite sure whether my 'Greetings from Pisa' pen fell into that category. 'Greetings from Pisa' was embossed in gold—I'd hazard a guess it wasn't real gold— at the top of the pen. The middle of the pen carried a photo of a Latino-looking lady with a one-piece bikini on. When you pointed it down to write, the bathers would drop down (which was now up) to reveal a totally naked Latino-looking lady.

The best souvenir ever bought has to have been the one snapped up by a French naval officer who was holidaying on the Greek island of Melos way back in 1820. He was down by the port scouring through the souvenir stalls, more than likely looking through the MY FRIEND WENT TO GREECE AND ALL I GOT WAS THIS FUCKING T-SHIRT T-shirts and cheap ceramic statues, when he came across a large marble statue of a woman. It was a bit dodgy—it had no arms for a start—so the proprietor gave it to him for about

50 bucks. A bit expensive, the French guy thought, but, hey, it was a pretty big statue.

That statue was the *Venus de Milo*, from the second century BC. It is now a star attraction at the Louvre in Paris, worth zillions.

You never know, my pen could be worth a small fortune. I wonder if they were cheaper by the dozen…

After a week in Italy, we would wend our way west through the Italian Riviera along the 200-odd kilometres of autostrada that hug the coast and cut through 147 and a half tunnels to the French border.

I would offer a very expensive bottle of French champagne to any passenger who could tell me how many tunnels we would pass through before we reached the French border. No-one would get it right, though, because everyone would have counted 144 tunnels by the time we reached the large Italian/French customs building at the border. But the official border, which is only marked by a small sign announcing FRANCE, is actually halfway through the fourth tunnel after the customs border. It kept the buggers amused for a few hours, and it meant I got to keep the bottle of very expensive champagne for myself.

On one occasion a Japanese girl had her bag, with cash and her passport in it, stolen in Florence. Because there was no Japanese Consulate (the nearest was in Rome), I had to try to sneak her through the border without a passport. She would then be able to get a new one in Paris.

Ten minutes before we reached the border, I took her

upstairs to the top deck, hid her under a pile of about twenty sleeping bags and told her to remain perfectly still. That wasn't difficult: she suffocated to death. Only joking. The poor girl was petrified she'd end up in jail or be mauled by savage guard dogs. I calmly flashed my bag of passports and showed my paperwork to the French border guard. He gave them a quick glance, grunted at me, spat on the ground, on my passports and at me, and waved us through. We were safely in France, where we would spend two nights before making a flying visit to Spain and Barcelona.

PAELLA
PORRONES
& PRYCA SUPERMERCADO

Colombian drug barons come in handy sometimes.

Only one day before we were due to enter Spain, an Australian fellow came up to me brandishing his passport.

'Hey Brian, do I need a visa for Spain?'

'No,' I replied confidently.

'Well, how come Peter's got one in his passport?'

'Has he?' I asked warily.

Peter did have a visa and he informed me that, as of two weeks earlier, all Australians now needed a visa for Spain. I rang the office in London. 'Is it true Australians now need a visa, prior to arrival, to enter Spain?'

'Um...yep.'

'Gee, well thanks for telling me. I'm going to Spain tomorrow and I've got eighteen passengers without visas.'

There was nothing the office could do. And all I could do, or try to do, was bluff my way into Spain. If that didn't work, I would have to leave eighteen people on the border at the mercy of a band of murderous gypsies.

Arriving at the border, I waltzed confidently up to the border guard, said one of my six words of Spanish— '*Hola!*' (hello)—and handed over my pile of passports. All the passports with visas were at the top of the pile, in the hope that the guard would look at the first few, get bored, and wave us through. But no. He wanted to look at every single one and have a good perve at the passport photos of all the girls.

When he discovered the passports without visas, he started ranting and raving at me in Spanish. I'm pretty sure he wasn't enquiring about the well-being of my family or inviting me to his place up in the hills for homemade paella and a few glasses of nice sherry.

It was then that I walked back to the bus and got the Colombian drug baron. Carlos (he couldn't have had any other name, really) was a sweet-natured and charming cocaine dealer. Well, that was my theory anyway. His extra large and (initially) very heavy suitcase seemed to get lighter as the trip went on, and I would jokingly ask him if he was unloading cocaine along the way. He would laugh, put a gun to my head and tell me to keep my fuckin' mouth shut.

Only joking.

He never used to swear.

I dragged him off the bus to talk to Jose, my good friend and border guard. They talked for about five minutes, by which time both Jose and Carlos were smiling. Jose then threw me the passports and waved us all through. Walking back to the bus, I asked Carlos what he'd said.

'Oh, not much.'

Now, I didn't actually see any transaction, so I could only assume that Carlos had arranged to meet up with someone like Jose's brother in Barcelona to hand over half a kilo of cocaine. But hey, I didn't mind. It got us into Spain.

Just outside Barcelona we would stop at Pryca Supermercado, which I reckon sounds a bit like a Spanish superhero. 'Look, up in the air! Is it a plane? No, it's SUPERMERCADO.' Pryca is another one of those ridiculously large Euro hypermarkets, and I loved visiting the place for two very good reasons.

One was that the receipts were non-itemised, listing prices only, so I could buy anything I desired (and usually did). The other reason was that Pryca had the most beautiful checkout chicks in the entire world.

First on our shopping list were the ingredients to make that devilish Spanish drink sangria, for our sangria party (read debauchery) that very evening. The traditional recipe consists of red wine, oranges, pears, Cointreau and brandy, but I had conjured up my own brain-numbing concoction.

Next time you invite a small group of your closest friends over for an orgy, try this.

Buy a large shiny plastic rubbish bin and carefully place a black garbag inside. Now fill this with ten litres of red wine (bought in convenient and so-cheap-it's-a-bit-of-a-worry tetra paks) and three litres each of lemonade, orange juice and Fanta. Then add a bottle each of rum, vodka and gin—which is so cheap it could only be made from effluent from the nearby petroleum plant—a bottle of peach schnapps and, finally, some chopped-up apples, oranges, pineapple and pears. Put the lid on the bin and leave it sitting in the hot sun for a few hours to encourage further fermentation. Then *voilà* (or whatever they say in Spain), you now have a drink that would not only kill a black dog but would make passengers fall over, throw up and have sex with anyone (but not necessarily in that order and sometimes all at the same time).

I would also buy two *porrones*. These traditional Spanish drinking vessels are a bit like a small glass jug, but the spout is about twenty centimetres long and funnels to a very narrow tip. Filled with sangria, they are emptied from a great height into one's mouth and, inevitably, ears, eyes, nose and belly button. Hence the name. They also have the added charm, given the copious amount of sangria being poured down people's throats, of making partygoers get pissed twice as fast, fall over twice as fast, throw up twice as fast and have sex with anyone twice as fast.

The emphasis is on quantity, not quality.

In the course of this flurry of alcohol buying, we would still manage to fill a trolley or two with food, including Barcelona's most famous national dish: the Chupa Chup ('suck-suck' in Spanish). First created by Enric Bernat over 40 years ago, Chupa Chups are now sold in 167 countries, with a 700 million dollar turnover and 4 billion sold every year. God, that's a lot of lollipops! There wouldn't be a second that goes by when someone around the world hasn't got a mouth full of Chupa Chup. As I handed the passengers Chupa Chups from my large plastic tub, I would justify it as a cultural experience because the logo was designed by one of Catalonia's favourite sons, Salvador Dali.

In some ways the Chupa Chup story maintains a venerable tradition.

In the sixteenth century, Spain introduced Europe to a lot of strange and exciting food that we now take for granted. Tomatoes, potatoes, corn, peppers and (most important of all, see Chapter 3) chocolate were brought over from South America and landed at Barcelona on their way to the tables of Europe. I can't even imagine what the world would have been like without a bucket of chips smothered in tomato sauce, with a chocolate chaser.

According to a worldwide medical report on diet a few years back, Spaniards have the healthiest diet in the world. Even though they eat lots of seafood, olive oil, fruit and vegetables and all that healthy shit, I find that very hard to believe. Breakfast ('the most important meal of the day', nutritionists and Kelloggs are always telling us) for a lot of Spaniards is *churros con chocolate*. This is churros, which are long, deep-fried doughnuts covered in sugar, dipped in the thickest, sweetest hot chocolate drink you could imagine. Even an incurable chocoholic like myself found it all a bit too much first thing in the morning. And this from a man who once had, for main course in a restaurant, ostrich covered in chocolate sauce!

I have to admit I would sometimes get a little too excited about the prospect of shopping at Pryca with those unitemised receipts. I went crazy one day and bought four pairs of ski socks, a matching pair of cacophonously loud shorts for my driver and me, a couple of T-shirts and— this is when I knew I'd gone too far—a cassette tape of Linda Rondstadt singing soppy Spanish songs. What can I say? It was a rush of blood. I was all caught up in the Spanish thing and thought it would be cool for the bus. It lasted all of one and a quarter songs on the bus stereo before it was unceremoniously booed off. Oh well, it could have been worse. I could have bought the *Julio Iglesias Sings Songs of Spain* tape instead. Or, worse still, *David Hasselhof's Love Songs*. Ready for a really scary statistic? David Hasselhof has had over twelve European Top Ten albums. Unfortunately this is not a misprint.

So much for music being a universal language.

Finding our bus in the gigantic car park at Pryca was supposed to be easy. Each small section of the car park was signposted with a different animal. So if you parked in, say, the elephant section, which had a silhouette of an elephant on the sign, you knew you'd find it among the hippos and lions, just like the eagle was near the duck and toucan, etc., etc. The only problem was that the car park was so vast that they had to use many animals, and they ran out of ones that look completely different. You may be able to tell the difference between the silhouette of a spiny-tailed bandicoot and a blue-nosed aardvark at 40 paces, but I can't. So I always made sure we parked in the shadow of an unmistakable animal, like a giraffe. After shopping, we'd head straight to the Laughing Whale—no, not another section of the car park, but the name of our campsite and venue for the sangria party.

Once we pulled up to the Laughing Whale late in October only to find the gates padlocked shut. The place seemed deserted. While my passengers sat in the bus glaring at me, I unsuccessfully tried to find a way to get in. Eventually I sauntered nonchalantly back to the bus, grabbed Carlos and casually led him to the gate. Pointing to a sign written in Spanish, I calmly asked him what it said.

'It's-ah...um...clos-ed for ze summ-er.'

I stepped back on the bus. 'Sorry, everyone. It looks like it's...um...closed.' Robbo, my driver, leaned over and whispered to me, 'We passed another campsite about ten minutes ago. Shall I try there?' We did. It was open.

I felt so embarrassed I got all the passengers cabins—at considerable expense to the office—and told the office that's all they would give us. They couldn't complain about the bill; after all, they were the ones who not only didn't tell me about the visas, but sent me to a closed campsite.

In the event, the passengers made such a noise and such

a mess of the cabins, the campsite owner told me (at the top of his voice) we were not welcome in his campsite ever again. Unlike the mob at the Laughing Whale, he was just not used to seriously intoxicated Aussies and Kiwis screaming Cold Chisel songs, throwing up all over the grounds and bonking in the shower blocks.

On my first ever trip to Spain, I decided I would cook dinner on the first night. To be more accurate, I decided I would do my very best to fuck up Spain's national dish, paella (pronounced, by the way, py-yay-yar). It seemed easy enough. A bit of saffron-flavoured rice with a few choice bits of seafood, chicken and, for some reason, peas. Beside the fact it cost five days worth of food kitty money for one meal, it turned into a marathon and never seemed to get past that so-gluggy-it-looks-like-someone-vomited stage. Following Spanish tradition, we finally ate at eleven o'clock. I planned it that way. Honest. Speaking of which, I still have trouble coming to terms with the fact the Spanish don't eat dinner till ten, eleven or even midnight. If 'me dud'(Yorkshire for dad) didn't get his chops, mashed potato and peas by six o'clock, he'd just about have a seizure. I remember when we were kids, as soon as Harry ('me dud') walked in the door at five-thirty, our nightly dinner of chops, mashed potato and peas would be on the table ready to go.

Anyway, my paella ended up tasting horrible, and was nothing like any paella I'd ever eaten before. But luckily most people already had half a belly full of sangria and, really, I could have served them someone's gluggy vomit with a few mussels thrown in and they wouldn't have noticed the difference.

I only have vague recollections of sangria parties. I even asked other tour leaders if they could remember any funny stories from their sangria parties, but they'd just give me a blank look and say, 'No, sorry. I can't remember a thing.' I mainly remember watching people fall over a lot, covered in sangria and bringing up something that looked like a fresh serving of my paella. And I do remember sitting near the driver, Robbo, watching as he tried his charming and drunken best to pick up one of the girls. His pick-up line went something like this: 'I usually don't try to pick up girls on a trip, but I really want to make love to you.' *She* didn't fall for it, but when I bumped into Robbo naked in the shower block half an hour later, he was with another girl who obviously did.

On a couple of occasions I walked—well, staggered— some of the group fifteen minutes down the road to the local disco. Most times, though, the passengers would be lucky to stand up, let alone make it to the disco. A lot of nightclubs in Spain don't even *open* till two in the morning. We'd rock in late (or should I say early?) to find the place full of Pryca checkout chicks and sleazy Spanish senors. The Latino lads would try to pick up our girls, but they seemed to have dropped out of Mafisto's 'How To Pick Up Women School' on the first day.

We would attempt to dance to that excruciatingly annoying thump-thump-Euro-Latino-pop-house-music which, thank God, has never made it out of Spain, while the hot-blooded young Spanish men leered at our girls. One guidebook says, 'Some women report annoying cat calls, overly insistent Don Juans and obnoxious groping all night', while another suggests, 'If the hassling gets too much and you want to offend a Spanish man, say something unpleasant about his mother.' I searched countless Spanish phrase books, but nowhere could I find how to say, 'Your mother wears army boots.' The best (or worst) I could come up with was '*Tu mama es un buñuelitos*', which translates into 'Your mother is a small fritter with a variety of fillings.' I taught this to the girls, but they told me the only response they ever got from Spanish men was a rather confused look.

The passengers probably blamed their hangovers for the church looking so odd, as if it was melting in the hot Barcelona sun. But no, it was Antonio Gaudi's still-unfinished Expiatori de la Sagrada Familia. After starting it in 1882, Gaudi obsessed over it for 43 years until the poor sod was hit by a tram as he crossed the road. Unrecognised and a bit smelly (he used to wash himself with breadcrumbs), he lay in a paupers' hospital for a few days before he died.

I love Gaudi's wavy, elaborate and fantastical buildings, which are dotted across Barcelona. When a couple on one of the trips also showed a keen interest in his work, I told them they had to visit Parc Güell. This park represents Gaudi at his finest. It's like entering a fantasy land, with winding paths, lavish gardens, weird, rough stone tunnels and the famous lizard made of broken glass and tiles. Boy, there must have been some good drugs going down in Barcelona at the end of last century. I'm certain there must have been some LSD involved.

So anyway, the couple caught the public bus way out into the suburbs of Barcelona, walked into Parc Güell and within minutes were mugged at knifepoint. When they returned, they informed me it was my fault. Naturally. Yeah right, like I rang up the mugger and told him, 'Look, I've sent two over your way; the guy's got a money belt on and the girl has an expensive camera and some cash in her handbag. Then meet me in some dark alley in town and we'll split the profits.' Actually, that's not such a bad idea...

'Not another bloody leather demo!' the passengers would groan as we headed across to Mestre Piel, home of Spanish leather. I would tell them that the Spanish use a very different technique to treat their leather and make their jackets, when in fact the stuff was identical to Florentine leather, and so was what they made out of it. However, I liked the demo. The shop had air-conditioning and, I'm sorry to be so rude, but I found Juan's accent an absolute scream.

The Catalonians—Barcelona is the capital of the region called Catalonia—speak a similar-but-crucially-different language to official Spanish (Castillian). The citizens are almost militant in their use of their own language, with street names, museum exhibits, newspapers, radio programs and movies all in Catalan. Naturally, the Catalonians all speak Castillian Spanish as well, along with the rest of the 230 million people in 22 countries who make Spanish the fourth most spoken language in the world, behind Mandarin Chinese, Hindi and English. But like the South Americans, the Catalonians make damn sure they don't speak it properly. They pronounce 'c' when it sits in the middle of a word as 'th', hence 'Barthelona'. And when Juan pronounced any English word with an 's' sound in the middle, it made him, along with the whole population of Barcelona, sound as camp as the proverbial row of tents.

'So. Firtht today, I would like to show you thome leather and thome of the betht leather jackets.' Juan would put on a video for the demo and within seconds most of the group would be fast asleep, lying on the cool carpet. This would be a little embarrassing, because when the video finished no-one would move. I would have to clap my hands and shout, 'OK, that's it everyone', wake them from their slumber and take them on a short walking tour of the city.

By the end of a trip, and particularly after a big night on the turps, the walking tours resembled a scene from *The Living Dead*. They would stare at me with glazed eyes and groan exactly like the zombies in the film as they shuffled ever so slowly down the street.

Las Ramblas has been called the best street in the world and each time I wandered down the sweeping, shady expanse, I could almost agree. It's hard to believe this famous street was once nothing more than a drainage ditch.

I would walk the passengers the whole length, from Plaça de Catalunya, only veering off briefly to wander the cool, narrow alleys of the Barri Gòtic, then back on to Las Ramblas and its many parrot shops—every house in Barcelona must have a parrot by the look of the usually crowded stalls—before finally ending up at the port and, as Dave from Dandenong so eloquently called him, 'that Marco Polo cunt'.

The group would then have the afternoon free while I went searching for the ultimate in tapas, those wonderful little tidbits of squid or olives or prawns or sardines or marinated mushrooms or things I didn't have the faintest hope of identifying, but which tasted good anyway. I would then quite often spend an hour or two lazing about over a beer in Plaça Reial. Just off Las Ramblas, it's a splendid nineteenth-century square fringed by arcaded houses, palm trees, a couple of cafés, the odd prostitute and drug dealer, and lots of lampposts designed by that man Gaudi when he was just a wee lad back in 1879.

By afternoon, most of the Spanish folk would be at their siesta, which would have to be one of the greatest ideas of all time. No wonder the Spanish look so deliriously happy over their tapas and wine at lunch when they know they can go home straight after it for a bit of a kip before heading back to the office. It is such a wonderful idea. I've even tried to carry on this fine tradition back home in Australia. After a couple of beers and a large plateful of food at lunch, I have sometimes snuck down to the toilets at work for a quick nap. The Spanish really have it sussed.

One afternoon, before I went hunting tapas, I had a chore to do. It should have been relatively simple. During a trip we have 'money pick-ups' from Thomas Cook offices along the way, so we don't have to carry a whole trip's worth of traveller's cheques around with us. I was due for a pick-up in Florence, but the money wasn't there. I rang the office. 'Oh shit, someone forgot to send it,' they said (this someone person always got the blame, the poor sod). 'We'll have to send it to a bank in Barcelona.' (There were no Thomas Cook offices in Barcelona.) They faxed me the bank's address in Plaça Catalunya, but I did seventeen laps of the square and couldn't for the life of me find the damn bank. Frustrated, I went to see my friend Juan. When I showed him the fax, he said, 'No, thith ith Platha *de* Catalunya, you want Platha Catalunya, which ith out of town a bit.' Out of town was right. Just not *this* town. I jumped in one of Barcelona's ubiquitous yellow and black Renault cabs and headed out towards Madrid.

I think it's really cool when a city has its own recognised and distinctive taxis. And quite often they reflect the personality of the people in that city. New York's yellow cabs are big, brash, noisy and bright, while London cabs are old, conservative, stylishly black, and you can never get one when you want one. Barcelona's cabs are zippy, flashy, cheeky, slow in the heat, and not very good at picking up women.

Anyway, when I finally reached Plaça Catalunya without the *de* and the bank, I decided to eat first. I found a lovely suburban tapas bar and sat munching sardines and things I didn't have the faintest hope of identifying, but which tasted good anyway, with a group of local thugs. I walked into the bank feeling happy, full and rather content. All of a sudden I didn't mind the fact I'd travelled all afternoon to get there. Possibly the most beautiful girl in the world served me—things were getting better—and, through skillful use of her broken English and my six words of Spanish, managed to figure out I was there to pick up some money. She returned with a large pile of forms, all written in Spanish, and I signed them all while she kept smiling at me. I had no idea what the forms said. For all I knew I could have just signed over my first born son, and I wouldn't be at all surprised if, when my first born son eventuates, two large Spanish fellows arrive at my door to take him away.

Then she disappeared for about ten minutes. At first I thought she'd forgotten about me, but then I thought she was more likely just collecting up all the traveller's cheques. The love of my life finally returned with a huge wad, fifteen centimetres high, of pesetas. Notes! My eyes widened. 'Um...trav-e-ller's...cheque...s?' I said, while drawing the shape of a traveller's cheque with my fingers. She just flashed me the most gorgeous smile and handed me the biggest wad of cash I'd ever seen in my life—all, by the way, in small notes, like someone's ransom money. ('Make it up in small notes or I'll kill the bitch.')

I was petrified.

Barcelona is the undisputed pickpocket capital of the world, and here I was about to step out into the street, in a rather seedy suburb, to hail a cab, carrying £2000 ($5000) in Spanish pesetas. If a mugger got me, it would be like all his Christmases, birthdays, Easters, Father's Days and bar mitzvahs had come at once. Terrified, I just hung out near the front of the bank until a cab came along, then I headed straight back to camp and hid the cash in my bag of dirty and soiled underwear: no-one in their right mind would look there. On top of this, I had to carry this pile of what looked like drug or laundered money all the way through France, runner-up as pickpocket capital of the world.

At the end of a hard day's work I would go for a quick dip in the camping ground pool, lounge about poolside and share an ice-cold bottle of San Miguel with a few thousand mozzies. During our training trip, one of the trainee drivers strolled over to me while I was lounging by the pool having a three and a half minute rest from study, and said, 'Brian, you have to have a look at this. Come with me.' I followed him into the toilet block—a little worried now as to *exactly* what he was going to show me—and he pulled out a three page fax that had been sent to head office. It was all horribly creased. 'I found it in the bin, in the office of the campsite. Check it out!' It was a list of all the trainees on the trip, and against each name was a progress report from the tour leader trainer. Mind you, this was only day five of the training trip.

Next to my name it said, 'Has a very good general knowledge, but have yet to test his organisational skills. A bit of a smart-arse.' I was happy with that. You should have seen some of the others. Scathing, to say the least. 'He has no chance of getting a job', was one, while another said, 'He has zero personality and his spiels are boring.' At least all I got was 'a smart-arse'. I could live with that. We dared not show anyone else, as most of the trainees were bagged in one way or another. By the way, the fellow 'who had no chance of getting a job' was the other Brian, who lost it in Florence and was sent back to London the following day.

On our last night in Barcelona I would take the group up to Montjuic, past the Olympic stadium, to Poble Espanyol. This mini-Spain-in-a-bottle is made up of narrow alley-ways and tiny squares, and is filled with buildings representing different regions of Spain. The architectural style of each building reflects Spain's different influences over the centuries. It's amazing to think that Spain was ruled by the Romans for 600 years, then ruled for another 600 years by the Moors (or as George Costanza was sure they were called, the *Moops*). Spain's Spanish name, *España*, is Phoenician—they were the rulers before the Romans—for 'the land of the rabbits'. Which is odd, because I'd have to say I can't recall ever seeing one of the buggers, let alone a whole land of them.

I had read somewhere that the bars in Poble Espanyol really go off at night, with the locals taking over from the hordes of tourists that visit the area during the day. It was a Wednesday night the first time we visited, and the place was a little quiet. But I soon discovered this great little bar that had a flamenco dancing class in progress. What a great idea to hold it in a pub. We would sip our cold drinks while watching the local, so cool twenty-somethings strutting their stuff on the dance floor to the accompaniment of castanets and racy flamenco guitar.

Spain's greatest gift to the world of music is the guitar. Originally introduced by the Moops as a crude and rather useless four-stringed instrument in the twelfth century, the Spanish craftsmen of the sixteenth century refined it into its present form. So you can thank the Spanish every time you see a busker strumming a guitar and singing 'I'm Leaving On A Jet Plane' or 'I'm Being Followed By A Moon Shadow'.

At the end of the flamenco class we would join in. Well, at least some of us would attempt to, trying not to look too clumsy. Quite often the flamenco students would hang around and teach us a few steps.

One particularly balmy evening we arrived to find Poble Espanyol a virtual ghost town. Even the flamenco class in my favourite little bar wasn't on, and I had to bang on the bar and scream '*Hola!*' for five minutes just to get the barman's attention. Wandering around the totally empty streets—empty, that is, except for the odd German tourist planning their forthcoming attack on Europe—

I glanced into an empty café to see a group of about five people, who looked like the waiting and cooking staff, glued to a television set. Barcelona was playing AC Milan in the final of the European Cup and every citizen of Barcelona was glued to a TV, watching their beloved Barça with bated breath. The whole city is soccer mad. And I do mean mad. The team is the pride and joy of the fiercely Catalonian people and, if they were to win that evening, we were in for the party to end all parties. The locals would be storming out into the streets and bars, and I could even be lucky enough to fulfil one of my lifelong fantasies and pick up a Spanish girl, albeit a very drunk one, but a Spanish girl nevertheless. But no. Barcelona got an absolute hiding and were beaten 4–0. The locals stayed at home, sobbing or just contemplating slashing their wrists.

One time we were driving for an hour and a half down the autopista out of Barcelona on our way back to France. The air was perfectly still and the bright morning light dazzled our eyes as it reflected off the Mediterranean on the left-hand side of the bus, while the hills on the right... wait a minute... Mediterranean on the left? Shit, wouldn't it be on the right if we were heading north? We were driving south towards Morocco and the driver was blissfully unaware of his total balls-up.

I stuck my head through the tiny window of the driver's cabin (we were in a decker) and enquired calmly, 'Johnno, do you notice anything odd about the Mediterranean today?'

He turned around. 'Nope. Looks normal to me.'

'Well, what side of the bus do you think the sea would be on if we were, say, heading north?'

I was then hit with a barrage of choice expletives. About five kilometres up the road he turned off the autopista, went round and round the loopy-loopy bits and rejoined the autopista, pointed in the right direction.

Three hours after we left Barcelona, we stopped for our regular toilet stop, still ten kilometres south of where we started out that morning. None of the Hong Kong Chinese charter passengers seemed to have noticed that we were passing gigantic, bright green signs counting down the kilometres to Barcelona, and they didn't even blink at the fact that what had been a three-hour drive from the border to Barcelona two days before now took us over six.

SNAILS
SANISETTES
& SIXTY BAGUETTES

Shit! I forgot Napoleon.

It was only when I sat down after finishing my history spiel on France that I realised I'd failed to mention European history's most famous little man. I'd been standing up at the microphone talking about the French Revolution; the storming of the Bastille on 14 July 1789; how France had become a republic under Robespierre; and how for the next twenty years he led the reign of terror, with thousands losing their heads to the guillotine, including the king, Louis XVI, and his wife Marie Antoinette. Then I went blank. I didn't know where I was. Half the bus was staring at me as I stood there, in silence, for what seemed like minutes.

'Oh sorry, where was I? Um, right…then, by 1870, the Prussians had surrounded Paris during the height of the Franco–Prussian war…' and so on to the finish, without once mentioning that little bugger Napoleon. More than a slight oversight, I'm sure you'll agree. He not only marched his armies all over Europe and ruled most of it, but there have been about 50 000 books written about him and he stars in more movies than Lassie. He even has a bloody brandy named after him, for God's sake. Some of the passengers must have noticed, I thought. But no. No-one mentioned a thing, which either meant they were historically ignorant and thought Napoleon was just a character in *Bill and Ted's Excellent Adventure*, or they were asleep, or (sob) my worst fears were realised and no-one listened to a single word I said. As I said earlier, my spiels weren't boring. You have to believe me. I would not only talk about history in my spiels, but talk about things the passengers were actually interested in, like beer, chocolate and sex.

My spiels were nothing like those of the fellow on our training trip whose '*spiels were boring*', as the tour leader trainer had put it. Try reciting this in a slow mono-tone and you'll get the idea: 'France has a total area of 547 123.48 square kilometres, with a total population of 57 968 542 of which—and this is very interesting—

74.32 per cent live in urban areas. The birth rate is 1.3 per cent while the death rate is 1.1 per cent, which means the rate of population growth is 0.4 per cent. The legal system and judicial process in criminal cases in France are inquisitorial rather than adversarial...' And so it would go on. This fellow didn't get a job, by the way, and the last I heard he was working as a sleep motivator for Insomniacs International.

Unlike some other tour leaders I would briefly look at my notes, then stand up facing the passengers and do my fifteen-minute or so history spiel in a slightly different way every time. Others would sit in their seat and read from prepared cards, which is usually easier (if potentially less entertaining) but still isn't foolproof.

One tour leader (on her first trip) decided to do her spiel on the history of France in Italy, just before the French border. However, she'd forgotten about all those tunnels. Every twenty seconds the bus would enter one and be plunged into total darkness. So halfway through her spiel there would be a long pause. And another. And another: 'The heroine of the Hundred Years War was Joan of Arc who, in...
......1429, rallied the French together and led the siege of
....Orléans, but in.........
..............................1431, in the town of Rouen...'
It couldn't have been more obvious that she was reading from a card, and the longer tunnels must have left an almighty hole in the history of France.

Crossing the border into France, the coastal road soon turns into an inland, busy autoroute with no hint, beside a few Porsches and Rollers, that we were right in the heart of the French Riviera.

At the entrance to our camping ground in Antibes, Camping le Sourire, was a huge metal-grilled gate locked with a heavy padlock. My driver would have to beep the horn almost continuously for five minutes to get Jean Luc the gatekeeper's attention. You see, Jean Luc could never hear us because he was always inside his tiny, shabby 1950s caravan, just behind the gate, playing along with Dire Straits' 'Sultans Of Swing' with his electric guitar cranked up to stadium proportions. Every time I visited the Antibes campsite there he'd be, following Mark Knopfler's licks on his guitar over and over and over again. I would even joke about it to the passengers five minutes before we reached camp, and sure enough, we'd pull up to hear '...And the band played Creole...duh duhhduhh duh, duh duhhduhh duhhh...' The guy was undoubtedly a few *baguettes avec fromage et jambon* short of a picnic.

One evening he came over to our site carrying his guitar, amplifier and—I'm not exaggerating here—trailing an extension cord that stretched about 50 metres back across the camping ground and up the steps of his van.

I was having a little bit of a sing-a-long with my group at the time, merrily strumming the tune of 'My Bonnie Lies Over The Ocean' on my acoustic guitar. The delightful lyrics I was singing, which seemed wittier and more appropriate with each succeeding drink, were, 'Oh, peel back my greasy old foreskin, and I'll give you the juice from my nuts. Oh, peel back my greasy old foreskin, and I'll whitewash the walls of your guts.' The ever-smiling Jean Luc Le Fruitcake turned up in the middle of this moving love song with guitar in hand. He spoke little English and my knowledge of French ran to the extent of: 'Where is the train station?', 'I'd like a crépe with ham and cheese please' and 'Will you sleep with me tonight?' Which were by no means tailor-made for the occasion. He sat down next to me and plugged in his guitar: 'Er, 'ello…you… play Diyerr Straits?'

'*Er, non*,' I replied in perfect French.

We just sat there a minute, then I started playing a Beatles song. Jean Luc waited a couple of minutes, then came in with the lead break from 'Sultans Of Swing'. It was played beautifully and was note perfect, of course, but somehow it just didn't quite fit in with 'Let It Be'.

We played for a little while. I did 'Brown-eyed Girl' and he played the lead break from 'Sultans Of Swing'. I did 'Honky Tonk Woman' and he played the lead break from 'Sultans Of Swing'. It sounded fucking horrible. To put it mildly. I made packing-up motions and said one of the other sentences I know in French: 'I am very tired, so good night.' Forlorn, he trudged back to his caravan and started practising the riffs for the second line in the third chorus of 'Sultans Of Swing'. It sounded pretty darn good, I have to admit, but so you might hope, after practising the same song every day for about three years.

At the tiny supermarket in the campsite—no bigger than your average loo—I would order one-metre-long crusty baguettes in the evening for lunch the next day. One night I wandered in and, in what I thought was beautiful French, said to Jean Paul, *'Bonsoir! J'aimerais soixante grandes baguettes pour demain, s'il vous plaît.'* Jean Paul gave me a startled look.

'Soixante?!'

'Oui, bien,' I replied confidently.

'D'accord,' he shrugged.

The next morning I skipped down to the mini-market and greeted Jean Paul warmly: *'Bonjour, comment ça va?'* He smiled. *'Bien bien.'* And put a large paper bag filled with about ten baguettes on the counter, followed by another, then another, till six bags were sitting neatly on the counter. *'Voilà!'* he said. Rubbing my forehead for a second, I asked, *'Qu'est-ce que c'est?'* (What is that?)

'Soixante baguettes!'

Oh, shit. That's when I realised I had ordered not six-teen but *sixty* one-metre-long baguettes. I said, *'Non. Seize baguettes, seize!',* as if that's what I'd said the night before. Jean Paul then quickly taught me quite a few new French words. None, I imagine, suitable for use in polite company.

So every time after that, whenever I'd order my baguettes, he'd write my order on a piece of paper and shove it in my face to make sure I had the right amount.

My problem was that I pretended I could speak French, while really I had very little idea at all. Once, sitting in a restaurant, a very cute waitress greeted me in French and

I answered in French, asking how she was and commenting on what a beautiful day it was. She smiled and asked me ever so sweetly, '*Parlez-vous francais?*' Smiling back, I said in my best French accent, '*Ah, oui. Un petit pois.*' She laughed and said in English, 'Would you like to order a drink?' It was only when she walked away that I realised I'd just answered her question, 'Do you speak French?', with, 'Ah yes, a little pea', instead of, 'Yes, a little bit' (*un petit peu*).

But that wasn't as bad a faux pas as that made by one of my passengers, who wondered why he kept getting strange looks—and no answer—when he asked a few Parisians, '*Où est la gare?*' (pronouncing *gare* as 'gair'). Instead of asking, 'Where is the train station?' (*gare* pronounced 'gar'), he had been asking, 'Where is the war?' Which, I imagine, wouldn't go down too well with the locals, seeing their track record in wars has never been that good.

A few years back the French Government set up a special department to try and weed out English words that had snuck their way into the French vocabulary and to replace them with a 'new' French word. A little bit paranoid, I feel. The odd 'weekend' or 'hamburger' won't exactly destroy the French language, and anyway, English is full of French words. For example:

We had a *reservation* for *dinner* at the *restaurant*, but first we were to see a *premiere* at the *cinema*. My date was a *croupier* and looked *chic* in the *bikini* she'd bought from the *boutique* at the *hotel*. We had established a *rapport* in the *foyer*. *En route* to the *theatre*, the *limousine* broke down in the *boulevard*. Luckily we were in front of a *garage*. Our *chauffeur*, who was also our *chaperone*, seemed quite *blasé* about our missed *rendezvous*. I said, 'We've already *RSVP*ed for the *premiere*.'

'*C'est la vie*,' she said. 'Let's go into this *café*.' I lit a *cigarette*, asked for the *à la carte menu* and ordered some *hors d'oeuvres* and *paté* for an *entrée*. The *chef's pièce de résistance*, however, was an *orange* made of *papier-mâché*. I think he made a bit of a *faux pas* there. He bid us *bon voyage* and I took a *serviette* as a *souvenir*. He handed me a *condom* and asked, 'Would you like a *ménage à trois*?'

'Not with that *moustache*,' I said.

There you go! And you don't see us complaining. *Que sera sera* is what I say.

The tour brochure stated that the passengers' trip to the French Riviera included a day on the beach in Nice. However, I don't think a collection of golf-ball-sized, back-breaking pebbles really qualified as a beach.

When Nice first became a tourist destination, back in the 1700s, the Brits would travel for fifteen days to go to a beach that was identical to the one at Brighton in southern England, where at least they could get good fish and chips and a nice pint of warm beer. This was in winter, by the way, when it would have been a balmy 12 degrees. It wasn't until the 1920s that summer holidays in Nice took off, which was also when Coco Chanel returned to Paris from the French Riviera with the world's first ever trendy tan. Up until then it was fashionable to be white. Only peasants had a tan, and the rich, and rather silly, would even drain their blood before they went out for the evening to make themselves look even paler.

Today, Nice's winter population of 350 000 swells to just under a million in summer, with all the seasonal workers and tourists. In peak season you have to fight for a spot on a pebbly beach. Later, you need to spend an hour at a good chiropractor for every two you spent lying uncomfortably on those hotly contested stones.

Cannes, on the other hand, has fine sandy beaches, albeit imported. Most of the sand on the French Riviera is shipped in (from where, I wonder?), but still, it's better than ending up with chronic back pain from the overgrown pebbles. Cannes is both the Beverly Hills and Miami of Europe. Movie stars frequent the place—someone has to buy those god-ugly $20 000 dresses in the shop windows—but it's also the retiree capital of France. The retirees seem, in my experience, to spend most of their time in the queue at the post office, making my relatively simple stamp purchase into an all-afternoon affair when I wanted to be down at the beach gawking at bikini-clad beauties.

Driving down La Croisette, past swanky hotels overlooking the water, I would point out the Carlton, Martinez and Majestic hotels, with their own private beaches. In fact, most of the beaches along La Croisette were private. In the flash hotels they had a tunnel that went under the road from the hotel to the beach, so the rich and famous didn't even have to see us plebs as they headed off for a swim and to see who could get skin cancer the quickest.

Two of my passengers decided private beaches should be for everyone, so they swam around from the public beach and casually strolled ashore into the private domain of one of the most expensive and ritzy hotels on La Croisette. They plonked themselves onto lavish deckchairs and eyed off the bare breasts of the ladies next to them—maybe someone famous?

However, their faded Quicksilver boardies and the fact that they greeted the waiter with 'g'day mate' probably gave them away. Before long, large security men with no necks turned up. Preferring not to be beaten senseless, the passengers sauntered down to the water and swam back to the public beach.

I would quite often just wander around the old harbour to look at the boats—well, ships really—and stand there transfixed by some ludicrously large vessel with over-the-top trimmings and mumble to myself, 'Fuck, they must have a lot of money!' Then I'd move on to the next boat, stop, and say, 'Fuck, they must have a lot of money!' Just the leather lounge suites you could peek at inside a cabin door would be worth more than everything I owned. What the hell did these people do with so much money? Buy a ludicrously large boat and fill it with expensive lounge suites, I suppose.

On one visit to Cannes, a Hong Kong Chinese girl returned to the bus absolutely soaking wet. Clothes and all. I found it very hard not to burst into uncontrollable laughter when she told me what she'd done.

She and her friend had gone to a *sanisette*, which is one of the new-fangled public loos that replaced the old *pissoirs*. Instead of spending two francs each (about 50 cents), her friend held the door open so she could sneak in. What they didn't realise is that when you finish your business in one of these sci-fi portaloos and step outside, the whole cubicle is cleaned and disinfected. And I mean the *whole* thing: walls, floors and ceilings (in case someone somehow manages to piss that high?) are sprayed with jets of water. So when the second girl stepped in, she was given a good flushing and disinfecting.

I laughed so much I had to go to the *sanisette* for a piss. And to see if it was possible to hit the ceiling. It's not.

Three times now I've been in town during the Cannes Film Festival, and neither myself nor 40-odd passengers have yet spotted anyone even vaguely famous. On a couple of occasions I've seen a large group of paparazzi and general hangers-on surrounding someone and going crazy with microphones and cameras. On both those occasions I've tried to push my way to the front and jumped up and down a lot, only to see a complete stranger who just happened to be dressed rather nicely. I asked some sleazy-looking paparazzo who one of these 'stars' was and he told me she was a famous soap star called something like Gee Gee Le Prat. Yeah, probably from France's version of 'Home and Away'. During the festival itself, you can't get tickets to any of the films, and the restaurants are either full or they cost you the equivalent of Mel Gibson's pay packet. The whole place is full of tossers in convertible Rollers and fur coats carrying those tiny yappy dogs you'd love nothing more than to kick into the Mediterranean. Really, why would you bother? Unless, of course, you had one of the above or were some arty-farty director from Slovenia, dressed entirely in black, with silly-looking facial hair and a ponytail.

That evening we would try to emulate the lifestyles of the rich and famous as I'd get my passengers to dress up in their best clothes (well, best flannelette shirts, anyway) and head to the land of glitter: Monte Carlo. But first I had to get them smelling nice—and make myself a sizable commission. My group would follow the very lovely Dominique around Fragonards Perfumerie in the town of Eze for a perfume-making demo followed by a perfume-buying demo. 'Look everyone, like this. Buy *lots*.'

Almost two-thirds of the world's perfumes are designed by Fragonards, including Oscar de la Renta, Anais Anais, Beautiful, Georgio, Paris and Opium. Then Fragonards takes out one of the hundreds of ingredients from these well-known perfumes, changes the name and sells it for a quarter of the price. So as you'd expect, the passengers came out of the place with armfuls of perfume and reeking of four or five different fragrances each.

Actually, the first designer perfume was unleashed on the world's nostrils in 1922. This was Chanel No. 5, created by the then very-soon-to-be-sunburnt Coco Chanel.

Napoleon, on the other hand, begged Josephine in one of his letters not to bathe for two weeks before they were due to meet so he could enjoy all her natural aromas. Quite a lot of French people carry on Josephine's washing regime today.

Our first 'national meal' in France—thank God this one really was French, as I got sick of trying to explain to the passengers that something like roast chicken was actually Italian—would be at the Italian-named but French-cuisined 'Bella Vista'. Beautiful view. It really was a magical place. I would book the tables outside, next to a low brick wall and an almighty drop of hundreds of metres down the steepest hillside. Nestled on the rocks on the water's edge far below was a cluster of villas. From the restaurant, it looked as though bungee-jumping was the only possible way to reach them.

When the sun dropped slowly into the Mediterranean, with the twinkling lights of the boats and villas around you and the soft cooling sea breeze caressing your face, it really was magical. Yet here's the remarkable thing. Some passengers would complain. There was the food for a start—well, more the price really. But listen to this. For just over $25 you got a buffet with at least sixteen different salads, meats, cheeses, marinated olives, etc.—which, by the way, was delicious—followed by a turkey escalope with cream, mushroom and white wine sauce, then chocolate mousse. And to wash it all down, we got half a bottle of red or white wine each. 'Bit expensive' some would say.

Unbelievable. For that view, with that food. You can understand why sometimes I just felt like throwing a couple of
them over the balcony.

I even had a girl who refused outright to go to the meal
and just sat in the bus. 'There's nowhere around here to
get any other food,' I said. 'That's alright,' she sulked.
I found out later in the trip that she'd brought $200 spend-
ing money for a four-week trip. That's $14.30 a day.
Astonishing.

It was the French who introduced the restaurant concept to the world. Originally it was a place for people who
had overindulged. The bourgeoisie of the day came to
these 'restaurants' to have a break from high-calorie, rich
food and eat a simple and healthy broth made of meat
and lots of vegies. Mind you, the traditional style of French
cooking, with its rich exotic sauces and herbs, was actually designed to disguise the poor man's food, like tripe,
brains, bottoms, guts and penises and any other part of
the animal that makes you squirm just thinking about it.
I'm pretty sure, though, that it was turkey hidden under
all that exotic rich sauce and those herbs at Bella Vista.
Even though pig ears are very similar in shape and size, it
was definitely turkey. I think.

With a few glasses of wine under their belts, the passengers would be in a jovial mood as we zig-zagged our way
to the Principality of Monaco. At only two square kilometres, the country is so small that the local golf club has
its clubhouse in Monaco and the fairways in France.

Sounds a bit like a Rodney Dangerfield joke: 'The country is so small that when you go to the bathroom, you clean your teeth in Italy, have a bath in Monaco and piss in France.' Then he'd fart and say, 'Hey, someone must have stood on a duck!' Boom, boom.

The reigning Grimaldis, headed by Prince Rainier III, trace their ancestors back over 500 years, making them the longest-reigning family in the world. Rainier was married to the drop-dead gorgeous Grace Kelly, who popped out Stephanie, Caroline and Albert. But I won't talk about them at all, because they're boring. Well, that's according to one of the would-be tour leaders on our training trip, anyway. His history spiel on Monaco failed to mention the Grimaldis once. 'Any reason why you didn't mention Prince Rainier, Grace Kelly or their children?' the trainer asked.

'Yeah, I think they're boring.'

That went down particularly well, as you can imagine. Not mentioning the country's most famous family because, well, he personally didn't like them. This, by the way, was the same fellow whose '*spiels were boring*' according to the trainer's fax to head office. Of course, he did tell us that the average annual rainfall was 758 millimetres and that Monaco has a stand-by electricity capacity of just over 8000 kilowatts of power. Riveting stuff.

Not long after entering the 'country' of Monaco we would join what is, for one day of the year, the grand prix track. I would make racing-car noises into the microphone (as you do), while the passengers would scream for the driver to put his foot down. Once Chris, the driver, got

242

just a little bit carried away. I think my rather too realistic racing-car impersonation went to his head. He floored it. We were literally racing around the streets, flying around corners and accelerating down the straights. And the whole time my now possessed driver had this scary grin on his face. 'Chris, Chris!' I screamed. He finally snapped out of it and dropped to a more appropriate speed. 'Chris, what were you doing?'

'Sorry, I just got a little bit excited.' I must admit, though, he was good. Probably would have given Schumacher a run for his money.

I would walk the group up to Monte Carlo's famous casino, stop at the front and just look at it. None of the passengers would be suitably attired to actually enter the establishment. They might have been wearing a brand new 'I've been to Rome' T-shirt and a freshly polished pair of thongs, but that wouldn't get them in. Back in 1857, though, they probably would have let us inside in our underwear. When the casino first opened, the roads into Monaco were so bad, hardly anyone came at all. In fact, in the whole of November 1857, *one* person stepped into the place. Even then he walked out with a two franc profit.

With the main casino a no-go, I'd walk the passengers down to Loew's Casino, by the harbour. There they'd happily let us in to pay the equivalent of Monaco's GDP for a beer, and to throw whatever money we had left into pokie machines. I would allow myself exactly 50 francs to gamble.

Three and a half minutes later I'd leave to get a drink

at Rosie's bar. Rosie was about 60 but looked more like 120, while her husband, Jean Louis, seemed permanently pissed off his head. Rosie's bar was a favourite haunt of grand prix drivers and the walls were adorned with their photos and signatures. It also served by far the cheapest beer in Monaco. (I have to say, I could never understand why grand prix drivers were after cheap beer when they'd get at least $10 000 for just turning the ignition on.)

Most of the group would inevitably end up there after they'd lost the rest of their spending money for the trip at the casino. I once made the terrible mistake of playing Jean Louis' acoustic guitar after finding it behind the bar, so every time I dropped into Rosie's after that I hoped Jean Louis would be too pissed to recognise me. But alas, it didn't matter if he was a blithering wreck: his face would light up when he saw me and he'd say, 'Ahhhh, you...play...now!' Then he'd hand me the guitar and spend five minutes trying to set up the simplest of microphones.

I would sing a few songs with Jean Louis leaning on me and holding another microphone at the guitar, which he'd jab painfully at my fingers. When my fingers had finally been jabbed numb, I would hand the guitar to Jean Louis. It was then I felt like I'd just stepped back to my high school French class with Madam Chopov. Jean Louis would break into a drunken version of *'Frère Jacques, Frère Jacques, Dormez-vous?'* and follow that with *'Alouette, gentille alouette, alouette, je te plumerais'*. Everyone would be boisterously singing along. I almost expected Madam

Chopov, with her jet-black dyed hair and half a kilo of make-up and smelling like she'd just done five circuits of the perfume demo at Fragonards, to step out and say, 'Brian, sing it properly, or don't sing it at all.' Jean Louis would eventually go off into some incoherent French folk song until he knocked the microphone stand over or just knocked himself over. But hey, I loved the place, and Rosie kept bringing me large and, more importantly, free beers all night. You've got to be happy with that.

Deckers weren't allowed into Monaco. I never knew why, probably something to do with low bridges, but I guessed it also had something to do with how old and ugly the buses were. You wouldn't see a car in Monaco more than about two years old, unless of course it was a \$200 000 1952 Silver Shadow Rolls Royce. Anyway, we would have to be dropped off at the top of the country. We then had to walk a couple of kilometres to the casino and back up the steep hill at the end of the night. Returning to the bus before midnight, the streets would be empty, and I mean *empty* empty. There was never a single person to be seen. Monaco has a population of 30 000. So where in the hell was everyone? I know it's a big tax haven and half of the 30 000 residents only stay in the country for a few hours a year to check their bank accounts, but you'd still expect to see *someone*. Anyone. Then again, Monaco has 34 000 television sets, so I guess residents were in their zillion-dollar apartments watching 'Le Home et Away' on the box.

Thankfully, the lung-busting and calf-aching journey

back up the hill to the bus was broken by conveniently placed lifts. Yes, lifts. A nondescript entrance in the middle of a street would take you down a long corridor to a lift, and a lovely one-minute, air-conditioned journey replaced a ten-minute, taxing, sweaty mountain hike. Monaco is full of these underground walkways and it never ceased to amaze me how perfectly and almost clinically spotless they were. On top of this, the walls, ceilings and even the floors are made of marble, and instead of those horrible fluorescent lights (usually covered in wire mesh back home so people with the IQ of a pet rock can't smash them) they have ornate brass lamps. Anywhere else in the world, these walkways would be covered with incomprehensible graffiti, the floors littered with empty Coke cans, McDonald's wrappers and one shoe (every walkway has these three things), and the whole place would reek of urine, decomposing bodies and, worse still, half-eaten Big Macs.

Walking through Monaco's walkways is like walking the corridors of Prince Rainier's palace, and I would ask my passengers to behave themselves because every walkway is under the scrutiny of countless closed-circuit video cameras and the 4000 strong Monégasque Police.

Unfortunately, asking the passengers to behave was like waving a red rag at a bull and, without fail, someone would do something stupid in front of the cameras. Nine times out of ten this would involve the dropping of pants and a show of bottoms. I have to confess that on one occasion, after a few too many beers at Rosie's, I put on what I thought was a very entertaining song and dance routine.

You have to admit, it had to be more entertaining for the police than a fat, hairy bottom wiggling about with someone shouting, 'Oi! Get a load of this!'

On my first trip to Monaco, Coach Captain Kevin Kelvin told me he would be waiting, as usual, at the 'top' of the country for our return. But when my hot and tired group reached the border, the bus was nowhere to be seen. Then I remembered. On our training trip we were picked up right on the border, but were told the drivers would normally park 'just up the road'. We would have to make our way to the bus. There was one small problem, though. I had never found out exactly where 'just up the road' was. With a steep, winding road heading off both left and right, I didn't know which way to go. But I was relieved to see stone stairs directly in front of me, hopefully leading straight to my bus. So, with 22 passengers in tow, I began the perilously steep and dark climb up the cliff face. After a slow 200 steps, the vegetation around us was getting thicker and hanging precariously over the stairs. But undeterred, I kept on moving up in what was, by now, almost total darkness. All of a sudden, after another 50 steps or so, we came upon a massive brick wall. The steps just stopped at the base of the wall and there was no way of going left or right. Twenty-two huffing and puffing passengers stopped behind me. 'Sorry guys, this is a dead end,' I panted. With a few 'oh fucks', everyone turned around and headed back down into the dark, with me saying over and over, 'Why would they build steps that lead fuckin' nowhere?' At the bottom, I finally had to admit to my group that I had no idea where the bus was. I split the passengers up into two groups and sent one left and one right to find the elusive bus. Naturally I went the wrong way. Ten minutes later, off in the distance, we could hear the horn blaring from the bus as the other search party reached it. As a tour leader, it really is terribly embarrassing to have to say to your passengers, 'Look, I'm sorry. I'm lost. I've got no idea where I am.' This instils great confidence.

Some legs of a European bus tour have long, and I mean *bloody* long, stretches of solid driving between cities. For example, the drive from Antibes to Barcelona is about twelve hours, as is the trip from Avignon to Paris. In fact, there are no fewer than eight drives of six hours or longer on a four-week trip. On a decker, people could sleep in their beds, play cards around a table, cook scones, bonk or just sit around chatting over a nice cup of tea. But on a coach I would have to find a way to keep the buggers entertained. I would make up quizzes and all sorts of games in an attempt to prevent terminal boredom. One of my favourites was 'Dear Abby'. Each passenger would write his or her make believe—or in some misguided cases, serious—agony aunt letter. Then they would all be put in a pile, mixed up, and passed around so another passenger could write a reply. Originally I would get one of the passengers to stand up at the front of the bus and read them all out. Bad mistake. After what happened during my first go at 'Dear Abby' I started reading them out myself, so I'd at least have the chance to do a little bit of on-the-spot culling. Here's why. This one was read out at that fateful attempt:

Dear Abby, I am one of the male passengers on the trip [there were only seven, by the way] *and I know one of the girls has already slept with four of the guys, so I am just wondering, do you think I'll have a chance to get with her? Signed, Sad Lonely Guy.*

The answer was then immediately read out.

Dear Sad Lonely Guy, don't worry. She'll get around to you eventually.

The girl in the letter, along with everyone else on the bus, knew exactly who it was about. And while she really had already slept with four of the guys, she thought no-one knew. The whole bus was in hysterics, while this poor girl (who was, despite her exploits, very shy and quiet) bawled her eyes out. The sobbing went on for about three hours and me apologising to her only made matters worse. 'Sad Lonely Guy' wasn't too happy either, because he really was a sad, lonely guy who'd made no friends during the trip. The whole thing was a debacle. Thank God there were only four days to go.

After our long drive from Barcelona to Avignon one time, I realised I'd made another mistake. Never, and I mean *never*, teach passengers how to swear in a foreign language. And particularly don't tell them the worst swear words you can say in that language. Most of all, never ever teach them to someone like Dave from Dandenong. I had taught him and a bunch of other rowdy lads the delightful

French saying '*Enculer!*' (pronounced 'on koolay'), which roughly translates into English as 'Go fuck yourself!' Dave and his sweet bunch of mates would then take every opportunity, whether walking down a busy French shopping street, sitting in a quiet restaurant or standing in the middle of a large church, to shout out in perfect unison, '*On koolayyy!*' Pardon my French, indeed.

To them, of course, it was just a funny sounding foreign word, but how would you feel if six French tourists walked through your quiet local shopping centre screaming out 'Go fuck yourself!' every couple of minutes?

When I was doing my one year of French at high school with Madam Chopov, we would plead with her every week to teach us a French swear word. Finally she gave in and said, 'I won't tell you the word or what it means, I'll just write it on the blackboard.' She wrote *merde* neatly on the board. 'What does it mean?' we asked, but she would never tell us. It wasn't until three or four months later that we discovered what it meant. As spotty fifteen-year-olds, we thought it was so cool that our teacher had written 'shit' on the blackboard.

But learning how to say 'shit' in French in the outer suburbs of Melbourne is not quite the same as teaching a bunch of larrikins how to say the worst possible swear word in a language that 59 million people in the immediate vicinity just happen to speak and understand.

We would generally arrive in Avignon late and, after doing the setting-up and eating dinner thing, I would march the group across the Rhône River, through the ramparts of the old walled city and up to the Papal Palace. One passenger was perplexed: 'It's brown! So why's it called the *Purple Palace?*'

In 1309, fleeing political turmoil in Rome, the popes established themselves in Avignon and hung out there for 68 years. What they got up to, however, made an 18-to-30s tour of Europe look like the Mormon Tabernacle Choir's Sunday Picnic & Family Day. They would have even put Club Hab to shame. There were more prostitutes per head than anywhere in Europe. The popes had more mistresses than Warren Beatty—not that they could probably remember them, since they were pissed off their heads most of the time. They partied all day and night, probably playing Cold Chisel songs really loudly and annoying the neighbours. As some contemporary commentator called Petrach so nicely put it: 'Avignon is a sewer where all the filth of the world gathered.'

To be fair, the locals couldn't really complain that much about a bunch of drunk Aussies and Kiwis staggering through the streets of Avignon at two in the morning screaming out '*On koolayyy!*' We had nothing on the popes.

The drive from Avignon to Paris was the longest of the trip. Miles and miles and miles of autoroute through predominantly flat fields were only broken up by the occasional huge services plonked down in the middle of nowhere.

One day in September 1992, as we stopped for the first of many services stops that day, I rang Melbourne to find out which team had won the Aussie Rules Grand Final. The game had only finished half an hour before (it was about 10 am French time) and I had eight very excited Western Australians on board who were dying to know how their beloved West Coast Eagles had fared against the Victorian team Geelong. My parents weren't home, so I rang my grandma. I had never called her from Europe before, so she was very surprised—and utterly delighted of course—to hear from me. But I just said, 'Hi Gran. How are you?...Good...Look, I have to get going, I've got a bus full of people. I just need to know who won the Grand Final and by how much.' She told me the score and then started going on about the Annual Ladies' Scone Day Bowls Championship and Pop's new hip. 'That's great, Gran, but I really have to go. Nice talking to you and say hello to Pop...Bye.' I hung up with her going on about how her azaleas were blooming late.

Back on the bus I got on the microphone and announced that Geelong had won with a record-winning margin of 123 points, or just over twenty goals. The Perth gang were devastated, while the Victorians on board cheered and screamed. Their own team might not have won the Grand Final, but at least an interstate team had not won the premiership.

About seven hours later, when only a short distance from Paris, I turned off the Cold Chisel tape, stood up and said, 'Oh, by the way, everyone. You know how I said earlier that Geelong had won the Grand Final? Well, I was only joking. The West Coast Eagles won by 28 points.'

I then sat down, chuckling to myself as half the bus laughed while the other half screamed out something very similar to '*On koolayyy!*' It could have been a lot, lot worse though. *Adelaide* could have won the Grand Final.

I made my first major blunder as a tour leader on a stretch of autoroute just south of Paris. And quite a decent blunder it was too. My first ever tour of duty, after finishing the gruelling training, was a five-day decker trip to the 24-hour car race at Le Mans. If I could survive 24 excruciatingly tedious hours of noisy cars going round and round and round in circles and the roars of the accompanying rev-heads, I could survive anything. I had all of six passengers to look after. It couldn't possibly be too difficult. At least that's what I thought.

After a night in Paris we did a 'rolling start' at six in the morning in order to be in Le Mans before lunch. While all of my passengers lay asleep upstairs, we stopped at a services for fuel at around eight o'clock and then continued our drive south. With only eighteen kilometres to go before reaching Le Mans, the last few passengers made their way downstairs for breakfast. A bleary-eyed fellow called Mark was the second last to appear, and asked casually, 'Where's my brother?'

'Upstairs asleep, isn't he?' I said.

'No, I don't think so!'

We bolted up the stairs and checked his bed, under sleeping bags and under tables and found nothing. Somehow, somewhere, we'd lost Mark's brother, Wayne. I'd counted all the bodies upstairs when we left Paris and he was on the bus, so where in the hell was he? 'Ah-hah!' I exclaimed. 'The services!' When we'd stopped for what should have been the most simple and uneventful pitstop, he must have snuck out the back door for a wizz. Ohh, shit! I asked Mark whether Wayne would try to hitch after us or just wait. Mark then told me Wayne had never been out of the small Victorian country town of Koo-Wee-Rup before, and this was only his third day overseas. Wayne would wait at the services for days if he had to.

We turned the bus around and, just over two hours later, we passed the services. But now we were on the opposite side of the autoroute. There, standing outside the services, was Wayne—and, I'm not joking, he was standing there in his white baggy jocks and singlet with a toothbrush in his hand. He waved frantically then stopped suddenly in shock as we drove straight past. We had to continue down the autoroute for another half-hour before we could turn around. An hour later, and now on the right side of the road, we pulled into the services to find Wayne in a real state. He'd had no idea what to do when we passed him and then didn't turn up for an hour. He honestly believed we'd abandoned him, and he would live the rest of his life at a services at god-knows-where, France.

To be honest, it was very hard not to piss myself laughing as we pulled into the services. There was Wayne, who had been standing in that one spot for three hours, in the worst pair of jocks I've ever seen and a tiny singlet, clutching a bright purple toothbrush.

As part of the written test we did towards the end of our training trip, we were given a list of 22 problems that might occur during a trip. No. 6 was: 'After a service stop, you have a headcount and find that you have left young Johnnie behind.' We then had to write what we thought we should do if such a problem occurred. Poor little Johnnie had a bloody rough time on his trip.

On arrival at Antibes, young Johnnie tells you that he wants to see a doctor.

In Rome, young Johnnie gets run over by a car and is hospitalised for a week.

In Venice, young Johnnie is imprisoned for a week for breaking a shop window when drunk.

The morning after the night at the Red Garter nightclub, you find young Johnnie has stolen a painting from the wall.

Johnnie has his passport stolen in Amsterdam.

Young Johnnie has died of a heart attack.

I thank God young Johnnie was never on one of my buses. I consider myself quite lucky though. All of the examples above actually happened at some time on other trips. A few years back one tour leader went upstairs in a decker to wake up a passenger who'd slept through breakfast, to find him not just dead to the world, but dead. All the other passengers had been happily eating their cornflakes joking about the bloke upstairs who couldn't handle the pace. He certainly couldn't.

We would inevitably arrive late into Paris, having spent what seemed like 26 days of the 28-day trip driving from Avignon, and just have time to set up camp and hit the shower block to freshen up before dinner. I hated the showers and toilets in our Paris campsite, and I'll tell you why. Yes, the showers did have hot water, as long as you were no later than the fifth person to have a shower in the morning, which meant getting up at quarter past three. That's nothing. It's the stupid button thing I hated. You had to stand in the shower and wash all your bits while all the time keeping a finger pressed hard into a tiny metal button sitting just out of reach (unless you were Kareem Abdul Jabaar). If you released this bloody god-forsaken bastard shit of a button for a micro-second, the water stopped. You could *almost* manage to wash yourself with one hand, but sometimes you needed both hands (well, I did). Using my hip, I would lean hard into the button and, with my body at a 45 degree angle, try to wash my hair under a stream of water that was metres away. Even Houdini would have had trouble with this ridiculous contortionist act. In any case, I'd end up walking out of the place with bruises all over my bum and my hair matted with unrinsed shampoo.

Most important of all, I always made sure I did the toilet thing before I had my shower, because I would more than likely fall in the toilet or shit on myself.

The toilets, really nothing more than holes in the ground, were affectionately known as squats. Doctors will tell you the traditional squatting position is the natural way of emptying the bowel. As you squat, the thighs apply gentle pressure to the abdomen, which reduces the strain on your abdominal muscles. 'Pressing and squeezing is not healthy,' a doctor will tell you. That's all very well, but it means squat if you can't use the damn thing properly. For a start, you can't just drop your pants and go for it because, and I've done this, you end up shitting in the jocks that are stretched across your knees. I would have to take my pants and jocks completely off, which presents the problem of keeping them clean. Somehow, and God knows how, there always seemed to be shit everywhere in these squats. I can't for the life of me understand how on earth, if people are squatting only inches away from the hole, they manage to get poo near the door, in the corner, on the wall and on every square centimetre of the floor. Unless Europeans like jumping up and down and dancing around the cubicle while they shit, I can't figure it out. Anyway, taking off your pants without them touching any part of the floor was not easy. By the end, I'd just strip off outside first, then walk in semi-naked and begin emptying my bowel the traditional way.

One evening a girl from my bus came running back to camp squealing her head off. She had lost her footing on the slippery ceramic squat, fallen arse over tit into the toilet and dipped her long ponytail right into the hole. She ran out with her ponytail well and truly covered with... well, you can imagine. She grabbed her friend and screamed, 'Cut it off! Cut it off!!' With a pair of scissors her friend cut off in one fell swoop what probably took her at least five years to grow. I seriously doubted that any men would be keen to kiss the back of her neck that night, though.

Paris is just too big and all its major sights too spread out for a walking tour, so I'd take the passengers, or rather the driver would take them, on a driving tour. This basically involved me arming myself with the microphone and saying, 'On your left you'll see...' and 'on your right is...' a lot. I would start my commentary at Place de la Bastille, site of the old Bastille prison, revolutions, fraternity, liberty and all that, then turn into the long Rue de Rivoli where, luckily for me, the traffic was always bumper to bumper. There was a lot to point out and a lot to talk about on Rue de Rivoli, and the snail-paced journey up the street gave me plenty of time to do my spiels.

Except, as I discovered, on Sunday mornings. We reached Rue de Rivoli at around nine-thirty one Sunday and started off nice and slowly, giving me plenty of time to point out the butcher's shop with a big horse's head above the door and the word CHEVAL painted in large letters across the front window. Most passengers winced, while others, especially the girlies who just love horsies, recoiled in sheer horror as I told them that this butcher sold nothing *but* horse meat for human consumption.

Little did they know that I would be serving them up spaghetti bolognaise made from lovely fresh minced horse meat for dinner that very night. Hey, look, it's a quarter the price of beef, which is bloody expensive in France, and with all those tomatoes and onions and lots of garlic and basil mixed in with it, no-one could tell the difference. I would sit on my camp stool at dinner scoffing down my spag bol and say to the girl next to me, 'Can you believe French people actually eat horse meat?' She would screw up her face and say, 'Ergghhh! It makes me sick just thinking about it.'

'Yeah, same here,' I'd say, as I shoved another forkful of gee-gee into my mouth. The Koreans, on the other hand, told us they don't like eating pork or chicken. So the pork we served them in a thick, rich sauce somehow magically became veal. Chicken became, of all things, guinea fowl—our cook's idea there. They said they didn't like eating pork or chicken, but they still polished off their plates and came back for seconds.

Anyway, after passing the horse butcher that Sunday morning, the bus all of a sudden lurched forward and started racing down Rue de Rivoli. To make things worse, we seemed to get every green light. We were just flying past sight after sight. My spiel went something like this:

'On your left everyone is the Hôtel de Ville, built in 1874, it's the...whoops, quickly to the right everyone can see down the street to...well, you might have seen down that street back there the Georges Pompidou Centre, which has, which has...Ohhh! To the left is Tour St Jacques, which is the remains of...great shopping on your right, Forum des Halles of...there's Paris's largest department store, Samaritaines, on the left...well, that's actually the Louvre on the left, but back there was...and there goes the Palais Royal on the right…but the Louvre was started, was started ages ago, sorry, I forget when, it's got the *Mona Lisa* and…to the right is…well, that was a statue of Joan of Arc, who saved France and was burnt…to your left again are the Tuilleries Gardens, which was, which are, and this is…Place de la Concorde.'

Then, thank God, we hit traffic. I was a blithering wreck by this point, and most of the passengers had a severe case of whiplash.

When we finally pulled over in Place de la Concorde for a photo stop only a couple of minutes later, Robbo turned to me with a big dopey smile on his face and said, 'Hey, that was cool. I've never had such a good run down there before.' He was totally oblivious to the fact that I couldn't finish any of my spiels; he was just excited, as only a driver could be, that he'd caught a string of green lights. 'Maybe we'll get a good run down the Champs Élysées as well!' he enthused.

On another occasion we had just pulled into Rue de Rivoli and the traffic was the way it should be—standing still—when, halfway through talking about the horse butcher, my microphone decided to die on me. I tried the proper technical way to fix it, which was to hit it hard with my hand and smash it against the dashboard, but the 'fucking bastard of a thing', as I so lovingly called it, didn't want to work.

I then spent the next fifteen minutes shouting my spiels as loud as I could. By the time we reached Place de la Concorde I could barely speak, only being able to make a rather horrible rasping noise. I did, however, figure out how to fix the microphone. I should have known all along. It's so easy. Just call it a 'fucking useless pile of shit', throw it on the ground, kick it into the door of the bus and *voila!*—fixed.

On yet another occasion we couldn't get anywhere near the centre of Paris because the last leg of the Tour de France was riding into town. There were people everywhere, lining up to see the last few kilometres of the 4000 kilometre race. All together, 20 million spectators lined the route to catch a glimpse of the world's premier cycling event. Fair enough, I suppose, to just pop out your front door somewhere in the countryside to watch the lads cycle by, but you usually knew who the winner was before the race was anywhere near finished, so why wait for hours in central Paris, getting squashed by thousands of people, to see a three and a half second flash as the bikes zoomed by? In my view they had a much more enjoyable and worthwhile event to watch back in the good old days.

In the middle of the sixteenth century, cat burning was a regular and popular attraction. A special stage would be built and a large net containing 50 or so cats would be lowered onto a bonfire. The spectators, who included kings and queens, would shriek with laughter as the cats, screaming in pain, were roasted alive. Now that's what I call entertainment. If they'd thrown a couple of dozen poodles in there as well it would have been perfect.

What is it about Parisians and their dogs? Paris has more dogs than any other city in the world. With over

500 000 of them, there's one for every four inhabitants. Unbelievable, considering most people live in tiny dog-boxes (so to speak) with no backyards. On top of that, most of the dogs are those annoying, yapping things you'd love to kick the shit out of or feed to a Doberman or, even better, both. This all adds up to sixteen tonnes of dog *merde* on the streets of Paris every year. Even with 50 full-time doggie poo inspectors giving on-the-spot fines and the ubiquitous green pooper-scoopers scooping up poopers, you still have to play 'dodge the poo' when walking the streets. I have to admit, though, it's a lot better than it was ten years ago, when my companion on a Parisian stroll said, 'Hey Brian, check out that building!'

'I can't,' I said. 'If I take my eyes off the footpath, I'll step in dog shit.'

Then again it could have been worse.

Halfway through the seventeenth century, Paris was the wealthiest and most populous city in Europe. And in those days there was a lot more than just *dog* shit on the streets. The locals would relieve themselves wherever and whenever the need arose. Maids would empty chamber pots out of windows onto the street. Most houses didn't have any sort of toilet. You couldn't walk down the street without seeing a gentleman defecating behind a door or down an alley. Most pedestrians had to walk around holding their noses because the stench was so bad. It must have been horrible, but at least they had the cat burning to look forward to.

At the end of the Champs Élysées, in the middle of the world's most chaotic roundabout, stands the Arc de Triomphe. Every driver I worked with took a rather unnatural delight in doing laps around this, the world's largest triumphal arch. Grinning like Cheshire cats, they would go around and around while the passengers squealed with delight as the bus came within centimetres of squashing some Renault that could easily fit into one of the luggage bins under the bus. All along the drivers would be mumbling to themselves, 'I'm bigger than them, I'm bigger than them.' After fourteen or fifteen laps everyone would be feeling a little dizzy. The passengers' ecstatic expressions would slowly change into the dazed, spaced-out look of someone who had overdone the scary rides at an amusement park.

Finally, around the time they started frothing at the mouth, I would ever-so-calmly suggest it was time to pull over. Whichever maniac was behind the wheel would suddenly swerve across five lanes of traffic, sending Peugeots and Citroens shooting off into a street they'd had no intention of going down until they were given no choice in the matter.

We'd eventually pull up into one of the thirteen streets that converge into Place Charles de Gaulle and, while the passengers headed through the tunnel underneath the roundabout to have a closer look at the arch, I would bolt down the Champs Élysées to the tourist office and pick up a pile of city maps for my group.

The city maps were sponsored and paid for by either

one of two Parisian department stores, Galeries Lafayette or Au Printemps, and the back of each map was covered with ads for French perfume, champagne, Hermés scarves, Grand Marnier, Lacoste and other French goodies. Which, I might add, was fine by me because both department stores were well worth a visit—Galeries Lafayette for the world's largest perfume department (which sits under a vast and stunning turn-of-the-century stained-glass dome) and Au Printemps for the spectacular views from its rooftop cafeteria.

But one day, all of a sudden, the tourist office was handing out Plan de Paris maps sponsored by that well-known French institution...McDonald's.

I couldn't believe it.

Each McDonald's store was shown as a large red box with a big yellow 'M' in it. These were placed over almost entire city blocks, even covering major sights like churches and museums. All up, there were 35 McDonald's 'restaurants' shown in central Paris. Frightening. But what's even more frightening is that all those McDonald's would be full of French folk. I couldn't understand it. Not only is France world-renowned for its fine cuisine, but its cafés and brasseries are at the heart of French culture. There's nothing better than sitting down to a *croque monsieur*— even if it is just a flash name for a toasted cheese sandwich—and watching the world go by. In 1910 there were 510 000 cafés in France. Today there are less than 50 000 and they are closing at a rate of 3000 every year. Trade has been cut by 40 per cent, and this is blamed solely on fast food restaurants. There are almost 600 McDonald's in France alone. They'd tell you, of course, how French they are. I mean, gee, they've even got a 'French burger' that features sauce made with pepper and mustard, non-shredded lettuce (this makes a huge difference) and onions. How French! They can't fool even me with such cunningly disguised names as Le Filet-o-fish, Le Chicken McNuggets and Le Cheeseburger.

Instead of ads selling French goodies, the back of the McDonald's map showed seven recommended walking tours that, conveniently, passed at least one well-marked McDonald's on the way. Promenade Walk Number Six managed to wend its way past all of six McDonald's in an hour-long walk. That's a McDonald's stop every ten minutes. Even a fat American who eats in one sitting as much as the entire country of Eritrea eats in one day would struggle to polish off a McDonald's McHappy Meal every ten minutes for an hour.

On one trip I was late back to the bus after browsing through some restaurant brochures and then having to join a long and slow queue to get my maps. I had to sprint down the Champs Élysées to make it back to the bus on time. When I arrived, everyone was sitting on the bus except for one couple, who were still standing across the roundabout underneath the Arc de Triomphe. I shouted to them, over the whirring motor-mower engines of all the small French cars, 'Hey, you guys! Hurry up, we're leaving!' Assuming they'd come back through the tunnel, I was shocked to see them take the direct route and run out across six hair-raising lanes of oncoming traffic. Somehow, by the grace of God, they made it to the middle of the intersection. Then they just stopped dead as the realisation of what they'd just done hit them. I was positive they were going to die. Cars were missing them by millimetres and drivers were waving their fists and screaming, 'On koolayyy!'

This daredevil, death-defying feat wouldn't have been attempted by even Evel Knievel. I was already trying to figure out what I was going to say when I rang their parents to inform them that their children had been run over by no fewer than twenty cars. But somehow they made it across. I didn't actually see the last bit of their crossing as I had my hands over my eyes. Watching blood and guts and bones being reduced to a pulp by rampaging Renaults was not something I wanted to see. The lunatics were welcomed back onto the bus with rapturous applause. There can't be too many people in the world to have made that crossing and survived.

Then there was the time we couldn't stop at Place de la Concorde or the Arc de Triomphe because of out-of-control traffic, and I had a handful of passengers begging me to stop so they could go to the toilet. Coach Captain Kevin Kelvin pulled up into the only space available, a bus stop in Avenue Kléber, and ten passengers, tightly clutching their groins, jumped off the bus, pushing and shoving to be the first into one of the two space-age port-a-loos available. Two minutes later a local Parisian bus pulled up behind us. The driver, naturally, was pretty keen to pull into his spot. He began abusing the hell out of us, reacquainting me with some of the words Jean Paul had taught me at the mini-mart in Avignon. There was one small problem, though. Kevin had joined the toiletees and was nowhere to be seen. The French bus driver got on his mobile phone and within minutes *les flics* (French slang for the police) turned up with sirens blaring. We were only stopping for a quick piss, for God's sake.

Our friendly *gendarme* began bashing on our front door and then, thankfully, Kevin turned up. Still waiting for more passengers to return, we tried to stall the cop, but he was getting rather irate by this point. Captain Kevin, on the other hand, was calm as can be. The *gendarme* screamed at Kevin. Kevin just smiled. Nothing, and I mean *nothing*, fazed our fearless Coach Captain. When two of my passengers returned and tried to get in the front door, our lovely *gendarme* wouldn't let them in. He stood there, arms at full stretch, blocking the door. The pair ran around, unnoticed, to the back door of the bus. Realising they were getting aboard, he ran around to the back door after them, only to see two more passengers jumping in the front door. It was all starting to look like a Keystone Cops set-up.

Before the now fuming cop got out his gun and started shooting randomly into the nearest window, Kevin slowly and calmly started moving the bus along the road. We were still two passengers short, so I screamed at Kevin to stop. That left us stopped in the middle of an extremely busy road 40 metres from the toilets and just out of range of the long arm of the law. The last two passengers came bolting up the street with *les flics* hot on their heels. When they were just metres away Kevin lurched forward and we pulled the passengers one at a time onto the now fast-moving bus. Just as the last passenger jumped on, Kevin floored it, leaving our friendly *gendarme* standing in a cloud of thick black smoke. I watched in disbelief as one of my lads, who thought this was hilariously funny, bared his bottom out the open back door to the *gendarme*, who would have loved nothing more than to beat the living daylights out of this bunch of obnoxious tourists. Luckily for the mooner, and me, we lost him in the busy Paris traffic. Nevertheless, I was paranoid all day. Even in a big city like Paris, a garishly painted, English-registered double-decker bus couldn't be too hard to find.

When its ten-year concession expired in 1909, the Eiffel Tower almost became 7000 tonnes of scrap metal. Only the invention, a few years earlier, of the wireless radio saved it. The Eiffel Tower became, well, basically nothing more than a rather ornate radio mast. Today it's probably the most well-known landmark on earth. At 320 metres high, it's pretty bloody hard to miss. So imagine my surprise when, after spending over an hour parked in Champs de Mars a couple of hundred metres away from Gustav's Tower, a passenger paused as she reboarded the bus and asked me, 'Brian, when are you taking us to the Eiffel Tower?'

'What do you think *that* is?' I asked. 'A block of *flats*?'

(It's very difficult not to be sarcastic in this job at times.)

Another time one of the shy, quiet girls was sitting nearby on a park bench waiting for everyone else to return to the bus when a well-dressed Frenchman sat down next to her. '*Bonjour*,' he said, with a charming smile.

'Oh…hello,' she replied sheepishly.

'You…are Ingleesh, no?'

'Australian, actually.'

'Ahh, very nize. Mar name iz Pierre. Would yew lark to 'ave your own personal tour guide to Paree? I would lark to be your guide.'

'Err, no thank you, I'm already on a tour.'

'Ah well.' He shrugged. 'Would yew lark to 'ave sex wiz a Frenchman instead, then?' he asked, ever so politely.

I tell you, the French aren't shy when it comes to sex. In fact, in a recent worldwide survey, the French people were noted for having intercourse more often than any other people on earth (well, besides bus drivers, of course).

Oh, by the way, the girl refused the young Frenchman's kind and generous offer.

We would also stop at the Eiffel Tower as part of our 'night driving tour', which followed essentially the same route as the day driving tour except that it was…night. On a decker trip that started in Paris, the first night would include dinner at possibly the best restaurant in all of Paris. We would park the bus in Champs de Mars, overlooking the vast green lawns with an uninterrupted view of the Eiffel Tower, and as twilight approached and the lights of the Eiffel Tower lit the whole skyline, I would serve up my award-winning *coq au vin* to candlelit tables inside the double-decker bus. One *could* pay hundreds of dollars for a view like that, and with my culinary marvel plus a few bottles of choice French wine, we had a restaurant that rivalled Maxims. In fact, it was probably better because after dinner you got a free guided tour of Paris without leaving your seat. Then it was only a three-second walk upstairs to bed.

Our night driving tour also included a stop at Pigalle and a walk up to Montmartre, with the rest of the 36 million tourists. I can't even comprehend the fact that 36 million people visit Paris every year, and that 67 million visit France. That's seven million more than its whole population. Compare it with Australia (a country that's at least ten times bigger), which has around four million overseas visitors a year.

France is the most visited country in the world and Paris is the most visited city, and they're both leagues ahead of other countries and cities. But Pigalle is a poor excuse for a red-light district.

There are the usual sleazy bookshops and tacky peep shows. Then there are the *belles du nuit* (beauties of the night), as the locals call prostitutes. That description could hardly be less true of the Pigalle girls; they all looked like Madam Chopov with fishnet stockings on. It was enough to turn you off your crêpes.

When we'd finally found a spot to park among the thousands of tour buses, I would walk the passengers up the steep, steep hill to Place du Tertre, where portrait artists outnumbered tourists about three to one. After saying, 'What part of "I don't want a portrait done" do you not understand?' for the seventy-third time, I would head to the steps of Sacré Coeur to take in the magical view of Paris and be offered a small can of beer by a guy who looked suspiciously like the Italian video camera hawker for the bargain price of only $8. 'Gee, at that price give me two! I would have to walk nearly half a block to the mini-mart to buy an identical can of beer for two dollars.'

In mid-winter, minus the throngs of tourists, Place du Tertre becomes a quiet village square, where you will probably only be asked to have your portrait done once or twice. Even the overpriced tourist restaurants that cluster around the square begin to seem charming and delightfully French. On one particularly cold and grey winter's evening I had dinner in one of the restaurants and not only was my waiter friendly and attentive, but I actually saw him smile. Twice.

On Bastille Day, the fourteenth of July, the Parisians really whoop it up. The whole of Paris is one giant party, and when one of my trips happened to be in Paris for France's biggest day, we weren't going to miss it. Parking in central Paris was out of the question, so I dragged 22 passengers onto the local SNCF train service into the Gare de Lyon, only five minutes' walk from Place de la Bastille. The night went well, with lots of drinking in bars, fireworks, drinking in the streets, shouting '*On koolay!*', drinking in the parks, singing Cold Chisel songs, and more drinking. By around two in the morning we'd had enough frivolity and the trains had finished running a couple of hours ago, so we thought we'd simply jump in cabs back to the campsite.

Bad mistake.

There wasn't a single cab to be seen. The cabbies had more than likely left their cabs at home and were staggering drunkenly around the streets with the rest of Paris. If I had been by myself or just with a friend, I would have thought, Oh well, can't be helped, and found a nice bus shelter to kip down in for the night.

But I had 22 passengers with me, with every one of them looking to their all-knowing tour leader for a nice, simple way back to the campsite. We wandered the streets for almost an hour. Then, as we crossed the River Seine near the Gare d'Austerlitz, I stopped the group. Pointing at a grassy area on the banks of the Seine, I said, 'Down there looks like as good a place as any.'

'As good for what?' someone asked.

'For sleeping,' I said.

Yes, here I was, a trained and highly professional tour leader, bedding down my ever-trusting passengers on the banks of the Seine like a bunch of deros. Thankfully, most of the group were seriously intoxicated and they were asleep in minutes. Just try to picture the scene. Twenty-three people lying next to each other in a neat line, all fast asleep, only metres away from a busy Paris street.

I awoke abruptly at six-thirty to see what seemed like

the whole of Paris streaming past us on their way to work. The army of men in suits walking along the banks of the Seine didn't even give a passing glance to 23 people sleeping *al fresco, en masse.*

The passengers had two free days in Paris to do whatever their little hearts desired. One time I had a group of four people who spent the whole of the first day in bed asleep. For them, this was nothing new. Earlier that trip they had managed to sleep their way through Munich, Rome, Florence and Venice. So it came as a big surprise when, on their very last day, they crawled out of bed and set off to see Paris. Wonderful, I thought. Maybe they'd visit the Louvre, the Georges Pompidou Centre, Notre Dame Cathedral or the Latin Quarter. Maybe they'd even take a guided tour of the Opéra Garnier. But no. With hundreds of wonderful sights to see in Paris, they jumped on the Metro and rode it to the outer suburbs to visit the resting place of France's greatest son: Jim Morrison.

When they returned I asked, 'Did you see the graves of Chopin, Edith Piaf, Oscar Wilde or Delacroix?'

'Who, who and who?' they chorused.

'It doesn't matter,' I said.

They had spent four weeks in Europe and visited ten countries without bothering to look out the window. Now they were as happy as Larry to see nothing more than a drugged-out hippy's grave.

I have visited Paris more than twenty times and every time I visit I still find new and exciting things to do or see.

Whether it's simply an undiscovered square with a splendid little café, some small out-of-the-way gallery holding one or two world-famous pieces of art, or just some interesting shops to scour, I can keep myself amused for hours. I could spend a whole day just checking out the goodies in Fauchon, the world's largest deli (with my deli fetish, I am in heaven there).

Indeed, I'd have to say that Paris is my favourite city in Europe. Yeah, I know the Parisians can be bloody rude, the city gets too crowded and you have to pay a small fortune for a toasted cheese sandwich, but I love the place.

I have to confess, though, I've never been to the Louvre. I find it all a bit daunting. If you looked at every piece of art in the museum for just one minute, it would take four months to see it all. If you tried to see everything in one day, within opening hours, you would have to devote approximately 1.62 seconds to looking at each piece, and that's not even allowing for walking time between each one. But the good thing is that it gives me an excuse to return to Paris. It's amazing. All those times I've been to Paris and I haven't seen the *Mona Lisa*. I mean, even Dave from Dandenong went to visit the *Mona Lisa*.

I swear this is true. Dave from Dandenong and his mate strolled up to the information counter just inside the entrance to the Louvre and asked the elegantly dressed lady behind the counter for directions. 'Yeah, g'day. Can ya tell us where we'd find the *Moaning Lisa*?' The woman, I believe, didn't even look at him. She pointed off in some vague direction and spat on the ground. I made that last bit up, but you get the picture. Anyway, Dave from Dandenong finally found the *Moaning Lisa* and stood looking at it for about thirteen seconds until his mate said, 'OK, you've seen it now. Let's go find a pub.' Dave told me later that his mum would have been very disappointed in him if he'd been to Paris and not seen the *Moaning Lisa*.

In my wanderings, probably the most bizarre place I've visited in Paris is the Natural History Museum in Jardin des Plantes. Inside, the place seems unchanged since the turn of the century. The first exhibit I came across was so peculiar I didn't know whether to laugh hysterically or be sick all over it. Neatly laid out, ranged from small to large and labelled with delicately handwritten cards, were...jars of penises. There were penises that at one time had belonged to tigers, baboons, hyenas and aardvarks. There was even a rather frightening looking elephant's donger. The scary thing was that one or two of them looked unsettlingly like the fillet of veal that had been served to me for lunch earlier that day, only metres from the museum.

But it got even better, or worse, as the case may be.

Next up was a long procession of dead animals nailed onto boards. They had been cut open with what looked like a butter knife and all their guts and squirmy bits were spread out across the boards. Each display was then freeze-dried and all its organs were painted in bright, exaggerated, happy colours. Fluorescent orange lungs, for instance, and a delightful mauve heart. Mmmm, what was for dinner again?

The pièce de résistance, however, was the freaks section. In any other country, these exhibits would be banned.

Among the utterly delightful pieces on show were a freeze-dried two-headed lamb, a six-legged pig and the skeleton of a two-headed baby. A fine collection, I must say.

But that museum has nothing on some of the other 'kooky' museums around Europe. In Bergen, Norway, you can visit the Leprosy Museum. What does that contain, I wonder. A few arms, ears and fingers on display? People all over Europe are just *dying* to visit the Funeral Museum in Barcelona. Then there's always the Matchstick Museum in Jönköping, Sweden. 'Wow, look. Another matchstick!' What the hell they have in the German Hygiene Museum in Dresden is anybody's guess, but they do have changing exhibits: a recent one was called *The History of Elastics and Rubber in Hygiene*. 'Oh, look, there's a yellow pair of rubber gloves, and gosh, there's a pink pair.' Just take a wild stab at what type of museum they have in the French town of Condom. Hopefully, though, no jars of penises.

By far my favourite belongs to those wacky Dutch: the fabulous Poop Museum. This exhibition travelled around Holland to great acclaim. The main attraction was an exhibit subtly entitled 'Pooh'. This was an interactive exhibit that consisted of boxes filled with animal drop-pings that can be smelled but not seen. Visitors had to guess the animal responsible, then press a button to find out if they'd chosen the right one. I was thinking about visiting the museum, but I heard it was a load of crap. (Sorry about that. I couldn't help myself.)

One of my favourite haunts in Paris is Jardin du

Luxembourg on the Left Bank. I have spent many a pleasurable afternoon sitting under a plane tree in one of the ubiquitous green chairs, reading, writing or eyeing off the elegantly dressed Parisian women. In the centre of the park is a large fountain where ducks fight for space with an armada of radio-controlled toy boats. One warm afternoon I was watching an eight-year-old boy in a designer sailor suit concentrating fiercely on his radio-controlled submarine. Just near the centre of the fountain was a tiny wooden platform, and mummy duck and her two chicks were standing on it, absolutely petrified. The submarine was on the surface and circling the platform as the ducks watched its every move. One of the chicks jumped in when it thought it was safe, but within seconds the submarine launched a full-scale attack, ramming into the poor little thing until it jumped back onto the platform. The submarine then went back to patrol duty. I watched for a couple of minutes and moved on. When I walked past twenty minutes later, the boy was still at it. If he'd been born 300 years earlier, he would have most likely been the head cat burner, which must have been one of the choice jobs of the era.

Returning to the bus when it was parked behind Notre Dame Cathedral one afternoon, I noticed something very odd. I was probably 50 metres away when I noticed that our decker was totally surrounded by the usual hordes of tourists, and it was rocking. It was rocking up and down like one of those trick cars from the fifties that, well...

rock up and down. I couldn't believe my eyes. I fought my way through all the check pants and Instamatic cameras and unlocked the back door. Cups and stuff were falling off the bench. I walked upstairs and there was one of my female passengers bending over with her pants down. She was holding onto the rail while who else but Coach Captain Kevin Kelvin was—how can I put this nicely?— doing what dogs do when they get excited.

'Whoops! Sorry,' I said. 'I've just come to get…this, um…left shoe.' Walking across Pont St Louis, I glanced over my shoulder to see the bus still merrily rocking away.

On our final night in Paris, the twenty-seventh night of our 28-day tour, I would take the now very weary group to our last 'national meal' in the Latin Quarter or, as it should be renamed, 'The Greek Quarter'. Between the very 'Latin Quarter' streets of Boulevard St-Germain, Boulevard St-Michel and the River Seine, on prime restaurant real estate, was 'Little Athens'. And, as in the Plaka area of Athens, each one of the rows and rows of identical Greek restaurants has a rather sleazy-looking and always moustached Greek fellow standing in the doorway trying to coax you inside. As you walk by, someone just inside the door will smash a plate and yell a lot, as if to say, 'Gee, look how much fun we're having!' The Greek man would be almost down on his knees, begging me to come in, as he eyed the 40-odd people trailing behind me.

I'd have to say, they're a smart bunch, those Greeks.

A large sign outside a restaurant would be advertising

a set menu for the bargain price of 55 francs. Then, when the place (or at least the section facing the street) was sufficiently full, they'd change the sign to a 95 franc set menu. The punters walking by see that the restaurant is quite full, even though it's more expensive than the others. They assume it must therefore be good and go in. They take the 95 franc menu—even though they could have the 55 franc menu, but strangely enough it's nowhere to be seen—and Hercules Dimiakis, the restaurant owner, makes himself a huge pile of drachma.

I would take the group to one of the three French restaurants I frequented: La Petite Hostellerie, Restaurant Le Saint-Séverin or, my favourite, Le Grand Bistrot. This was your typical French restaurant, with authentically rude waiters and everything. The group had a choice of one of five entrées, five main courses and five desserts. The alternatives included Frenchy things like snails, onion soup, breast of peppered duck, sorbet, tarte tatin and the most popular dish in all of France: *Châteaubriant avec pommes paille*, known in English as...steak 'n' chips. Everything is served with chips. In fact, it wouldn't surprise me if your $200 lobster mornay from Maxims came with a side-serve of fries.

I would warn the passengers about the steaks. Here, let me show you how quickly the French cook a steak:

Throw it on a hot grill... Tsssssssssssssssssssssssssssssss...

Turn it over, then...Tsssssssssssssssssssssssssssss...and it's done.

As quite a few Aussies and Kiwis like their steaks

cooked for at least a week, I would ask the waiter, who'd look at me as if I had the culinary expertise of an orang-utan, for the steaks to be *bien cuit* (well done). This meant—and I would warn the passengers—that the steak would come out medium rare. I could just imagine the waiter walking into the kitchen and saying, 'Hey, Jean Paul, zere's a bonch of *orang-outans* on Table Seex oo wont their steaks wull doon!' Jean Paul would grunt and say, 'Peeg-dogs!' as he spat on our soon-to-be-eaten steaks. Every trip, without fail, people would complain about how undercooked their steaks were. 'I told you eighteen times,' I'd say, 'the French won't cook steaks well done, they just will not do it!' After 28 long days, I was always tempted to just shove the whole steak—roquefort cheese sauce and all—down their throats.

Most of the group would try snails—well, we were in France—and once a girl was so horrified when she saw the green and slimy buggers that she was almost sick and screamed, 'I can't eat it! I can't eat it!', at which point one of the lads chimed in charmingly. 'You should be an expert at this...just close your eyes and swallow!'

While we're on the subject of horrible looking food, I once ordered an entrée called *tête du fromage*. My French was good enough to figure out that the name meant 'head of cheese' and I guessed, given that we were in France, which has over 400 types of cheese, that it would be a lovely selection of choice regional cheeses. After I'd ordered, two French friends of the mate I was visiting in Paris turned up. When my entrée arrived, I screwed my face up in disgust and said, 'Erghhhh, what the hell's that?' When he finally stopped laughing to draw breath, one of the French guys told me, 'It's um…cold…'ow you say… jellied brains of ze pig.' I wasn't even game to try it.

But then again, it could have been worse.

After five months the siege of Paris during the Franco–Prussian war of 1871, the city was totally surrounded and running out of food. Five thousand people were dying of starvation every week, but somehow the restaurants were managing to do a roaring trade. Your average run-of-the-mill restaurant was serving, cleverly disguised by exotic sauces, dogs, cats and rats, while the more salubrious establishments were slowly clearing out the city zoo. Two elephants went, a herd of zebras, giraffes, camels…the whole bloody lot. It must have seemed bizarre even at the time, but they even ate the kangaroos.

After dinner, it would be back to camp for a final knees-up. On one trip this was a 'divorce party'. The couple who I'd married in Venice had split after a 'breakdown in communication'. I thought it probably had more to do with the fact that the recently married bride had bonked half the guys on the bus.

The sad thing was, I really did have a divorce on one trip. With only two days of the trip to go, the whole group was sitting on their little camp stools in front of the cook tent, quietly digesting their dinners, when the announcement came. The wife of a soon-to-be-totally-flabbergasted husband stood up and said, 'I would like to announce to everyone that I'm getting a divorce.' She promptly sat on the knee of the fellow next to her who, unbeknown to the husband, had been bonking her for the last week. The poor husband had no idea at all, and the rest of the group, including me, sat there dumbfounded. What on earth could you say?

Back to the divorce party, though. Darren, the newly dumped husband, was getting quite inebriated in the campsite bar. After returning from the loo to find his pint of beer stolen for the third time, he stormed off to the bar to get another. When he returned, he put his full pint of beer on the table and announced loudly to the crowded bar, 'OK, everyone. Can I have your attention, please?' He then delicately pulled out his John Thomas, dipped it in his beer, swirled it around, took it out, shook it, and plopped it back in his pants. 'Now steal my beer, you bastards,' he said. Then he casually lifted his pint, took a mouthful, smiled and sat down.

One night there were two other deckers in the campsite. They were both on the first night of their respective trips, while I was on the last night of mine. It was the first trip for one of the drivers and he had a bunch of Hong Kong Chinese on board. Tired after his first big day of driving, he'd snuck off to bed early and within minutes he was fast asleep in the big double bed upstairs, which the driver always had to himself. Now this driver was a nice, sweet, shy country lad, so when in the middle of the night a young lady stumbled up the stairs and stood next to his bed and stripped off every article of clothing in front of him, he lay dead still, horror stricken. She then jumped into his bed and cuddled up to him, rubbing her more than ample breasts in his face.

He told me later that he'd lain awake most of the night, too scared to move and much too scared to do anything. I told him he was insane. It was a gift from God.

He quietly crawled out of bed at 6.30 the next morning, having realised by this stage what had happened. He went next door to Rocky's bus, walked upstairs, woke Rocky out of his peaceful slumber and said, 'Rocky, I think I've got something that belongs to you.' Yes, she had got up in the middle of the night from Rocky's bed to go to the loo and had returned to the wrong bus, oblivious to the fact that it was a totally different guy.

It was the first night of Rocky's trip as well. As usual he'd picked up on the first night, which was nothing strange because he was good. Even Coach Captain Kevin Kelvin came a distant second to Rocky. He was the King, the Doyen, the Master of picking up. I'd almost have to say he was as good as, if not better than, the Italian master, Mafisto. Rocky's had more bonks than I've had pints of lager, and his perfect combination of charm and sleaze never failed to work. I was jealous, of course. But he's probably got five or six sexually transmitted diseases now and is making maintenance payments to support the 36 children he has scattered around the world.

Boiled eggs, peanut butter and Branston pickle.

That was one of the combinations of ingredients we

had for the last meal on the last morning of our trip. We would try to use whatever food was left over to make breakfast. I was over the moon one time to find a large box of pancake mix left over, but sadly our choice of toppings let down what could have been a delicious breakfast. They included Vegemite, sugar, tomato sauce and Branston pickle. (There's always a large jar of Branston pickle left over.) Mmmmmm. Tasty.

There would always be plenty of bags of things left over, but it's rather difficult to make breakfast with ten kilos of rice, three litres of raspberry cordial, a kilo of Spanish onions, seven taco shells and a large bag of Birdie Num-Nums.

The final leg of the journey to Calais then London would generally be a quiet affair. After 28 long days and 27 even longer nights, everyone would be well and truly shattered. On one occasion, though, the passengers decided they hadn't done anywhere near enough partying. So they stocked up with cheap booze, cranked up the bus stereo and, as we headed north up the A1 to Calais, they were literally dancing in the aisles.

With all their piss-farting about that morning, we had left the campsite very late and the driver insisted we didn't have time to stop for a toilet break if we were going to make the ferry connection. He would drive the four hours to Calais straight through. Needless to say the passengers, who had been pouring copious amounts of liquid down their throats, needed a wee-wee and were soon begging me to stop the bus. I asked Coach Captain Kevin Kelvin. After initially suggesting I tell them all to fuck off, he suddenly had an idea. I went to the tool cupboard, got out a screwdriver, and began undoing the screws holding down a metre-long metal plate on the floor in the centre of the bus. When I pulled it away it revealed a large hole, with the motorway zooming by underneath. It was simple, really. The guys would get down on their knees and wizz onto the road, while the girls went upstairs, did it in a bucket and emptied that out through the hole as well. It was a very classy service I offered on my tours.

It was always nice to see the smiling and welcoming faces of the passport control people at Dover as we disembarked after our one-hour ferry crossing from Calais. I have a British passport and I would just flash the front cover of my passport as I walked through the EC PASSPORT checkpoint and be greeted with, 'Good morning, sir. Lovely to have you home. Would you like a nice cup of tea and maybe some scones with jam and cream?' Meanwhile, across the room, there would inevitably be a long queue for NON-EC PASSPORT HOLDERS. The Aussies and Kiwis would be grilled by sour-faced officials—I wonder if they take it in turns being Mr Nice Official (for the Brits) and Mr Nasty Official (for the rest)—with questions like, 'How long are you here for?', 'How much money do you have?', 'What is your quest?' and things like that.

Once I had to wait over two hours for my passengers to come out because they'd been stuck behind six coachloads of Poles in shell suits, who were being checked for shower heads and smelly sausages.

The first time I ever arrived at Heathrow Airport over ten years ago, there was a line for UK PASSPORT HOLDERS and another line for ALIENS. I was looking out for little green men with five eyes, but could only see the horrendously long queue filled with people in turbans, robes, loin cloths, kimonos and assorted odd hats. And stuck in the middle of them all were the Aussies and Kiwis in board shorts, T-shirts and thongs, which, by the way, was rather silly. Even though it was 32 degrees when we left Melbourne, it was a balmy three degrees outside in sunny London.

On the transfer back to Central London, I would be doing my very best to remember everyone's name for the inevitable goodbyes. For the entire trip I had been their best friend, mother, father, brother, confidant, nurse, advocate, referee, oracle, babysitter, therapist, teacher and drinking buddy, so they'd expect me to at least know their names. However, I'd be racking my brain trying to remember them all. I'd have most of the names, but there would always be two girls who had been quiet as mice the whole trip, and both would invariably have red hair and glasses. It would be so embarrassing as we said our goodbyes when I'd say, 'Bye, Karen. I hope you had a great time.'

'My name's Louise.'

'Oh... sorry.'

After seeing off my flock one by one, I would wander downstairs at head office to finish my accounts, while most of my group would hit the pub—you'd think they would have had enough, wouldn't you? The joy of doing my accounts would include sorting out a shoebox full of receipts, all of which I would hopefully have clearly marked. I would stare at any stray ones for a second, then just write, 'Fruit and veg shop. Heidelberg markets', or something like that. Eventually it would all add up, sort of. I'd have a quick beer at the pub to catch up with the other crew in town then crash—absolutely, mind-numbingly knackered—at around midnight.

My alarm would SCREAM at me at 5.30 the next morning and I would be up as bright and cheerful as I could possibly be to meet 42 new passengers and, yes, do it all again.

Tonight, we would be off to see the sex show and my good friend the Banana Lady.

Yippeee!

AFTERWORD

So, what happened to everyone? Well, I'm back working in advertising, which is much the same as life on the road—lie a lot, get drunk a lot, scam a lot and go to lunch a lot. Sadly, I still regularly break rule no. 3 (*don't get lost*) a lot, too.

Coach Captain Kevin Kelvin now works down the mines in Western Australia somewhere and, last I heard, he'd taken a *two week* holiday at Club Hab (read two weeks of nipple suctions and dancing the Nutbush in your underwear).

Rocky's drinking expertise came in handy. He now runs a liquor shop.

Robbo married one of his DAFs and traded the cold Yorkshire dales for the sunny climes of Adelaide. In fact, it seems most of the drivers married their DAFs (or the cook, if they couldn't find a DAF to marry).

Chris still drives but has replaced the screaming passengers with the slightly more subdued parcels and letters of Australia Post. He is so used to long drives now, he thinks nothing of driving eight hours to go to a party then driving back the next day.

Terry is still a miserable git.

And finally, Dave from Dandenong. He's now a Member of Parliament. Liberal Party, I believe.

I'd like to take the opportunity here to thank a few people. First of all I have to thank the tour company I worked for. What other job lets you travel all around Europe, drinking, eating and partying and pays you for it. (Oh, besides being an Australian government minister, of course.) The crew I really enjoyed working with, who not only made my job easier but made it fun, included Chris, Johnno, Colin, Nial, Jo, Libby, Heidi and Trudy. Thanks to the crew who helped me fill in the beer-affected, hazy bits I would otherwise have missed, including San Khoo, Mark Calleja, Chris Davies, Julie Thompson, Mick McDonald and, especially, my lovely wife, Natalie.

Thanks to most of the passengers for all the good memories, and to the rest of them for providing so much material.

Jim Richardson patiently fixed up most of my shocking grammar and curbed my tendency to use punctuation at random. My darling sister Tracey patiently deciphered and typed up the whole manuscript from my extremely messy scribbles.

My friends Ant, Tim, Mat, Paul, John, Nick, Deb and Mark, who read the first draft and gave me some very helpful observations like, 'Brian, you're a sick man!'

I would also like to thank my agent, Anthony A. Williams, who was always confident someone would publish my ramblings. Sandy Webster for making the book read much better. The gang at Allen & Unwin, including Simone Ford and the lovely Sophie Cunningham who has shown nothing less than bubbling enthusiasm for my book.

If you'd like to find out where the best gelati in Italy can be found, where the Banana Lady performs, where to find a park full of naked Germans, where the best place to nap in Venice is and where the greatest collection of penises in the world resides, visit www.brianthacker.tv